GRT | LENGTH 1035 FEET (315 METERS) | FOUR SCREW STEAM TURBINE | SERVICE SPEED 30 KNOTS

JOHN MAXTONE-GRAHAM

FRANCE/NORWAY

FRANCE'S LAST LINER/NORWAY'S FIRST MEGA CRUISE SHIP

W. W. NORTON & COMPANY · NEW YORK · LONDON

For Sarah, Ian, Emily and Guy,
who all cherished S.S. France

France/Norway
John Maxtone-Graham

Copyright © 2010 by John Maxtone-Graham

Manufacturing by Mondadori Printing, Verona
Composed in Stellar, Electra, and Metro
Book design by Robert L. Wiser, Silver Spring, MD

Library of Congress Cataloging-in-Publication Data

Maxtone-Graham, John.
    France/Norway / John Maxtone-Graham. — 1st ed.
        p.   cm.
    Includes bibliographical references and index.
    ISBN 978-0-393-06903-7 (hardcover)
    1. France (Ship)—History. 2. Norway (Ship)—
History. 3. Ocean liners—History—20th century.
4. Cruise ships—History—20th century. 5. Ocean
travel—History—20th century. I. Title.
    VM383.F69M39 2011
    387.2'432—dc22   2010038083

W. W. Norton & Company
500 Fifth Avenue, New York, NY 10110
www.wwnorton.com

W. W. Norton & Company Ltd.
Castle House, 75/76 Wells Street, London, W1T 3QT

1   2   3   4   5   6   7   8   9   0

Display Photographs

p. 1: Emblem from an issue of special china for the
France cruise of 1989. (Author's collection)
pp. 2–3: Outbound *France* seen between Piers 88
and 90. (Tee Adams Photo)
pp. 4–5: *France* in St.-Nazaire. (Philippe Baudry collection,
courtesy Patrick Depelsenaire)
pp. 6–7: Rolls-Royce emerging from after hold.
(Tee Adams Photo)
pp. 8–9: *France* alongside in Le Havre. (Tee Adams Photo)

387.2432
MAX

CONTENTS

ACKNOWLEDGMENTS

First, a word about this volume's remarkable exterior. I shall always be grateful to my editor Jim Mairs for suggesting that Donald Stoltenberg's twin portraits of *France/Norway* should share the jacket's front and back. This is my first Stoltenberg cover and Don's unerring taste and talent have wrought perfect postmodernist images. One marvelous Norton continuum linking *Normandie* with *France/Norway* is Robert Wiser's impeccable design. The Wiser imprimatur has spoiled this author badly for any other. I must also thank Austin O'Driscoll, Jim's irreplaceably efficient assistant editor, without whom we would all have been adrift and bereft. Wayne Mazzotta has once again been kind enough to execute some glorious endpapers, enriched by digital designer Nick Burkett. Front and back are different, each dedicated to *France* and *Norway*, respectively. Additionally, Messrs. Mazzotta and Burkett contributed two port maps. Triple thanks are due my Norwegian comrade Bård Kolltveit: for the profiles centering each endpaper, his superb *Norway* cutaway, and unerringly useful nuggets of Norwegian research, promptly volunteered.

As for the text, there are legions on both sides of the Atlantic whose help and expertise must be acknowledged. In St.-Nazaire, my thanks to two staunch Bretons, Hubert Chemerau and Jean Cévaër; their incomparable local knowledge and guidance were irreplaceable. *France*'s retired commandant Raymond Kervedo was extremely helpful, as were two men pivotal to *France*'s design and construction, both now, alas, deceased: *France*'s naval architect Jean Coune and senior Chantiers de l'Atlantique engineer Philippe Guitart. Old friends Jean-Noël d'Acremont and Jean LeTutour, retired Chantiers de l'Atlantique president and project manager, respectively, offered useful input as well. St.-Nazaire's EcoMusée director Daniel Sicard allowed me extensive use of the museum's library and Thérèse Dumont led me through her beautifully organized film archive. At St.-Nazaire's other maritime museum, L'Escale Atlantique, housed in one of the city's fourteen U-boat submarine pens, director Andrea Klose was extremely generous with her time and help.

In Le Havre, Aymeric Perroy, director of the French Line archives, put a unique trove of French Line ephemera at my disposal. Special thanks must be extended to archivists Cecille Cailleteau and her colleague Thomas Forlen. Melinda Guettier handled the archive's collection of photographs and films.

Also from France I am indebted to Monique Auriacombe, *née* Croisile, daughter of *France*'s first master Georges Croisile. She shared some excellent photographs and presented me with a rare copy of her father's memoir *En Route pour la Mer*.

In Oslo, I am indebted to Knut Kloster, founder of both Norwegian Cruise Line and, indeed, Miami's cruise industry. Retired now, Knut served as an invaluable resource and adviser, enormously and unstintingly helpful.

For supplying encyclopedic details about his conversion of *France* into *Norway* and the later deck additions, I am grateful to Danish naval architect and conversion specialist Tage Wandborg. He provided fullest answers to too many authorial queries and cannot be thanked enough.

Other kind contacts who helped with *France* included Catherine Braendel, Gildas Buron, Jacques and Ethel Cachot, Chris Choa, Yannig Coraud, John and Mary Cranston, Odette Escolier, New York dealer Richard Faber, Richard Haslam-Jones, Jacques l'Heritier, Pine Hodges, Yann Joncour, William Jory, W. Stirling Kenny, Robert Lapin, M.D., Jack and Marianne Sauter, Marcel Texier, and John Tsui. How fortunate that Kenny had retained and shared perhaps the only extant copy of the mutineers' manifesto.

In Miami, Jeff Macklin was instrumental in connecting me with a host of Norwegian Cruise Line personnel, most now retired. Retired himself, Jeff's working life was with Miami's Tropic Oil Company, a division of Exxon. Macklin was instrumental in supplying fuel and lubricants for NCL's fleet. A *Norway* aficionado, his enthusiastic help and wide-ranging contacts were exemplary.

I must extend multiple thanks to two more old friends, Captain Svein Sleipnes, vice president of nautical and port operations/CSO for Norwegian Cruise Line, and Per Sopp, *Norway*'s superintendent port engineer for eighteen years. Per was a gold mine of technical information, always ready with bountifully useful detail. So too former NCL vice president for marine operations Jan Trollerud and a veritable flotilla of *Norway* masters: Jan Fjeld-Hansen, Hans

Meeg, Aage Hoddavik, the late Geir Lokøen, Sverre Sovdsnes, Gunnar Øien and Tommy Stensrud; gratitude as well must go to Staff Captain Gunstein Langset, hotel director Bjorn-Erik Julseth, and chief engineer Steinar Hammervold.

Thanked, too, must be Rolf Skjong-Nielsen, director of hotel operations for NCL for many years, and Peter Compton, the company's director of entertainment at the time of *Norway*'s Miami debut. Both signage wizard Tom Graboski and Jean Ann Ryan, NCL's reigning choreographer/producer, shared vital conversion recollections. Chip and Anne Slevin Hoehler also provided invaluable data, as did Hank O'Neal.

For additional *Norway* input, I thank, alphabetically, Richard Bergman, Maryvonne Cadieu, Sherry Donghia, (Texan) Richard Faber, Commander Steve Ferrario USN, Brad Hatry, Bill and Marsha Johnson, Peter Knego, Alison Kraus, Sissel Lokøen, Stephen Macey, David McFarland, David Monteith, Helge and Nini Narstad, Bruce Nierenberg, Henrich Nissen-Lie, Jon Persson, Stephen Sea, Jan-Olav Sorli, David Trevor-Jones, Kaushal Trivedi, Masaru Suzuki, and Susan Vinas.

If, peradventure, names have been omitted, my most profound apologies. One final name is mandatory, however: I cannot close without thanking my dear wife, Mary, who remembers so well, vets every chapter, and has once again provided an enviable index.

John Maxtone-Graham
New York, October 2010

Somewhere in a limpid nordic fjord, *Norway* is pictured tendering passengers ashore over a ghostly reflection of former *France*. (Author's collection, artist unknown)

11

PREFACE

The lives of ocean liners follow different and sometimes unpredictable courses. Their sea days over, the scrap yard seems inevitable. But some retirees never get there: *Caronia* ended up on a Guam reef under tow to Taiwan, fragments of *Amerikanis*-ex-*America* still adorn Mediterranean rocks, and, most recently, *Stella Polaris* sank while being returned from Japan for Stockholm restoration.

A fortunate few are quasi-preserved at alien berths. First *Queen Mary* endures a twilit afterlife in California's Long Beach. Consort *Queen Elizabeth* failed in Port Everglades before conversion to *Seawise University*, only to be torched by disgruntled Hong Kong shipwrights. Withdrawn in 1969, *United States* has anticipated redemption ever since, awaiting Star Cruises' announced intention of converting the moldering record breaker into a cruise ship. After only a decade of service, *Michelangelo* and *Raffaello* were withdrawn, later brutalized while serving as floating barracks for Iranian soldiers. Transatlantic veteran *Queen Elizabeth 2* will end her days at Dubai.

France, an amazing exception, survived. After a dozen years and 377 North Atlantic crossings, escalating fuel prices precipitated her withdrawal in 1974. Following a 1980 transformation into cruise ship *Norway*, she would embark very different passengers in the Caribbean for more than two decades.

One ship became another ship, each unique: *France* was the French Line's last ocean liner and *Norway* the Caribbean's first megaship. Save for *Queen Elizabeth 2*, she boasted the North Atlantic's last exquisitely wrought hull, preceding the fleets of slab-sided, balconied giants that sailed in her wake. *Norway* succumbed to balcony mania in 1990, returning to Lloyd Werft for installation of additional decks' worth of terraced cabins. Though revenues were enhanced, the profile was not.

Readers of this volume might find it useful to peruse my book *Normandie* of 2007. Time and again, she reappears throughout these pages, a ghost forever haunting her successor. Though *France*'s hull was the more graceful of the two, she boasted none of *Normandie*'s internal daring.

Normandie readers will note a shift of focus, documentation buttressed by multiple, firsthand accounts with the author as passenger/participant. Since *Normandie* was a 1930s-era ship, few passengers or crew survive; moreover, she sailed for less than four years. Conversely, *Norway*-ex-*France* steamed ten times as long. Recollections abound.

St.-Nazaire is the cradle of France's merchant marine and, in Britanny's collective memory, *Normandie* and *France* are mourned to this day. Regardless that dozens of French Line immortals steamed from the port, none achieved the status of these two iconic finalists, one's career truncated by war, the other's by jets and a vengeful crew.

Throughout St.-Nazaire's maritime museums, crowding bookshop shelves, adorning faded posters in restaurants and bars, and preoccupying old shipyard hands, surviving *France* crewmen, and what I describe fondly as the Breton mafia, *Normandie* and *France* are inextricably paired and lamented.

Books are written for an infinity of reasons—for money, mainly, but also by way of confessional, apologia, expiation, propaganda, self-justification, exposé, or proselytization. Why this volume? Merely a heartfelt memoir of two vessels, aboard which this maritime historian sailed many times.

Just as *Norway* meant a great deal to me, conversely, my name and voice came to mean a great deal to her crew. When she was new, I was asked to produce four half-hour programs, culled from my book *The Only Way to Cross*, each episode encapsulated by locations shot on board in April 1981. Three decades later, they are still broadcast weekly in every NCL cabin. Subject to years of repeated viewings, most *Norway* officers and crew members came to recognize my voice and face. Now that *Norway* is no more, those location shots evoke perfectly her interiors.

I was fortunate to have enjoyed a special and enduring linkage with *Norway*, with not only the vessel but also her captains, crews, and a host of congenial fellow passengers.

CHAPTER ONE

EXTRAORDINARY COMMITMENT

It was the best of times, it was the worst of times.

Charles Dickens, *A Tale of Two Cities*

. . . a body blow to decency and authority or . . . a trippy carnival of raised consciousness and experimentation.

Charles Taylor

The world is disgracefully managed, one hardly knows to whom to complain.

Ronald Firbank, *Vainglory*

Opposite: *France* in her home port. (Compagnie Générale Transatlantique)

Americans cherish the 1960s in fond retrospective as a time of liberation and love. During that decade

the nation sought to rekindle adolescent innocence. A benign plague infected the land, nurturing a new breed of celebratory youth—tie-dyed, jeaned, hirsute, and defiant. These were the articulate proponents of a bold, greening society, determined to establish new boundaries of permissiveness.

Nothing abetted their cause more expediently than birth control pills, first available by easy prescription in May 1960. Formerly proscribed but now relaxed sexual parameters were all of a piece with changed informality, attitude, social dynamics, and clothing. For hippies and beats, repression was out, weed was in. Tripping on LSD became a commonplace experiment, be-ins a spontaneous cultural phenomenon, and psychedelic everything the norm. On Broadway, the musical *Hair* celebrated the Age of Aquarius and—pubic shocker—in-your-face nudity. From overseas, four talented young Liverpudlians revolutionized popular music. Typifying the dawn of dizzying possibilities to come, men walked on the moon in 1969.

Yet darker pigment stained the canvas of that ostensibly luminescent landscape. The 1963 assassination of a popular young president and ensuing assassinations five years later of his brother Robert as well as Martin Luther King Jr. tore the nation apart, fostering a climate of abrasive violence.

That ugly mood was juxtaposed against the familiar but already numbed threat of nuclear annihilation. Americans had learned to duck-and-cover, to thrive despite the Soviet Union's ubiquitous, missile-laden polemic. Though an uneasy peace was sustained, amended to that unchanging cold war was a new kind of half-assed war, offering none of the inspiring heroism of the big one but the divisive pursuit of smaller-scale conflicts in Korea and Vietnam. A guns-and-butter mentality prevailed as that remote but increasingly fierce warfare coexisted with home-front indifference and excess.

At the same time, transatlantic carriers were in frantic pursuit of passenger market share. Peacetime's battle of the Atlantic was about to be won decisively as jet aircraft humbled the ocean liners. The struggle's inevitable outcome had long been foreshadowed. In the summer of 1956, Grace Kelly

and her Philadelphia family sailed aboard *Independence* to Monaco for her fairy-tale wedding to Prince Rainier. But their halcyon love story paled beside a sinister milestone: that summer, more transatlantic airplane seats than cabin berths were booked. As millions flocked to airports, pier-side embarkations diminished. "Look, up in the sky! It's a bird, it's a plane, it's *Superman!*" ran the television promo, but it wasn't a man of steel, it was a jet of aluminum, and no mid-twentieth-century shipowner could ignore its import.

First casualties were year-round transatlantic crossings by sea. Postwar tourists saw little reason to spend a potentially rough and unpleasant week heaving across a stormy ocean when the same journey could be achieved aloft in hours.

Coincidental with that airborne surge, shipboard niceties began to pall. Rituals established since the mid-nineteenth century were perceived as increasingly quaint. Distaff passengers' embarkation wardrobe—gloves, girdles, hats, heels, veils, and page-boy bobs—were discarded. Husbands' and fathers' double-breasted suits, waistcoats, watch chains, pince-nez, toothbrush mustaches, and homburgs and fedoras seemed relics.

Equally old hat were wardrobe trunks, evening dress (and dresses) for mid-ocean evenings, subservient stewards all of one nationality, bingo, horse racing, and two-stepping and fox-trotting. Some tried embracing the youth-oriented culture, but when the middle-aged did their awkward best twisting and frugging a cruel parody was perpetuated instead.

What remained on the sea-lanes connecting old world with new? We must find out, for the sixties' social upheaval was disrupting the old Atlantic order just as efficiently as was the aircraft. Flying both Cunard and White Star house flags, the two venerable *Queens* were approaching the end of their profitable lives. Was "Getting there is half the fun" still a viable catchphrase when winter crossings found those creaking giants a quarter full? Worse, increasingly sulky, unionized crews and home port dockworkers were bleeding the company dry.

Crossing/cruising hybrid *QE2* entered service in 1969. Second *Mauretania* was painted green to ape 1947's now aging *Caronia*. Smaller Cunarders *Saxonia*, *Ivernia*, and *Carinthia* were deployed on Canadian service or experimented with cruising itineraries. *Media* and *Parthia* appeared in 1963, sailing between Liverpool and New York and, occasionally, Bermuda. *Scythia* and a second *Samaria* entered service two years later.

By the early 1950s, the French Line was in desperate need of replacement tonnage. Former flagship of 1927 *Ile-de-France* (postwar, hyphens were added) sailed in tandem with Germany's former *Europa*, entering service in 1950 as *Liberté*.

First of the company's postwar newbuildings was 20,000-ton *Flandre* of 1952. She would be dubbed, unofficially, *Flounder* following maiden voyage electrical troubles and would be sold off to Costa as *Carla C*. Her sister *Antilles* came to grief in January 1971, burning off Mustique.

Holland-America was represented during the sixties by a fifth *Rotterdam*, entering service in 1959, sporting novel, side-by-side twin stacks like factory chimneys. Smaller *Veendam* and *Volendam* took up the company's cruising slack.

Though supplying the majority of transatlantic passengers, America had few ships in service. *United States* had co-opted the blue ribband forever in the summer of 1952 but had no running mate; look-alike *America* was smaller and slower. Also crossing the Atlantic were *Constitution* and *Independence*, linking New York with the Mediterranean.

The former Axis adversaries rebuilt but never achieved their prewar glory. North German Lloyd had to make do with conversions. Swedish-America Line's *Gripsholm* was renamed *Berlin* in 1955, joined four years later by the ex–French liner *Pasteur*, which sailed as *Bremen*. Italian Line latecomers of 1965 were *Michelangelo* and *Raffaello*, graceful sisters with twin, caged funnels, the first of the company's vessels sporting white hulls, cruising's unmistakable stigmata. *Andrea Doria* was rammed and sunk by *Stockholm* in the fog off Nantucket in August 1956.

That was the dwindling maritime context into which the next French Line flagship would be committed. Contravening twin portents—the deterioration of mores ashore and the inescapable supremacy of flight—the French Line decided that a huge new ocean liner would restore France's maritime prestige.

The vessel's keel would be laid a year before General Charles de Gaulle assumed the presidency of the Fifth Republic in June 1958. Although he had not been in power at the time the decision was taken to build *France*, her projected debut suited his jingoist agenda. The 1954 capitulation at Dien Bien Phu precipitated the loss of France's Far Eastern colonies, and Algerian instability and bloodshed augured for additional problems nearer home. De Gaulle urged liberation for Algeria despite bitter opposition from military diehards and the colony's settlers.

In bleak contrast to the general's optimism was the despair of old-line shipping men. Shrinking passenger loads and depleted revenues mandated compromise, retrenchment, consolidation, or subtropical exile. A North Atlantic Götterdämmerung was frightening: if ocean liners were to vanish completely what would replace them? The early sixties constituted a kind of maritime dead zone—liners at risk, a resurgent cruise industry unformed. No one could have imagined that three decades later giant, white-painted ships would surpass Atlantic liners' tonnage and capacity.

On October 7, 1957, a long steel plate was laid down atop a row of keel blocks lining the center of berth number 1 at St.-Nazaire. *France* would be too long for Panama's locks, the first of many "post-Panamax" vessels that would proliferate near twentieth century's end. (Panamax ships can fit through the Canal; post-Panamax cannot.) Exhibiting more than a hint of de Lessepsian hauteur, de Gaulle made light of the vessel's excess. "*France* is not too big," he proclaimed. "The Panama Canal is too small."

In sum, building *France* was an extraordinary commitment. A quasi-anachronism would be launched into a sea of uncertainty in a gallant attempt to repair an unraveling fabric. Woven with familiar warps of speed and woofs of *luxe*, the French Line hoped to perpetuate a transatlantic *nostalgie* perhaps already outmoded. Government funds would guarantee completion.

And, of course, the Frenchmen's damn-the-torpedoes determination offered one consolation that no one in 1957 could have foreseen: without *France*, *Norway* would never have come into being.

CHAPTER TWO

FOURTH OF THE THOUSAND-FOOT CLUB

If you want to build a ship, don't drum up the men to gather wood,
divide the work and give orders. Instead, teach them to yearn for the vast and endless sea.

Antoine de Saint-Exupéry

Each era in which ships sail and carry passengers is a golden era.

Greg Straub, 2007

Le paquebot de luxe fait place au paquebot fonctionnel.

(*The luxurious ocean liner makes room for the functional ocean liner.*)

Armelle Bouchet Mazas, *Le Paquebot France*

Opposite: It is 24 October 1959. G19's hull rises atop the same wedge-shaped *cale de lancement* from which *Normandie* slid into the Loire. Ganged cranes are lowering the penultimate prow section into place. (**Compagnie Générale Transatlantique**)

The third and final France *was born at Chantiers de l'Atlantique, an historic shipyard at the mouth*

of the Loire River from which all French Line immortals were launched. It is often called Penhoët, the name of the original fishing village now subsumed by a vast shipbuilding enterprise. Reflecting a Norwegian financial infusion, Chantiers de l'Atlantique was first renamed Aker Yard, then became Stxeurope, a Korean entity.

For years before *France*'s keel was laid, the company agonized about what kind of vessel they wished. Although a final decision was reached in 1956, during that interminable gestation dozens of suggestions sought consensus regarding the most efficacious displacement/speed/capacity formula.

One postwar marvel was already on a drawing board in Manhattan. In 1946 Vladimir Yourkevitch, the Russian expatriate who had designed *Normandie*, completed plans for a large ocean liner accommodating four thousand—double the capacity of *Normandie* or *Queen Mary*—at 35 knots. The project, alas, progressed no further.

Meanwhile, Yourkevitch's former French colleagues set to work. In 1946 their first newbuilding memorandum, stamped in red PERSONNEL ET SECRET, was circulated throughout the French Line's Parisian headquarters. Detailed therein were two choices, Vessels A and B. Vessel A—229 meters (751 feet) overall, displacing 36,350 tons—steamed at 24

knots and accommodated 430 in first class, 450 in second, and 410 in third for a total of 1,290. Larger Vessel B displaced 43,300 tons, was 275 meters (902 feet) overall, capable of 30 knots carrying fourteen hundred passengers in prewar's three classes. (A hint to observant handicappers: keep your eye on that filly Vessel B.)

On March 10, 1953, more alphabet soup, all with two classes. Vessel A would replicate rival tonnage on the order of *America, Nieuw Amsterdam, Mauretania II,* and *Caronia,* steaming at 25 knots for six-day crossings carrying fourteen hundred passengers. Vessel B would also be a six-day, 25-knot vessel but accommodated two thousand passengers. Bringing up the rear was Vessel C, capable of 31 knots and five-day crossings. (Seven years later, note that 1946's Vessel B has segued into Vessel C. Keep your eye on C.)

Then Vessel C underwent revision. In January 1954, the "eighth solution" emerged with a new moniker: PR 1066. PR stood for *Paquebot* (ocean liner) *Rapide*. (It is, of course, our old friend Vessel C.) On this list, choices included *Paquebots* B, C, and D only; Paquebot A, the midsized imitative option, had been pipped at the post. *Paquebot* B, 60,000 tons and steaming at 25 knots with 1,725 passengers, was described as "*lent*" (slow) whereas *Paquebot* C, "*rapide*" (fast)—31 knots, 68,000 tons, 1,910 passengers—remained in hot contention. *Paquebot* D, a 24-knot also-ran of 35,000 tons and nine hundred passengers, would be scratched. *Paquebot (Rapide)* C still led the field.

Further tweaks: *Paquebot* C was renamed C *bis* (second C) after undergoing tonnage diminution and increased tourist capacity. Invited to examine the C *bis* proposal, Penhoët weighed in with a preliminary price of 25 million new francs.

On June 16, 1954, the company offered *Paquebots* C and B, now with propellers factored in. *Paquebot* C (C *bis* yet again) boasted a length of 307 meters (1,007 feet); driven by four propellers, she would make five-day crossings at 31 knots carrying 1,910 passengers. Vessel B was less ambitious—288 meters (945 feet) overall and twinscrewed—and would require six days to ferry 1,795 passengers at 25 knots to New York.

Paquebot C, the favorite, was nearing the starting post. Whether original Vessel B, subsequent Vessel C, subsequent *Paquebot* C *bis*, or final

The three prior members of the thousand-foot club were together only once in New York during March 1940. *(From left to right)* Brand-new *Queen Elizabeth* just in from Scotland, *Queen Mary,* a New York prisoner, and *Normandie,* also imprisoned and still in peacetime livery. (Cunard White Star)

Paquebot Rapide 1066, the almost identical blood-lines of emergent *France* are glaringly apparent.

After four years of deliberation, it seems a retrospective no-brainer that the largest and fastest would waltz past the winning post. Hallowed *Normandie* haunted Penhoët's design ateliers and French Line headquarters alike. Her tragically brief career cried out for compensatory resurrection. A large, fast *France* would complete nearly the incomplete, fulfill that broken promise, and make amends for the loss of the company's—nay, the country's—prewar masterpiece. Only a *Normandie réchauffé* would stir the hearts, galvanize the will, and win the endorsement of France's maritime establishment.

The French Line's order was submitted formally to the yard on July 26, 1956. *France*'s three comparable predecessors were *Normandie*, *Queen Mary*, and *Queen Elizabeth*. Classic North Atlantic express liners, all exceeded a thousand feet (304.8 meters). *Normandie* and *Queen Mary* were

at one time the world's fastest and a different pair—*Normandie* and *Queen Elizabeth*—succumbed to fiery ends.

During their latter years, *Queen Mary* and *Queen Elizabeth* were occasionally dispatched to the subtropics, deployment that seemed twilight-of-the-gods desperation. But *France*, fourth of that select sorority, would prove a singular cruising exception, as we shall see. From 1962 until 1974 she thundered between Le Havre and New York, completing two hundred voyages as a traditional express liner only intermittently dispatched on cruises. Post-Panamax excess notwithstanding, two were global circumnavigations.

To build and launch *France*, existing infrastructure spared Chantiers de l'Atlantique years of toil and expense. Her hull would take shape on berth number 1, the same purpose-built wedge atop which *Normandie* had been erected in 1932. Constructed specifically to dispatch history's first thousand-footer into the water, it could now serve

By early April 1960 the hull is painted and primed and superstructure has been added. To the left stands the yard's earliest section gantry, far lower than the prow it was too short to help complete. (Chantiers de l'Atlantique/Cliché Ecomusée de Saint-Nazaire)

the yard's second. Its companion piece, nearby *entrée/forme* (entry/lock) *Forme Joubert*, would permit admission of newly launched *France* from sea level up into the waters of the protected *Bassin de Penhoët* for fitting out.

France's keel was laid on 7 October, 1957. Signaling the start of construction, the ceremony involved lowering a single steel plate onto the keel blocks. It was, as yard draftsman Yann Joncour terms it, a "keel laying on the sly." Since the unions were agitating for a raise and labor relations were prickly, *France*'s keel went down almost surreptitiously.

But if its placement was traditional, ensuing construction capitalized on different techniques. Hull components would be prefabricated. Called sections in English and *blocs* in French, those cubic chunks of ship had their interiors crammed with plumbing, tanks, and wiring more easily installed through accessible open ends rather than shoehorned 'tween decks inside a finished hull.

The practice had started because of World War II's urgent demands, pioneered throughout Henry John Kaiser's complex of American west coast yards. Churned out were fleets of what Kaiser called Liberty ships. Bow sections began life inverted, simplifying their construction for a semi-skilled workforce trained on the job, many female: Rosie the Riveter worked hand in asbestos gloves alongside Wanda the Welder. Conceived as almost expendable, 5,500 Libertys were ultimately delivered from eighteen yards.

In 1944, Kaiser followed Liberty ships with 551 larger and faster Victory ships. All his tonnage was welded and prefabricated. For *Normandie* individual steel fragments were delivered to the hull for attachment, but *France* sections prebuilt elsewhere could be married to the hull on demand, Lego-like components that visibly expanded the nascent vessel.

France's assigned hull number was G19. Hull numbers suffer a curiously evanescent existence. Whereas *Normandie*'s final name choice had been a cliff-hanger, *France*'s was established from the outset. Yet yard personnel always referred to berth number 1's occupant by number rather than name. Immediately after christening, G19 became *France*, number metamorphosing instantly into name. The hull number became outmoded and passé, surviving only as a quaint builder's plate footnote.

To assemble the hull, six whirly cranes, three per side, bracketed the *cale de lancement*; the picturesque French term for their solicitous profiles is *grue giraffoise* (giraffe crane). A new lifting mechanism was constructed to facilitate section attachment. Perched atop four girdered legs tapering down to wheeled trucks, it rode parallel tracks bracketing the launchway, raising, transporting, and then lowering *blocs* in place. In fact, that primitive gantry served only for preliminary construction; near completion, the vessel's bows surpassed its height.

Twenty-seven thousand tons of expensive, high-tensile steel (an acknowledged de Gaulleian extravagance) were delivered to the yard. It was a mixed bag—I-beams, solid or hollow columns, stanchions, and channel steel, the original flat plates folded or pleated for strength. But most arrived as they had emerged from the mill, rolled red hot into flat plates. From the latter, spreads of deck and shell plating would be created. In addition, a great deal had to be shaped. Every vessel's profile element has been fashioned from essentially two-dimensional elements: hull, bulbous bow, intricate superstructure, towering funnel, and mast all began life as flat plates.

That steel accumulation lay in open-air acreage near G19, within reach of whirly cranes. If a piece was needed in the Plate & Angle shop, it was delivered by an expert operating from the elevated cab of a specialized vehicle. Driving atop four long legs and steering wheels individually, he positioned himself over the requested plate, which had been rusting in place for months.

Electromagnets were lowered, betrayed by spiraling electric leads paralleling their lowering cables. Once they touched the topmost plate an activated current glued it to the discs. Then the steel was winched up, ready to travel. The driver departed along shipyard roadways with several tons of steel swaying beneath him.

At the Plate & Angle shop sliding doors were open. The driver entered, positioned his vehicle above a roller-topped table, and, lowering his payload, switched off the electromagnets, slightly *earlier* than necessary. The resultant crash combined deafening rebuke with farewell as the driver winched his magnets up, exited the shed, and jounced back to await his next delivery.

To give that plate a bilge's curve, a plate bender suspended it from chains in order to maneuver it into a powerful machine. He sent it back and forth between three hydraulic rollers—two beneath and one above—that gradually curled one side into the preordained curve his wooden template ordained.

The plate bender's most demanding task is creating a bulbous bow, that rotund knob destined for the base of the stem, like building a giant steel soccer ball from scratch. Paradoxically, that knob projecting in advance of a hull's forefoot ensures smoother passage through the water. It is a measure of every bulbous bow's vulnerability that, when a ship ties up, the bosun suspends a warning red flag from the prow to deter small craft from the semisubmerged protuberance beneath it.

In the old days, plates' overlapping margins were perforated with matching holes to be riveted together. The holes were skewered by a red-hot rivet before its protruding shank was battered

Almost ready for launch in early May 1960, G19's cradle has been built. Its forward-most element, the fore poppet, clutches the hull. The grand-stand is under construction beneath the bow. (Philippe Baudry collection, courtesy Patrick Depelsenaire)

noisily by a riveting gun until it had been shaped into a simulacrum of the rivet's button head. Once cooled and contracted, the plates were drawn tightly together.

But since almost all of G19's plates were welded rather than riveted, their edges were not perforated but trimmed and chamfered (beveled). Once two adjacent plates were positioned flat, a V-shaped ditch separated them; it had to be filled with successive beads of molten weld material heated to 3500 degrees centigrade.

Between the spring-clamped jaws of his electrified holder, the welder clasped a steel rod coated with titanium oxide or rutile. Dozens were used daily; the underfoot crunch of cast-off rutile fragments is symptomatic of weld-rich work throughout all shipyards.

Though large flat plates can be machine welded together, hand welding is necessary in tighter quarters. Clad in a helmet with a protective glass window, steel-toed boots, gloves, and apron, the welder attaches a live electrode to the piece. Once he brings his rutile-covered welding rod close to it, the two power sources produce a hot electric arc and the rod begins to melt. Methodically, the welder tracks the ditch back and forth, "mowing the lawn," laying down consecutive molten beads until the valley is slightly overfilled. A cooled weld is stronger than the steel it unites.

In summer, welding is hot, demanding labor, requiring that the welder crouch intently, assuming the attitude of a graven image. The dome of his helmet is silhouetted by a succession of intensely hot, spasmodic flares, destructive to observers' eyes; unprotected exposure to those green flashes must be avoided.

Some steel plates were cut to produce multiples, replications of specific brackets, stringers, rails, railings, clips specified by the drawings. Contemporary shipyard equipment includes automated, computer-guided cutting heads that, passing over steel, can create infinite numbers of identical shapes. Since that convenience did not exist in the 1960s, G19 duplicates were completed patiently by gloved hands.

Once welders had finished, plumbers and electricians were turned loose, packing the section's interior with preordained conduits, pipes, valves, switchboards, junction boxes, and tanks. Then the piece, elevated on temporary legs, was parked against the moment of its summons to the hull.

On the day, a flat-bedded transporter is steered beneath the raised section and the legs are replaced by extended jacks so that it can be lowered onto the waiting vehicle. Its driver is confined within a claustrophobic pod suspended beneath the deck, similar to a World War II B-17 gunner; short, agile men were invariably recruited. Directing multiple sets of rubber-tired wheels, the operator maneuvered his load to the *cale de lancement* where it can be picked up by the gantry for delivery and attachment to the hull.

Nowadays, at Penhoët, preassembled *blocs* are much larger. For *Queen Mary 2* 's construction in 2002–2003, component size had grown tenfold to 600 tons. And her hull was assembled not on *Normandie*'s vanished wedge but at the bottom of *Forme* B, a nearly kilometer-long dry dock. Building a vessel on a dock floor offers several advantages. First, shorter cranes can be used; second, building on the flat rather than a slope is easier; third, rather than sliding the finished hull into the water, water is brought to the hull.

Called the float-off, followed by a float-out, it can happen anytime, in anonymous silence with neither crowd, band, godmother, champagne, nor, most lamented, drama. Water floods in and, once it has achieved sufficient depth, the hull is suddenly and stealthily afloat.

The following table compares the respective building, fitting out, and trial schedules of *Normandie* and *France*.

	Normandie	France
Keel laid	1/31/31	9/7/57
Launch	10/29/32	5/11/61
Time elapsed	22 months	32 months
Start fitting out	10/30/32	5/12/60
First sea trial	5/5/35	11/19/61
Time elapsed	30 months	18 months
Entire delivery	52 months	50 months

Interestingly, the total time for both was nearly identical. And whereas *France*'s construction consumed almost a year more than *Normandie*'s, conversely, *Normandie*'s fitting out required an additional year. Given that first vessel's challenging debut—worrisome launch unknowns, refinement of her turboelectrics, rethinking decor after fires had ravaged Penhoët tonnage, labor unrest at the yard, and bicameral wrangling in Paris—perhaps it was to be expected. *Normandie*'s fitting out was also delayed by Penhoët's workforce dragging its feet; extending a lucrative contract was and still is, alas, common yard blackmail.

Regardless of the fact that newfangled prefabrication abetted *France*'s construction, traditional launch practice prevailed, albeit for the last time, at Penhoët. High into the air on berth number 1, every graceful contour was revealed, from stylish clipper stem to conventionally rounded counter. Lengthened to 1,035 feet (316 meters) to maintain 30 knots, *France* became the world's longest liner until it was superseded by *Queen Mary 2*'s 1,136 feet (346 meters) in 2004.

Another record: *France*'s launched hull displaced 33,500 tons, heavier than *Normandie*'s and the largest shipyard mass ever moved. For the launch, it was finished with the company's standard livery, black below, white above. A breakwater had been installed below the bridge, two decks' worth of superstructure was in place, and unoccupied davit rows lined the boat deck.

A *mat/radar* (radar/mast) rose immediately behind the bridge. Inside was an interior crow's nest, its ladder of ascent, a *corne de brume* (foghorn), and, higher still, two cantilevered radar platforms. Yardarms extending to port and starboard formed a giant white cross. In fact, that mast exhibited the kind of stylized profile design commonplace aboard today's newbuildings.

However apparently remote the estuary's far shore, G19's rearward surge would be strictly controlled. To that end, suspended from cabin portholes on both sides, tricing lines were rigged in eight looping festoons proceeding aft. They were attached to 150 tons' worth of U-shaped piles of drag chains, with the U's open end facing the water. Lines to the chains were laid out in a pattern of cushioning, whiplash curves across the sand.

Holding the vessel in place were fourteen *clés de retenue* (holding keys), locking devices with arms angled down and engaged within concrete slots. They would be raised and cleared for movement as yet another retention device would be eliminated, a substantial steel arm extending shoreward from the front of G19's cradle and hooked over the *cale de lancement*'s inland edge.

Though unfinished, the wheelhouse was enclosed. Only two consoles were in place, tangled cabling spilling from their pedestals. Neither radar scopes nor propeller indicators were installed and a modest wheel had no function because G19 was

still rudderless. Aft, a steam boiler would activate the trumpet-shaped Typhon whistle protruding from the radar mast.

Though Croisile is credited as the vessel's first master, he was actually the second. For the launch, retired Hervé Le Huédé would be in charge. He had been the first officer to board *Normandie* at

From the water, G19's stern rears above the launchway. Tail-shaft openings have been capped and, silhouetted on the port side, "sky hooks" have been welded onto the stern's upper strakes. (Philippe Baudry collection, courtesy Patrick Depelsenaire)

St.-Nazaire and the last to disembark in New York. After commanding *Liberté* and *Ile-de-France*, he submitted to obligatory Transat retirement in 1951. But nine years later, at age sixty-four, he was summoned to another bridge, brand-new *France*'s. Croisile described himself cheerfully as the *"père anxieux"* (anxious father) while Le Huédé was *"l'accoucheur"* (the obstetrician).

His appointment contravened tradition: shipyard masters normally handled Penhoët launches. But having grown up in the local village of Batz, Le Huédé knew well the estuary's war-torn waters, familiar with the reefs and wrecks littering the bottom, among them the capsized Cunarder *Lancastria*. Other hazards included unexploded bombs and shells; though many had been disarmed, others still lurked. A formidable hazard even at high water was the infamous Basse-Nazaire, a rocky outcrop sited just beyond the launch trajectory, delineated by harbor buoy number 14. Le Huédé's task was to ensure that G19 never reached that far: six tugs, drag chains, and that knowledgeable commandant had to stop the vessel.

On 10 May, launch day minus one, a hundred reporters were given an elaborate launch preview. A model hull was poised atop a miniature *cale de lancement*, surrounded by cranes, the entire set piece mounted on a trestle table. A white line painted across the Loire's "surface" indicated the vessel's path once it entered the water.

Although Le Huédé and Croisile were on hand, it was the engineers who starred. *Chef de lance* (launch chief) was Alfred Lafont, the yard's technical director. On his shoulders rested the dread responsibility of transferring G19 into the water. Her debut represented Lafont's seventy-first Penhoët launch. Two colleagues, naval architect Jean Coune and the engineer in chief Léon Vogelweith, were also in attendance, as were French Line director-general Edmond Lanier and its president Jean Marie.

As he discussed the launch particulars, showman Lafont stood, Gulliver-like, atop the table, his shoes dwarfing miniature tugs awaiting the model's descent. Cued by Lafont, two junior colleagues manhandled the model jerkily down the ways and maneuvered it across the tabletop "estuary." Photographers' flashbulbs dutifully exploded.

The next morning heralded launch day itself. May 11, 1960, was a freighted anniversary, commemorating not only Chantier de l'Atlantique's

Beneath the hull's starboard side, a U-shaped bundle of drag chain has been scrupulously laid out. Unique to the yard, every link has been scaled, painted, and impeccably aligned like guardsmen. A simple wooden retrieval buoy has already been attached to the tricing line. (Chantiers de l'Atlantique/Cliché Ecomusée de Saint-Nazaire)

Launch moment: Madame de Gaulle has snipped the restraining ribbon and the champagne is about to strike the hull. Lower right can be seen the cables for the welders who have already cut the *tôle de retenue*.

(Jean Coune collection)

Opposite: Racketing down the ways, the stern of newly named *France* has already entered the Loire, the drag chains not yet stirring. (Compagnie Générale Transatlantique)

centenary but also the fifteenth year since St.-Nazaire's liberation, the continent's last freed city.

Lafont prowled the *cale de lancement* well before dawn, marshaling his two-hundred-man launch team, almost the same number as the vessel's riding crew. A rigid countdown had begun. High water was scheduled for 4:45 P.M., producing a maximum estuary depth of 5.5 meters (18 feet). But that final thrust of tidal waters always produced an offshore current that would help keep *France* from the shallows. To capitalize on that beneficial assist, H hour had been advanced to exactly 33 minutes prior to the flood, 4:15 sharp.

A ship's christening combines industrial theater with *opera serioso*. An immense monument is suddenly engulfed by high fashion, steel and silk conjoined. For *France*'s debut, the highest echelons of the Gallic establishment had convened. President de Gaulle would be present and his wife, Yvonne, had consented to serve as *marraine* or godmother.

Tickets of admission had been printed in a patriotic blue, white, and red spectrum. By one o'clock, two thousand holders of the most coveted white invitations arrived at the station, disembark-

ing from chartered Parisian trains. A few *prominente* came by airplane while the de Gaulles whirred to earth via helicopter. Once they reached the specially erected grandstand, all faced an arduous climb, toiling up consecutive, interlocking staircase flights decorated with tricolor clusters. At grandstand level, those panting VIPs discovered there were chairs for only five hundred; the remainder would stand.

Shipyard families had been issued red tickets, entitling them to preferential vantage points nearby. Not so hoi polloi thousands who brandished blue tickets. They competed desperately for whatever viewing spots remained, jamming every promontory. Just as for *Normandie*'s launch, nobody ascertained an accurate head count and estimates varied wildly from about one hundred thousand to as high as two hundred thousand.

General and Madame de Gaulle took their places in the front row of the launch platform, surrounded by senior company and shipyard staffs as well as politicians and ministers from Paris. Yvonne de Gaulle wore a checked, blue silk shantung suit and a black straw cloche. Philippe Guitart, a senior launch team hand standing nearby, recalls how genuinely awed and delighted Madame de Gaulle was about everything, brimful of infectious enthusiasm.

Sitting or standing, the privileged and powerful surrounded the de Gaulles, kitted out with uniforms, gloves, hats, veils, and, always, medals. Below them, thousands of lesser mortals clustered within reach of that giant steel diva, jostling closer and craning for a better view. A contagious, fevered enthusiasm ruled the day as, talkative and restless, the crowd waited and watched in the hot spring sun for more than three hours, fretting impatiently yet relishing their presence.

A continual *tonk-tonk-tonk* echoed out of sight beneath the vessel, the noise of mauls driving wedges into the cradle's horizontal seam. Called setting up, G19 was being transferred from its original keel blocks to the support of that cradle beneath the hull. The cumulative introduction of hundreds of wedges did the job, expanding the structure like an activated hydraulic jack. The hull was raised only a centimeter or so but enough to ready G19's entire weight for unobstructed seaward movement.

Aural counterpoint to the rhythmic mauls was the clatter of falling timber. Gangs started toppling the forest of oak shores supporting both sides of G19's hull. Men attached lines to the top of each one while colleagues, manning 100-kilo (220 pounds) battering rams, dislodged the bases. Working in routine tandem, they attacked identically placed shores on either side at the same moment. Once down, long oak trunks were pulled clear and stacked in neat squares, like simulacra frontier forts, seven logs aligned north/south, then another seven positioned east/west atop them, and so on.

Flanking cranes were reversed, clear of the hull, their working jibs outboard; none was adorned with flags as for *Normandie*. But one feature of that 1932 launch, an unanticipated tsunami inundating dozens clustered along water's edge, would not recur. The floodplain to either side of the *cale de lancement* had been buttressed with high banks. But since thousands packed every vantage point, aid workers, ambulance men, and lifeguards of the Société Nationale des Hospitaliers Sauveteurs Bretons were stationed in readiness around every lagoon.

At 3:45, a diversion. Monsignor Villepelet, bishop of Nantes, flanked by acolytes, delivered a sonorous blessing into the platform microphone, only momentarily hushing the crowd. Press planes droned overhead, jockeying for the best aerial angle. Dozens of press photographers and newsreel cameramen stood atop the grandstand roof, lenses poised. The band—L'Orchestre de L'Air—was stationed down on ground level off of G19's port side, instruments ready.

Increments of preparation ensued. By three minutes past four, exactly on schedule, all supporting shores had been felled and G19, successfully set up, rested on her cradle. Oxyacetylene torches at the ready, four welders waited beneath the bow, not to join steel but to sunder it. Promptly at 4:05 they ignited their burners and, working toward the center from each margin, initiated cuts from both sides of the broad steel *tôle de retenue* (retaining steel) connecting cradle with *cale de lancement*. Completion of their cut would release G19's emergency brake. That moment would be preceded by the retraction of the fourteen *clés de retenues*.

At eight minutes past four, Madame de Gaulle was ushered up a staircase leading to a table positioned in the midst of the canvas-lashed platform protruding beneath the bow. To either side stood,

symbolically, builder and owner: René Fould, Penhoët's chief, and Jean Marie, president of the French Line, respectively.

Though *Normandie*'s starboard bow had been christened, the opposite flank served as focus for *France*'s baptism. Adorning every bow is a column of painted numbers ascending from keel to boot topping, the only means by which a floating hull's draft can be accurately assessed. *France*'s was measured in numbered tenths of meters and the integer column was made up of roman numerals because, on wooden hulls, they had traditionally been incised by carpenters' chisels.

"XXX" meters above the keel, a beribboned line was suspended from a welded bracket. Hanging from it was a double jeroboam of Piper-Heidsieck champagne. The blue, white, and red ribbon-wrapped cable on which it was suspended had been arbitrarily pulled out of the vertical and secured by ribbon to the far edge of the platform's table.

At the anticipated point of impact—roman numeral XII—a fail-safe steel spike lay in ambush. Thanks to that secret weapon and also that the bottle had been scored with a glass cutter, breakage was ensured. The dread negative connotation of a bottle that does not fracture haunts every launch: P & O's *Aurora*, christened by Britain's princess royal, and *Queen Victoria*, named by the duchess of Cornwall, are the most recent failures of note. In fact, Piper-Heidsieck's owners were disinclined to let the public see one of their bottles

shatter. Eschewing heaven-sent product placement, the vintner's identity was obscured by more ribbon shrouding the bottle into anonymity.

At ten minutes after four, Lafont's voice was heard over the loudspeaker: "The first part of the maneuver has been completed."

Five minutes remained. The crowd fell silent, so silent that the only noise heard was the persistent fizz/crackle from unseen cutting torches and the buzz of press aircraft overhead.

At exactly 4:12, Lafont's voice brayed over the loudspeakers. "Three minutes to go!"

Only 6 centimeters (2.5 inches) of *tôle de retenue* remained. Up on G19's bridge a sailor held a tricolor and halyard at the ready, to be hoisted the moment her journey began.

With thirty seconds remaining, Lafont's shouted command broke the silence one last time. "*Lachez les verrins!*" (release the jacks). Their deployment served to raise the bow slightly. As the four *béliers* (rams) fell, G19 was poised to move and Madame de Gaulle was alerted by Guitart. He had been issued with a small, battery-operated bell with which he summoned the *marraine* to her post. Then he handed her the ceremonial scissors.

Lafont commanded Madame de Gaulle to snip the ribbon; promptly, she did so. The cut ends of the tricolor fluttered free and the released bottle swung in a short arc toward the sheer of G19's bow, shattered by the concealed spike and anointing the bow with a deluge of champagne. Adhering to French christening protocol, the *marraine* spoke not a word.

After no more than two seconds' immobility, at 4:15 precisely, *France* started—almost grudgingly, it seemed—to move. In fact, motion was initiated by the abrupt, anticipated rupture of the slim steel remnant still holding the hull in place; it was snapped apart by the movement of the rams no less than by the overpowering, downhill yearning of impatient G19.

There is no more dramatic moment of a plunging launch than the spectators' first perception of movement. What had been an apparently fixed structure for so many months was suddenly, electrifyingly, thrillingly in motion. A great cry arose, buttressed by a joyful chorus of ship's whistles offshore and the ponderous opening chords of "La Marseillaise." At the same time as the seaman beneath the yardarm hurried his tricolor aloft, Croisile triumphantly activated his Typhon whistle.

Traveling at 21 miles an hour, maximum launch speed, *France* is almost afloat, her stern plunging into the depths.

(Compagnie Générale Transatlantique)

portside ways before the whiplash curves of lines connecting tricing ropes to drag chains were snatched from their sandy bed, snaking through the air as *France* thundered into her nascent element at maximum speed of 35 kilometers (21 miles) an hour.

As their attached cables tautened, drag chains twitched momentarily before erupting into vengeful life like the furies—rattling, jangling, and sending up clouds of sand and then water as they pursued their fugitive charge into the depths. Suddenly vacated, an empty launchway extended to the water.

It was at that moment that General de Gaulle's voice, echoing over the loudspeaker for the first time, delivered a presidential benison: "Vive le *France*, vive la France!" That pungent couplet was typical de Gaulleian showmanship, always a weakness for the general. Then, momentarily abandoning the microphone, he strode to the platform's seaward margin, posing exultantly with upraised arms in salute as the French Line's last flagship lay offshore, triumphantly afloat. In that commemorative photograph, *marraine* Yvonne de Gaulle is nowhere to be seen.

Never mind; the general's dream ship was not only launched, she was beautiful as well. A paraphrase of de Gaulle's subsequent remarks provides an epic, macho conclusion to the day's spectacle.

Ocean liner *France* has been launched and has married the sea . . . Her mission will be to carry, from one side of the Atlantic to the other, men, that is, their thoughts and activities, their fount of knowledge and their source of work, of art and riches . . . This is how this vessel will achieve her destiny; carrying men towards men!

I am more moved by a subtler, visual addenda, an unnoticed but memorable launch vignette. As the ship raced down the ways, many of her riding crew hung over the forepeak railing, waving giddily to friends below. But one man—presumably naval rather than shipyard—stood braced to attention. He wore a uniform cap and his upraised hand was locked in a presidential salute. The man remained resolutely in place as *France* careened down the ways to her destiny.

To my mind, that isolated and, for the informal sixties, rare gesture, conveying both gravitas and pride, offered a splendid promise: that this particular thousand-footer carrying him steadfastly into the Loire would, in the fullness of time, deliver French Line perfection.

Postlaunch refrain: lone platform occupant President Charles de Gaulle addresses the crowd. (Chantiers de l'Atlantique/Cliché Ecomusée de Saint-Nazaire)

Through the open windows of his Boulevard de Lesseps apartment half a mile away, Monsieur Albert Cam clearly heard that salutary chorus and, knowing exactly what it signified, began to weep. He who had directed *Normandie*'s launch twenty-eight years earlier had now, enfeebled by his eighty-one years, confessed that his health would not permit his attendance; Madame Cam appeared in his stead.

The hull's rate of movement escalated briskly as it approached initial launch speed of 29 kilometers (18 miles) an hour. As though a landbound pterodactyl yearning genetically for flight, *France* surged irresistibly seaward, racketing down the ways, cradle and poppets beneath her cracking and groaning.

The moment her rounded stern thrust into the Loire, she was no longer G19 but legitimately *France*. A trace of friction smoke rose from the

CHAPTER THREE

FRANCE IN STEEL

A ship is the result of a stupendous amount of compromises. . . . Sometimes it is very difficult to make land architects realize that the shifting of an air-trunk by one foot forward or astern will deprive boiler room No. 2 of its required volume of combustion air, or that the moving of a stanchion may have important repercussions on the whole structure of the hull.

Pierre de Malglaive, in a paper before the Royal Society of Arts, 1937

If you are too sophisticated, you lose courage.

Tan Dun

Opposite: *France* returned in mid-July 1961 to Forme Joubert for installation of tail shafts and rudder. Once the rudder was hung, courtesy of chain hoists, then tail shafts would be inserted into the four openings and propellers put in place. (Chantiers de l'Atlantique/Cliché Ecomusée de Saint-Nazaire)

Like bridesmaids at the church door, six attendant tugs, De Guesclin, Hoëdic, Guérande,

Pornichet, Pontaillac, and *St. Gilles,* converged to either side of *France* as she approached the zenith of her launch arc, having traveled 790 meters (2,591 feet) before stopping.

Immediately when the vessel had started moving, Philippe Guitart and his launch team had raced from the grandstand to a waiting tender that buzzed them out to *France*'s bow. Their job was not to assist the move but inspect the numerals indicating the vessel's draft. After studying his chart, Guitart discovered to his horror that less than two meters' clearance existed between *France*'s keel and the bottom.

On receiving that radioed intelligence on the bridge, Le Huédé decided that minimizing maneuvering was imperative. Capitalizing on *France*'s existing heading, he directed her into Forme Joubert sternfirst; towing tugs pushed instead.

First, drag chains were detached, impediments that would hamper the tugs. Since the onboard ends of the tricing lines were already buoyed, they could be dropped overboard. Tugs would salvage the chains for later reuse, but never as drag chains for no more plunging Penhoët launches would delight Nazairians again.

Clustered about their giant charge, four tugs entered the dock too, awaiting the fifteen-minute closure of the sea caisson. Once snugged, the water level rose. *France*'s wooden launch cradle would not be discarded onto the dry dock floor until the vessel's next entry, when it would be weighed down with salvaged drag chains.

Once the water level achieved parity with the Bassin's, the inner caisson was opened. With exquisite care, *France* was ushered from Forme Joubert and maneuvered alongside the projecting doorstep of the Quai d'Armement or fitting-out pier. Then the tug flotilla reentered Forme Joubert for descent to the Loire. Once gangways were rigged the riding crew disembarked. For the next year or more, matters on board would be supervised by interim yardmaster Albert Zanger. The second phase of *France*'s construction was now beginning.

Before heavy-lift cranes grind into action, however, we must pause. There is no better moment, while a vessel is in steel, to evaluate her G.A. (general arrangement). But first, another pause to carp about those words "general arrangement." Although accepted terminology, they convey, alas, an oxymoronic whiff: if "arrangement" implies or-

der, "general" does not. Far better that G.A. be renamed A.A. for "adamantine arrangement." Every cubic centimeter aboard *France,* from boiler room to bridge, from garage to gyrocompass, from wireless room to water pump, adhered to her G.A.'s ruthless demand. And any owner foolhardy enough to try and change things after he has signed off on his G.A. will find it painfully expensive.

The moment the company's latest G.A. was unveiled, it became clear that the French Line had remedied some egregious design misperceptions from the thirties. Then, the company's determination to pull out every decorative stop aboard *Normandie* produced paradoxical results: artistic accolades coupled with financial disappointment. *Normandie*'s ravishing first class was offset by an essentially meager tourist and third, creating a lopsided class imbalance. First class roamed public rooms, staircases, and lobbies like none ever seen before, so overgenerous that tourist class, exiled sternward, was disappointingly accommodated. Third class suffered worse, housed farthest aft in plebeian digs above four vibrating propellers. Small wonder that budget-minded travelers rejected those inferior quarters; it was the neglect of her bourgeois clientele that condemned *Normandie* to perennially unprofitable passenger loads.

To be fair, that injudicious ratio of grandeur to good sense was only partly to blame. No one foresaw the ruinous effect of the Great Depression. Suddenly and catastrophically, battered economies on both sides of the Atlantic curtailed passenger revenues alarmingly, throwing everything into a cocked hat. Despite breathtaking reviews, *Normandie* averaged a distressing 46 percent occupancy rate over her four-year existence. Doubly galling, archrival *Queen Mary,* blessed with superior tourist quarters, attracted the lion's share of the North Atlantic's diminished passenger pool.

Keeping that *Normandie* parable in mind, let us examine contrasting class fiefdoms aboard the company's first major postwar newbuilding. Those expecting *France* to emerge as a retro-*Normandie* were disappointed. She boasted none of thirties-era overscale interiors nor was *ruban bleu* (blue ribband) capability built into her turbines. Though fast, she would never break records. William Francis Gibbs's wonder ship *United States* had prohibitively raised the North Atlantic bar.

Subject to the company's reformed building philosophy, naval architect Jean Coune had arranged *France*'s G.A. for two rather than three classes, encouraging embarkation of hundreds of mass-market tourists. Her G.A. radiated a pragmatic realism, perfectly attuned to postwar demographics.

Compare the respective class numbers aboard the two flagships.

	1935 *Normandie*	1962 *France*
First Class	848	407
Tourist Class	665	1,637
Third Class	458	—
Total	1,971	2,044

Though their capacities were almost identical, note that *France*'s first class was half the size of *Normandie*'s and that *France*'s tourist class welcomed *four times the number accommodated in its first*. What an astonishing sea change from *Normandie*'s fatal, aristocratic hubris!

Save for Bordeaux Deck cabins, the lowest and least desirable, tourist class came up trumps. They enjoyed a sizable foothold on the *Pont Promenade Supérieur*. Amazingly, the forward reaches of that ostensibly first class deck housed tourist class exclusively, complete with two staircase ascents. So,

contravening the *Normandie* prototype, *France*'s G.A. surrounded first class with a dense hegemony housing inferior shipmates.

At the same time, *France* cosseted first class. Its public room dimensions offered spatial promise replicating the company's best. Though welcomed within Formica and tapestry rather than walnut and silk, service, food, and space aboard *France* represented, unequivocally, the North Atlantic's last giddy gasp. *France*'s only competitors were Cunard White Star's two aging *Queens* and the *United States*. Yet whereas all three were approaching the ends of their lives, *France*'s was just beginning.

The layout of her interiors profited from a new design wrinkle. Traditionally, transatlantic's three classes had always been confined within *vertical* hull segments: first amidships, tourist slightly aft and lower, while third was assigned the meanest leftovers. Sacrosanct within their own domains, they were spared slumming from above and hoi polloi intrusion from below.

A simpler two-class stratification emerged three years earlier aboard *Rotterdam*, enabling effortless conversion from segregated crossings to one-class cruising.

Aboard *Rotterdam*, 655 in first class numbered only marginally fewer than the 801 inundating

Just-christened *France* nears the end of her launch run. Lines connected to the drag chains are tautened and fully deployed. (Compagnie Générale Transatlantique)

Directed by Commandant Le Huédé from the bridge, tugs take control of the hull. Philippe Guitart is in the launch directly beneath *France*'s mast.
(Philippe Guitart collection)

case baffles were withdrawn, elevator controls reconfigured, and, *presto-chango*, the vessel commingled all passengers within one, democratic cruising class bound for Bermuda or the Caribbean.

As aboard *Rotterdam* of 1959, so aboard *France* of 1962. Jean Coune adhered to *Rotterdam*'s principle of accommodating each class within a naval architectural sandwich. First class on *Pont Veranda* (Verandah Deck) while, one deck below, tourist on *Pont Promenade*. Once again, the stage was set—no pun intended—forward in *France*'s Salle de Spectacle, or theater. Seating 660 overall, first class occupied the balcony, tourist the orchestra.

Let us track each class's after peregrination when leaving the Salle de Spectacle. As the credits rolled, first class exited the balcony, passing through Verandah Deck's lobby and *grande descente*, or main staircase. Once through the adjoining Grand Salon, first passengers had to choose one of two detours around obstructions.

Unlike *Normandie*, *France*'s uptakes—the chimneys connecting boiler room with funnels—were *not* divided; they were sited traditionally along the keel line. When uptakes are divided—shifted outboard toward either side of the vessel—a rewarding ease of passage obtains, permitting axial flow between public rooms. But when uptakes are not divided circumlocutions must be made around funnel casings.

Hence, divergent pathways confronted the aftbound first class passengers once they reached the number 2 funnel's uptake just behind their Grand Salon. To port, they could stroll through Jean Leleu's library and on through the writing and bridge room. On the starboard side, the path led past the Cabaret de l'Atlantique, a late-night hangout that included a minuscule dance floor, noisy combo, bar, and food counter.

In fact, the space was divided in half by a temporary wall. The forward half was first class, the after tourist. After midnight—the Cinderella syndrome in play—the wall was removed, like *Rotterdam*'s magic staircase baffles. There, at that hour, first and tourist class passengers intermingled, a singular Checkpoint Charlie that dissolved otherwise insurmountable barriers. "The French Line," North American manager Jean-Claude Potier once confided to me tongue-in-cheek, "was under no obligation to protect the livers of her tourist class clientele." Having penetrated the Cabaret de l'Atlantique, it was only a hop, skip,

tourist. Rather than separate them vertically, *Rotterdam*'s classes were spread *horizontally*. Spread was *le mot juste*: two adjacent decks emerged as a class sandwich, each assigned its own deck. Segregation was established forward in the ship's theater: first occupied the balcony, tourist the orchestra.

Maintaining class segregation en route from cabin to dining room and back, though, was more challenging. The answer was an ingenious staircase enabling passengers to ascend and descend without rubbing the wrong elbows or straying into alien territory. It replicated some famous fifteenth-century stairs in Chambord, the Loire valley Renaissance château. Designed for François Premier, palace levels were connected by twin, interlocking circular staircases, like intertwined but independent corkscrews, so the monarch could travel from floor to floor unobserved by his courtiers.

Rotterdam's main staircase duplicated the feat, albeit in scissors rather than circular configuration. On certain landings, sliding baffles were deployed, cutting off inappropriate deck levels and delivering each class, uncontaminated, to its correct destination. Similarly, six elevators bracketing *Rotterdam*'s staircase were restricted: numbers 1, 2, and 3 welcomed first while 4, 5, and 6 catered to tourist.

The beauty part was that *Rotterdam*'s class separation could be abrogated instantly. The moment she finished a two-class crossing to Hoboken, stair-

and lurch for those alien but black-tied intruders to exit the nightclub and roam throughout first class.

Another nearby crossover was necessary because, curious aberration, only one shop served the entire ship. Initially run by Paris's Printemps department store, it was later switched to Galeries Lafayette. Also divided into two sections, its after portion included a general *magasin* for shipboard sundries while upscale clothing and jewelry were offered forward. When first class passengers wanted to go shopping, they descended a glass staircase that carried them down one flight from the Cabaret de l'Atlantique and into the shop.

Final indoor first class destination along Upper Verandah Deck was the Fumoir, or smoking room. An impressive, double-height space, it was larger than the Grand Salon forward. The reason for the disparity was that promenades to either side had been wrought into smoking room adjuncts, port and starboard *terrasses*.

Earlier, I characterized the Fumoir as first class's aftermost indoor space. But not completely indoors: its after part extended outdoors toward the stern. Here, one exited through yet a third *terrasse*—athwart ship—a protected seating area partly shaded (and sheltered) by the Boat Deck's overhang above, sometimes referred to, mystifyingly, by crewmen as *la plage* (the beach).

On the tourist class spread one deck below, placement of its two largest public rooms was different from the position of first's. Whereas the Grand Salon *preceded* first's Fumoir, the very reverse characterized tourist class's arrangement. Walking aft, tourist class passengers passed through their smoking room *before* achieving their salon.

The switch was necessary because of larger passenger numbers. Maximizing the Grand Salon's capacity was critical. Whereas tourist's smoking room could fit between flanking promenades, its Grand Salon could not. It had to accommodate half—one eight-hundred-passenger sitting—of tourist's sixteen hundred clients. Occupying the full width of the vessel, it was blessed with generous fenestration.

The two rooms—tourist class's Grand Salon and first class's Fumoir one deck higher—were, in a sense, nested together: directly above tourist's dance floor was a raised ceiling cove, not a dome but a substantial, rectangular cavity that intruded vertically up into first class's smoking room floor.

After exploring their novel sandwich, *France*'s first class passengers would find that naval architect Coune had omitted three perquisites offered aboard *Normandie*. First, uptakes were *not* divided. Second, *France* boasted no forward-facing public room comparable to *Normandie*'s Winter Garden. Coune was well aware that the company's 1935 innovation often remained unoccupied because of severe pitching; moreover, after dark, it had to be shuttered to protect the night vision of bridge personnel above. As a result, no Winter Garden graced *France*. Indeed, no first class passenger was rewarded with any forward outlook at all but, oddly, a few—very few—in tourist class were.

The redoubtable steel bulkhead protecting the front of every deckhouse is called the bridge screen, usually wrought with a convex bulge for additional strength. Three decks' worth of windows penetrated *France*'s. Highest was the expanse of glass spanning the bridge; directly beneath that were horizontal windows illuminating senior officers' cabins; a third cluster of forward-facing openings was in tourist country down on Verandah Deck: four pairs of cabin windows had been cut through that otherwise impenetrable facade, offering splendid bow views. In fact, my family and I occupied the portside pair on our first *France* cruise over Christmas of 1968.

France's first entry into Forme Joubert.
(Chantiers de l'Atlantique/Cliché Ecomusée de Saint-Nazaire)

Coune's third and most significant change? There was no extra-tariff restaurant, no replica of *Normandie*'s Café-Grill overlooking the stern. First class passengers could never forsake the dining room to eat elsewhere. No alternative existed. This offered Jean Coune a splendid bonus: no space had to be set aside for either a supplementary restaurant or its galley.

The omission underscored the company's draconian resolve. The decision had been taken to offer unparalleled meals for every first class passenger. Remember, *France* embarked only 407, fewer than half *Normandie*'s 848; accommodated at one sitting, it was a manageable number to whom the chef himself could cater.

One drawback of indulging a well-heeled minority with superior fare is the perception of a hyper–first class. When Royal Viking's first extra-tariff facility—the Palm—was unveiled aboard *Royal Viking Sun*, one passenger demanded of founder/owner Warren Titus: "If your regular meals are supposed to be tops, then how come if we pay they get better?"

Aboard today's cruising fleets, multiple alternative dining rooms are commonplace. But back in the 1960s only the biggest liners offered one. Both *Queens* and the *United States* did but *France* did not. By eschewing it, the company set itself ingeniously apart. Unspoken but implicit was the perception that first class passage aboard *France* guaranteed incomparable cuisine.

In 1892, at the height of New York's gilded age, social arbiter Ward McAllister had compiled a list of what he considered the city's Four Hundred, its blue bloods, a number based on how many could comfortably be accommodated within Mrs. William Astor's ballroom. Exactly seventy years later *France* would inaugurate a transatlantic gilded age, embarking a fortunate Four Hundred (plus) to enjoy the same, selective distinction.

However *haute* the cuisine, galley and the dining rooms bracketing it were located as low in the vessel as possible. This was symptomatic of dining room placement aboard all transatlantic liners and the French Line in particular: *la grande descente* always terminated in the dining room. Aboard *France*, the only opportunity to proceed lower was to swim in D Deck's pool, down two flights of a claustrophobic staircase or pushing the lowest button on the portside elevator.

France's dining room, in steel, seemed a pallid replication of multistory grandeur, boasting neither the height nor the length of *Normandie*'s. To use a sports comparative that has become, alas, America's metaphorical crutch, the room's shape was more basketball court than football field. It was 78¾ feet (24 meters) long, fore and aft, and nearly 102 feet (31 meters) wide. Within those 744 square meters (893 square yards) were arranged sufficiently separated tables to seat 376 passengers; thanks to what the chief steward called "careful extensions," the entire first class complement of 407 could be accommodated at one sitting.

The room was as devoid of portholes as *Normandie*'s. Achieving daylight within *Normandie*'s Salle à Manger had been impossible because the room was insulated from the sea by first class cabins. But it would have been a cinch to cut portholes through *France*'s hull because the room extended to the shell plating.

It has never been clear why this was not done, although two blithe explanations were circulated. First, that air-conditioning rendered portholes redundant and, second, that passengers should be spared reminders of the threatening Atlantic. Spurious on both counts: dining room portholes were seldom opened at sea and, even during winter crossings, mid-Atlantic sun does shine. Even after *France* became *Norway* in 1980, opaque dining room walls in both classes remained stubbornly in place.

Elsewhere, things were different. Three small dining rooms were sited off the main one, a children's dining room to port and two Salles à Manger *particulières* to port and starboard. Their ten occupants, seated around an oval table, enjoyed no gastronomic advantage, merely the privilege of eating apart from their fellows while ordering from the same menu. The only bonus was porthole contemplation of the sea.

Two architectural features enriched *France*'s first class Salle à Manger. The first was an aluminum, navy blue dome rising 18 feet, 4 inches (5.6 meters) at its apogee above the floor, its diameter 54.5 feet (16.6 meters). Christened *la grande coupole* (the big cupola), it occupied the center of the room's rectangle, leaving numbers of surrounding tables beneath conventionally low ceilings. Although its surface was perforated with sound-absorbent openings, it remained acoustically lively; tables beneath it suffered intrusive echo and reverberation.

The other architectural feature appeared at the center of the room's after end, final elegant flourish

Opposite: The vessel reenters Joubert to have her cradle removed. (Chantiers de l'Atlantique/Cliché Ecomusée de Saint-Nazaire)

of *la grande descente*. It was made up of two broadening halves, in plan a trumpet shape nineteen steps high. The highest ten were separated from the bottom nine by athwart-ship glass doors. Once through them, in the dining room proper but not quite immersed, entering passengers stood on a landing. Their remaining descent was ceremonially reshaped by deeper, wider treads—a fantail leading the languid way to table.

France's debouching staircase was even more intimidating than *Normandie*'s. On the earlier vessel, the entry occupied one end of a long room; few saw latecoming passengers. But thanks to *France*'s rectangular configuration the stairs centered a long side and the entire room could scrutinize late arrivals.

That daunting slope would see its most telling use on gala evenings when, after every table was filled, the commandant, some senior officers, and the vessel's most prestigious passengers descended, bound for the captain's table along the forward wall. Intimidating for the nervous, perhaps, but for those inured to or rejoicing in public show a heaven-sent opportunity. Salvador Dalí, perennial *France* passenger, always made a late entrance for that very reason, sometimes leading his pet ocelot Babou.

If one were permitted (though passengers never were) to make a U-turn at the bottom of that staircase, one entered the galley through revolving doors. Proceeding aft, one then entered tourist class's dining room through another set of rotating doors. Because it had to accommodate exactly twice as many passengers for consecutive sittings, the room had more densely packed tables on two decks. Rather than a decorative dome, a surrounding balcony filled the space above. Accommodated around its rim were 196 passengers while, below, tables for 604 were provided.

Because of its two levels, separate entryways were required. Passengers could enter either from A Deck's after staircase or, for the balcony, through a supplementary entrance up a flight on Main Deck. The two levels were united only visually; no ceremonial staircase connected the two, although one of designer Marc Simon's renderings once suggested that possibility. No portholes illumined either level. Along the upper starboard side was a larger children's dining room and lining the balcony level to port were cabins.

Coincidental with *France*'s interior fitting out was installation of four propellers and a rudder, essential navigational components beneath the stern. A quartet of four-bladed propellers had been delivered to the yard for installation on 9 July, 1961.

It was a summer weekend of violent wind gusts out of the north and northwest. St.-Nazaire is famous for those phenomena, called locally *bourrasques*. Because of the wind, a five-tug escort was decreed for the move from fitting-out pier into Forme Joubert, where *France* had only once ventured since launch day over a year earlier.

The move took place on a July Saturday, a day off for countless Nazairians who, together with hordes of summer visitors, thronged both margins of Forme Joubert to admire, applaud, and photograph the new flagship's second outing. Shepherded within, *France* was moored carefully above cement keel blocks. Only then could the dock be drained, allowing the hull to settle in exactly the right position.

The following Monday, once the yard's routine workweek resumed, rudder and tail shafts were installed. The difficulties of both tasks were compounded because of the vessel's overhanging counter. Cranes could do no more than deposit heavy components outside that overhang. The rest of the job relied on rabbit ears, skyhooks, in effect, welded onto the underside of *France*'s counter. Old-fashioned muscle power, teams of riggers sweating at chain hoists and block-and-tackle, implemented the lifts.

First, it was the turn of the rudder, a balanced one of large area. All rudders float but, surprisingly, *France*'s was hung without the buoyant assist of water in the dry dock; brute force and chain hoists completed the job.

With rudder in place, the four tail shafts were suspended, one by one, from shackles hung on rabbit ears aligned in the precise, directional configuration of the shaft tunnels. Those tail shafts, final appendages of already installed shafts, were inserted like probes into the open ends of the four shaft tunnels. Only after each was inside and secured could propellers be mounted onto their after ends.

Just like *Normandie*, *France* suffered initial propeller problems, not vibration but cavitation, cumulative pitting and degradation of the blades' bronze surface. Jean Coune told me that the trouble originated, oddly enough, at the forward end of the vessel. During turns, *France*'s bulbous bow created a vacuum vortex that, traveling the length of the hull, impinged on the propeller blades.

Opposite: Lashed aboard a transporter, one of *France*'s eight boilers en route to the hull. Described as D-shaped, each was 30 feet (9 meters) tall. (Chantiers de l'Atlantique/Cliché Ecomusée de Saint-Nazaire)

Cast during the vessel's first summer of operations, five-bladed propellers replaced the four-bladed originals and cavitation was reduced if not entirely eliminated.

Fire safety and flammable precautions were high among *France*'s fitting-out priorities. There was no wood anywhere. A million and a quarter square feet (135,000 square meters) of fireproof Marinite insulated countless surfaces. Cabin furnishings were steel—beds, bureaus, dressing table, lamps, and furniture. No cork was employed save for passenger life jackets. Granular cork did not insulate bulkheads nor were cork sheets used for carpet padding. Instead, a double layer of cement and neoprene eliminated what the company described as "living-in noise." The hull was divided into eight fire zones and hundreds of fire prevention devices—365 hydrants and 470 extinguishers—were positioned throughout.

Although both *Normandie* and *France* produced 160,000 horsepower, in terms of engineering capability their power plants were different. *Normandie*'s turboelectric drive had represented, for Penhoët engineers, a bold departure, thirty-three boilers producing sufficient clout to rotate her alternators. *France* had eight larger, high-pressure boilers, producing steam for four sets of double-reduction geared CEM Parsons turbines. This was the familiar engineering standby that had driven prior flagships *France*, *Paris*, and *Ile-de-France*.

Whereas *Normandie*'s thirty-three boilers had filled four boiler rooms, *France*'s eight water tube boilers needed only two. Different from *Normandie*'s, they were described informally as "D-shaped" because their configuration of drums and headers rose in the form of a capital letter D. All were fabricated in Penhoët's Ateliers des Chaudières (boiler shops), enormously tall and rising 30 feet (9 meters) from base to top. Each boiler quartet occupied its own room, number 1 forward and number 2 aft. Number 1 delivered steam to the adjacent turbine room that, via immensely long, 215-foot (65.5 meters) shafts, turned two outboard propellers, while number 2, with shorter shafts, rotated the inboard pair. Because of their remarkable height, the boilers rose through three decks, from E up to and including C. The two lowest—D and E—were engine spaces; C Deck, the topmost, lay between rows of crew cabins.

Only after boilers, condensers, auxiliary alternators, and gear components had been lowered

Funnel number 2 is already complete and the wings for number 1 are in the process of being mounted atop the forward shaft. (Chantiers de l'Atlantique/Cliché Ecomusée de Saint-Nazaire)

45

In mid-July 1961, *France* returned a second time to Forme Joubert for installation of tail shafts and rudder. (Chantiers de l'Atlantique/Cliché Ecomusée de Saint-Nazaire)

Opposite: The only disappointment for crowds inspecting the finished profile were paint scaffolds surrounding her funnels. (Chantiers de l'Atlantique/Cliché Ecomusée de Saint-Nazaire)

could the funnel casings be closed, permitting erection of *France*'s smokestacks. Of all her profile elements, they were the most startling.

Selecting eye-catching funnels has always been a shipowner's prerogative. They are the first elements at sea to appear over the horizon; similarly, in port, a moored vessel's funnels tower over pier sheds. Small wonder that company livery—executed, like jockeys' silks, in bold, primary colors—always adorns every funnel's rotund skin.

Imperator's funnel trio of 1913 were so tall that they were shortened to improve stability; conversely, squat twin funnels aboard 1929's *Bremen* and *Europa* were heightened to loft smoke more efficiently. *Georges Philippar*'s twin white stacks of 1932 were square while *Caronia*'s solitary funnel of 1949 was larger than any aboard either *Queen*. But whether tall, short, square, or massive, all adhered to a classic, paint-pot prototype, their twofold purpose to identify the owning company and to disperse smoke and smuts.

Vessels steam within a unique aerodynamic envelope revealed by wind-tunnel testing. Smoke generators attached to a model's forward elements produce contrail paths delineating that envelope to perfection. Like an apparition from a séance, the superstructure is engulfed within an ectoplasmic shroud. Successful funnels must pierce that shroud, releasing stack gases above and outside it. Funnels that are too short or ineffectually designed retain floating detritus that fouls decks and pools.

Every nautical mile *France*'s furnaces consumed a ton of fuel so, predictably, her pollution dice were loaded. Steam turbines are prime offenders, worse than diesels, producing the most soot-rich smoke. *France*'s stack gases not only smelled unpleasant, they also carried soot aloft.

Two preventatives were devised, one unseen, the other blatantly on show. The first were a couple of cylindrical scrubbers concealed within each funnel's shaft, tall stainless steel aerodynamic centrifuges that should have extracted particulate matter from gases roaring up from below.

The second and very visible fail-safe emerged following two years of testing, starting in 1958 by a professor named Gabriel Valensi, head of the aerodynamic laboratory at the Centre-West Research Institute in Poitiers. Aware that even

The single winged funnel aboard Carnival's *Fantasy*. Farcus's design refinement includes a forward intake vent to help boost smoke up and out through both wings. (Author's collection)

Opposite, top: The first class smoking room, at the after-end of Verandah Deck, surrounded by three terraces. Proceeding to the right, the card room and library lie along the port side with the Cabaret de l'Atlantique to starboard. Next, the first class Grand Salon and, farther to the right, the balcony of the Salle de Spectacle. Beyond the auditorium and stage area is the chapel.

Opposite, bottom left: Down on Main Deck is the entrance lobby, surrounded by purser's desk, baggage master, telephones, and safe deposit boxes. The staircase descent leads down to the first class dining room on A Deck.

Opposite, bottom center: The floor of the dining room.

Opposite, bottom right: The first class pool down on D Deck.

scrubbed smoke could still be sooty, a fiftieth scale model of *France* 20 feet (6 meters) long was placed in the institute's wind tunnel, which was wide enough to permit a 45-degree diversion to either side. As generated smoke emerged from both funnels, miniature *France* was bombarded with simulacra ocean winds.

Years of meteorological records kept by watch officers indicated that east/west vessels invariably encountered north/south crosswinds. Whenever that athwart-ship assault impacted on paint-pot funnels, smoke was roiled indiscriminately over their leeward margin. Professor Valensi sought to redesign a stack that would dispel fumes abeam.

France's earliest funnel renderings were two unadorned, conical shafts. But after the company embraced Valensi's recommendations in December 1959, their design was amended, described as *cheminées avec ailerons* (funnels with wings). Never mind their mixed performance; their appearance created a sensation. Whereas *Rotterdam* had sported factory-like chimneys and *Queen Elizabeth 2* had a solo vertical pipe, *France*'s pair towered over the new flagship like no others seen before or since, save for one continuing exception.

Aboard Carnival Cruise tonnage, signature funnels are similar, enriched with a forward vent and wings flaring defiantly skyward. Carnival's resident designer Joe Farcus once told me that he had sketched the prototype on the back of an envelope. It was unveiled aboard Joe's first newbuilding, *Tropicale*, of 1982, twenty years after *France*'s debut.

In simplest terms, *France*'s funnels accomplished an elemental penmanship task: crossing two giant T's. Yet however simple the concept, how complex the resulting edifice. Assembling three sculpted elements into a five-story, aluminum-alloy structure necessitated history's most demanding funnel structure.

The after one—number 2—was installed first, a process that took twelve days. Its lowest element was a tapered cylinder of 24 tons and 40 feet (12 meters) high. Its ovoid base, measuring 46 by 21 feet (14 by 6.5 meters), was lowered by crane atop a white, also ovoid, plinth on Sun Deck. The cone's top horizontal plane was not flat but sculpted, the front end lower than the back so that it swept aft and upward with a jaunty flair. But that design fillip was not aesthetic; it was an engineering necessity, creating a secure resting place for the next funnel element, those celebrated wings.

Port and starboard wings were conjoined into one unwieldy unit spanning 62 feet (19 meters) and weighing 35 tons. Such was their awkward bulk that they could not even be delivered to the hull until the working day was over. Lashed aboard a transporter, the wings were inched along, their relatively short journey consuming two hours as potential obstructions were laboriously cleared from both sides.

Early in the still morning of 31 May, 1961, those first wings were hoisted aboard by a 180-ton crane. Lowered into place, the aerofoil configuration of the wings' underside married neatly with the shaft's curvilinear top; the gracefully shaped joint separating them essentially disappeared.

The third and final attachment was the also conical *capuchon*, or cap. Though some shipyard records described it as the roof, one wag compared it to black leather helmets worn by Spain's Guardia Civil. Funnel-top-as-hat comparisons are irresistible: long after the time when French Line clients had eschewed homburgs, two of them appeared to have been perched atop *France*.

Even painted they jarred. The shafts rejoiced in French Line red, primary cherry purposely dulled with what company aficionados called a "coal-smoke overlay." And since French Line livery mandated black funnel tops, wings and hats followed suit. No attempt was made to capitalize on the graceful joint where wings married shaft. Acknowledging that pleasing arabesque might have lightened the funnels' appearance, instead the final red/black demarcation remained stolidly and somehow unsatisfactorily horizontal.

Curiously, the wings' stance and angle were difficult to assess because their appearance depended on one's vantage point. From directly abeam they disappeared, revealed only by their shadow; from ahead or abaft, the wings seemed to have slightly different thicknesses or stick out in disparate directions.

Enough aesthetic nitpicking; did they work? I think not, having several times suffered an annoying 4-F: France Funnel Failure Firsthand. The *terrasse* aft of the smoking room was furnished with chairs whose seats and backs were upholstered in black leather, a presciently apropos choice. If one sat wearing white trousers, one found smuts adorning one's backside; soot particles that had rained invisibly onto the leather were only too clearly visible on light-colored clothing.

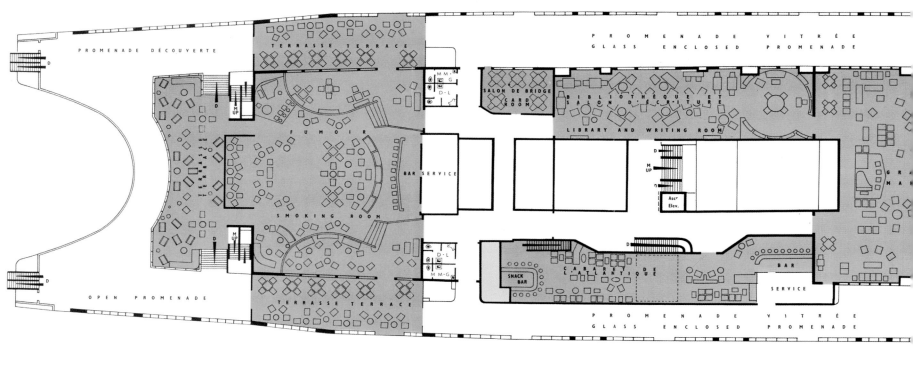

PROMENADE DÉCOUVERTE

TERRASSE TERRACE

PROMENADE VITRÉE
GLASS ENCLOSED PROMENADE

FUMOIR

SALON DE BRIDGE
CARD ROOM

BIBLIOTHÈQUE ET SALON D'ÉCRITURE
LIBRARY AND WRITING ROOM

BAR SERVICE

Ascr Elev.

SMOKING ROOM

SNACK BAR

CABARET DE L'ATLANTIQUE

BAR

SERVICE

OPEN PROMENADE

TERRASSE TERRACE

PROMENADE VITRÉE
GLASS ENCLOSED PROMENADE

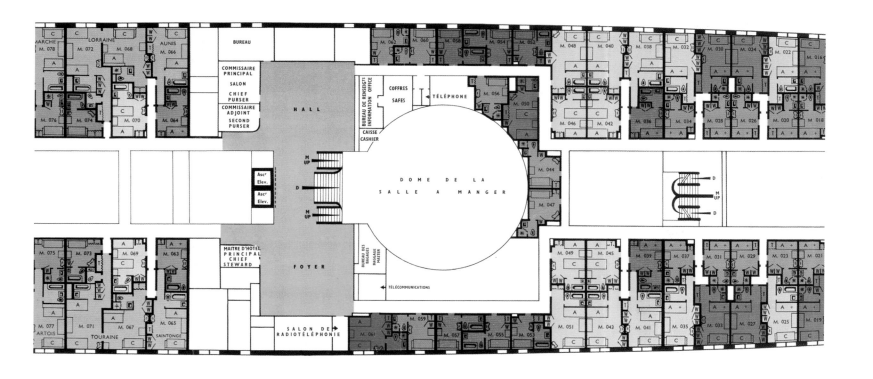

MARCHE
M. 078

LORRAINE
M. 072

M. 068

AUNIS
M. 066

BUREAU

M. 062 M. 060 M. 058 M. 054 M. 052

M. 048 M. 040 M. 038 M. 032 M. 030 M. 024 M. 022 M. 016

M. 076 M. 074 M. 070 M. 064

COMMISSAIRE PRINCIPAL SALON
CHIEF PURSER
COMMISSAIRE ADJOINT
SECOND PURSER

HALL

BUREAU DE RENSEIGTS
INFORMATION OFFICE

COFFRES
SAFES

TÉLÉPHONE

M. 056

M. 046 M. 042

M. 050

M. 036 M. 034 M. 028 M. 026 M. 020 M. 018

CAISSE
CASHIER

Ascr Elev.
Ascr Elev.

M. 044

DOME DE LA
SALLE A MANGER

M. 047

M. 075 M. 073 M. 069 M. 063

MAITRE D'HOTEL PRINCIPAL
CHIEF STEWARD

FOYER

BUREAU DES BAGAGES
BAGGAGE MASTER

M. 049 M. 045 M. 039 M. 037 M. 031 M. 029 M. 023 M. 021

TÉLÉCOMMUNICATIONS

M. 077 M. 071 M. 067 M. 065

ARTOIS TOURAINE SAINTONGE

SALON DE
RADIOTÉLÉPHONIE

M. 061

M. 059

M. 057 M. 055 M. 053

M. 051 M. 043 M. 041 M. 035 M. 023 M. 027 M. 025 M. 019

SALLE A
DES EN

CHI
DININ

D-L

Ascr Elev.
Ascr Elev.

A *France* cutaway, painted by Pierre Parreton and Michel Lezla in 1961

Decks	First Class Public Rooms	Tourist Class Public Rooms
1–22. Navigational Areas	23. Squash racquets court	71. Children's playroom
23–29. Observation Deck	54. Smoking room's after terrace	80–81. Grand Salon (later Salon St. Tropez)
30–47. Sun Deck	55. Smoking room (later Salon Riviera)	84. Smoking Room (later La Rive Gauche)
48–52. Boat Deck	64. Grand Salon (later Salon Fontainebeau)	86. Orchestra floor of Salle de Spectacle
53–74. Verandah Deck	68. Salle de Spectacle balcony	100. Swimming pool
75–97. Promenade Deck	69. Chapel	140. Dining room
98–119. Upper Deck	148. Dining Room (later Restaurant Chambord)	
120–37. Main Deck	173. Indoor pool	
138–50. A Deck		
151–59. B Deck		
160–65. C Deck		
166–76. D Deck		
177–84. E Deck		
185–86. F Deck		
187–232. Mechanical Areas		

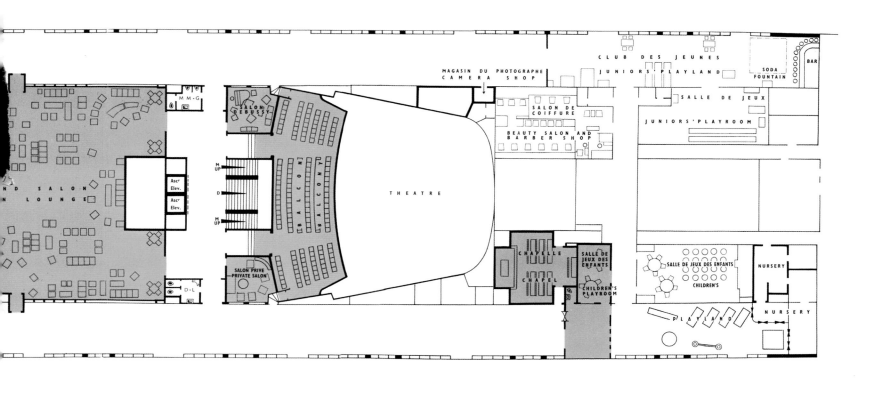

MAGASIN DU PHOTOGRAPHE
CAMERA SHOP

CLUB DES JEUNES
JUNIORS' PLAYLAND

SODA
FOUNTAIN

BAR

SALON DE
COIFFURE

SALLE DE JEUX

BEAUTY SALON AND
BARBER SHOP

JUNIORS' PLAYROOM

MM·G

SALON
DEBUSSY

BALCON
BALCONY

THEATRE

CHAPELLE

CHAPEL

SALLE DE
JEUX DES
ENFANTS

ND SALON
N LOUNGE

Asc'
Elev.

Asc'
Elev.

M
UP

D

M
UP

M
UP

D·L

SALON PRIVE
PRIVATE SALON

SALLE DE JEUX DES ENFANTS

CHILDREN'S

NURSERY

CHILDREN'S
PLAYROOM

NURSERY

PLAYLAND

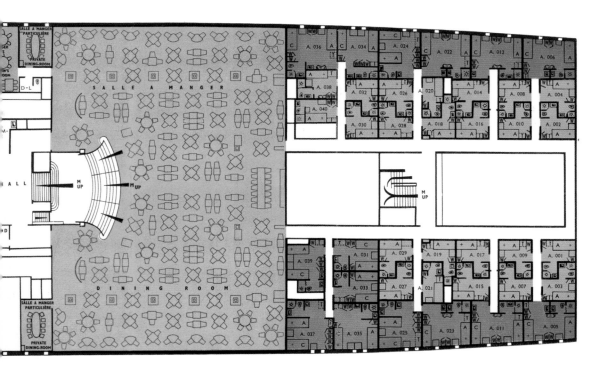

SALLE A MANGER
PARTICULIÈRE

PRIVATE
DINING-ROOM

SALLE A MANGER

SALLE A MANGER

DINING ROOM

PRIVATE
DINING-ROOM

SALLE A MANGER
PARTICULIÈRE

D·L

HALL

M
UP

M
UP

M
UP

A. 036

A. 034

A. 024

A. 022

A. 012

A. 006

A. 038

A. 032

A. 026

A. 020

A. 014

A. 008

A. 004

A. 040

A. 030

A. 028

A. 018

A. 016

A. 010

A. 002

A. 039

A. 031

A. 029

A. 019

A. 017

A. 009

A. 001

A. 033

A. 027

A. 021

A. 015

A. 007

A. 003

A. 037

A. 035

A. 025

A. 023

A. 011

A. 005

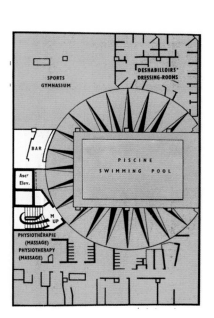

SPORTS
GYMNASIUM

DESHABILLOIRS
DRESSING-ROOMS

BAR

Asc'
Elev.

M
UP

PISCINE

SWIMMING POOL

PHYSIOTHÉRAPIE
(MASSAGE)
PHYSIOTHERAPY
(MASSAGE)

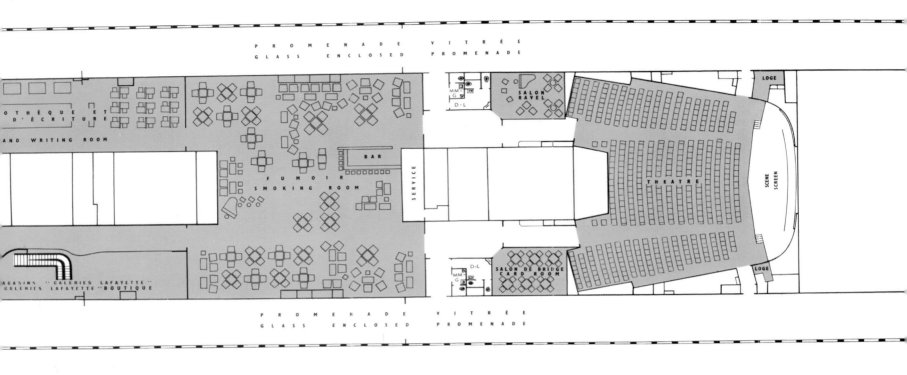

PROMENADE VITRÉE
GLASS ENCLOSED PROMENADE

LOGE

MM
G
D-L

SALON
RAVEL

OTHÈQUE ET
D'ÉCRITURE

AND WRITING ROOM

BAR

SERVICE

THEATRE

SCENE
SCREEN

FUMOIR
SMOKING ROOM

D-L
MM
G

SALON DE BRIDGE
CARD ROOM

LOGE

AGASINS "GALERIES LAFAYETTE"
GALERIES LAFAYETTE "BOUTIQUE

PROMENADE VITRÉE
GLASS ENCLOSED PROMENADE

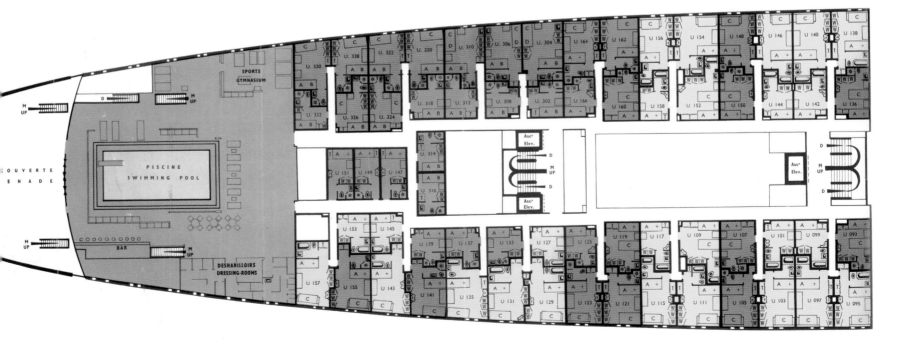

SPORTS
GYMNASIUM

D
M UP

M
UP

U 330   U 328   U 322   U 320   U 310   U 306   U 304   U 164   U 162   U 156   U 154   U 148   U 146   U 140   U 138

U 332   U 326   U 324   U 318   U 312   U 308   U 302   U 166   U 160   U 158   U 152   U 150   U 144   U 142   U 136

COUVERTE
ENADE

PISCINE
SWIMMING POOL

U 314

Asc'
Elev.

D
M
UP
D

Asc'
Elev.

U 151   U 149   U 147

U 316

M
UP

BAR

U 153   U 145

Asc'
Elev.

U 139   U 137   U 133   U 127   U 125   U 119   U 117   U 109   U 107   U 101   U 099   U 093

DESHABILLOIRS
DRESSING-ROOMS

U 157   U 155   U 143   U 141   U 135   U 131   U 129   U 123   U 121   U 115   U 111   U 105   U 103   U 097   U 095

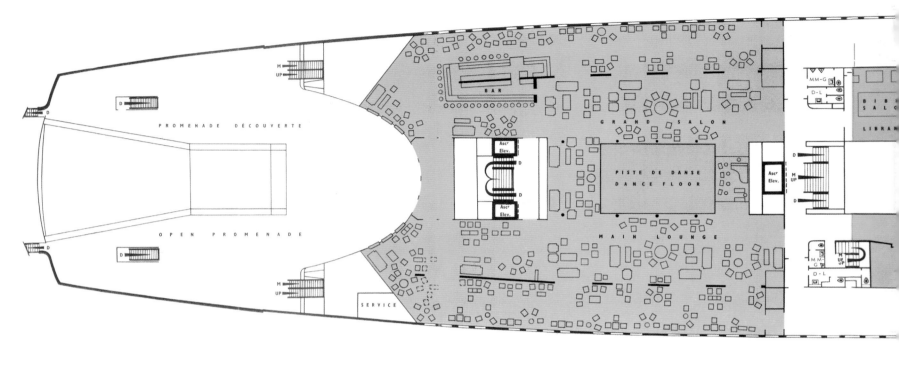

PROMENADE DÉCOUVERTE

OPEN PROMENADE

M
UP

M
UP

D

D

D

D

SERVICE

BAR

GRAND SALON

Ascr
Elev.

D

D

Ascr
Elev.

PISTE DE DANSE
DANCE FLOOR

MAIN LOUNGE

Ascr
Elev.

MM-G
D-L

BIB
SALO

LIBRAR

D

M
UP

D

MM-G

M
UP

D-L

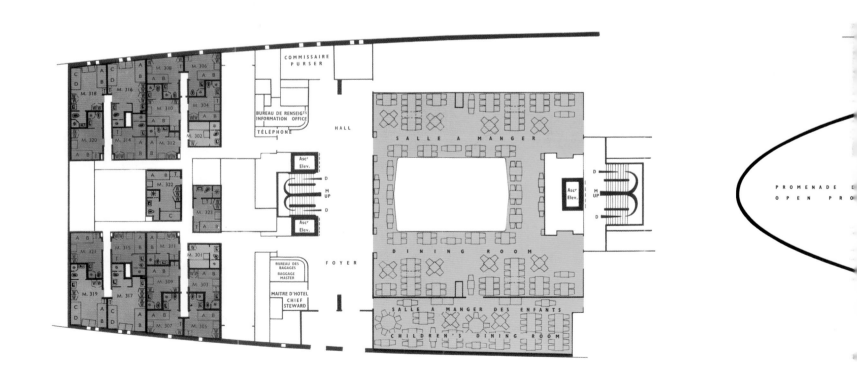

COMMISSAIRE
PURSER

M. 308   M. 306

C   A

D   B

M. 318   M. 316

W   M. 304

M. 310

B

BUREAU DE RENSEIG^ts
INFORMATION OFFICE

HALL

TÉLÉPHONE

M. 320   M. 314   M. 312   M. 302

M. 322

M. 323

Ascr
Elev.

D

M
UP

D

Ascr
Elev.

SALLE A MANGER

Ascr
Elev.

D

M
UP

D

FOYER

M. 321   M. 315   M. 311   M. 301

BUREAU DES
BAGAGES
BAGGAGE
MASTER

M. 319   M. 317   M. 309   M. 303

MAITRE D'HOTEL
CHIEF
STEWARD

M. 307   M. 305

DINING ROOM

SALLE A MANGER DES ENFANTS

CHILDREN'S DINING ROOM

PROMENADE D

OPEN PRO

In Havre, I unearthed a company document conceding that *France*'s smut attack was never repelled: "*Nous n'avons pu toutefois éviter les retombées des dépôts*" (We were not able to completely avoid the descent of deposits), confesses one report with a shrug.

Pity the poor illustrators trying to cope with those wings. Nobody got them quite right. Throughout advertising pages of the *France* souvenir issue of the *Journal de la Marine Marchand*, no two renderings portrayed the wings convincingly. They appeared as squashed triangles, square-ended protuberances, or pointed fins. Some artists, despairing of the task, merely fell back on the company's original conical stacks.

Albert Brenet was doyen of *France*'s maritime artists. For his first *France* portrait complete with funnels up and painted, he set up his easel on the far side of the Bassin de Penhoët. His resulting gouache portrays the wings' undersides as *red*. Presumably, that scheme was the company's earliest decision, later rescinded. Evidence is sketchy but I doubt that Brenet's expert eye would have been deceived.

Fitting-out details for hundreds of cabins preoccupied every decorator, executive, and even their secretaries. As opposed to complex engineering arcana, deciding the look of a cabin is every newbuilding's common design denominator, a field day for all comers.

For starters, early *France* mockups had projected cabin dimensions that were too small. In spring 1955, an exasperated memo from Albert Zanger was circulated.

It is useless to build them. We will fall into the same mistake we made when rebuilding *Ile-de-France* and a long time before that. It is necessary to suppress them as we did on the last ship.

That "last ship" had been *Liberté*. Indeed, throughout *France*'s cabin angst, she remained the bête noire, the scapegoat cited for invidious comparison. Formerly *Europa*, her design DNA was alien Teutonic. One persistent French complaint about *Liberté* cabins, for example, was that there were so many confusing light switches that passengers were never sure which one turned on what.

Worse, there were twelve *Liberté* cabins that had contained a conventional single bed paired with a convertible sofa. Though that "dirty dozen" proved consistently unpopular, the French never

remodeled them. Regular as clockwork, on every crossing's first morning, twelve couples would line up at *Liberté*'s purser's desk with the same request: "Can't we please have a real room with two beds?"

The fact that the 1929 *Europa*'s designers had experimented with bed masquerading as sofa dates the opening round of a battle that would vex shipboard designers throughout the century: should a cabin be more than a bedroom? Why not a living room as well? By the early 1960s aboard *France*, the temptation to adapt *chambre à coucher* (bedroom) into a *salon* had begun in earnest.

Hideaway beds, warned old lags at the French Line, were "extremely unpopular with Americans." A sofa concealing a bed, they opined, conveyed the impression that passengers were camping out in someone's living room rather than occupying a proper guest room. Additionally, it was preached that the mechanics of transforming sofa into bed would be too demanding for passengers to achieve by themselves, thus burdening the stewards.

Other French estimates of American mores were neither correct nor well observed. American businessmen, it was preached, hated to see telephones in their cabins because it reminded them of offices they were escaping. Cabin telephones should be designed to "fold out of sight when not in use." Nor should there, warned another, be any thermos in the cabins, this after inspection of a mockup at Penhoët.

Given those portentous warnings, it is interesting that almost every one of *France*'s first class cabins emerged with (a) one of its beds masquerading as a sofa, (b) the bureau separating *faux*-sofa from companion bed played host to a flagrantly visible telephone, and (c) parked in a rack on every cabin wall was a white thermos. All those agonized no-no's had made not the slightest difference.

Another cabin note of interest was the presence of wall murals, not scenic wallpaper but lithographic views cunningly reproduced on matte-finished Formica. Whereas today's cabins boast one framed lithograph for decoration, *France*'s sometimes had an entire wall portraying France's architectural patrimony.

Of course, upscale *appartements de luxe*, named after French *départmentes*, were decorated with legitimate artworks. In *Provence*, portside Sun Deck, Jean Picart Le Doux created an exquisite hanging tapestry of sea urchins and butterflies. And while we are in *Provence*, we should also note a

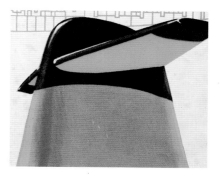

The covers of *France* deck plans showed the wings with red undersides. (Author's collection)

Thousands of souvenir ceramic ashtrays—labeled *The Funnel that Smokes*—were sold in the shop on board. (Richard Faber collection)

Opposite, top: This is tourist class country, aft on Promenade Deck. *France*'s largest public room, the Grand Salon seats 800. To the right, to port, tourist class's library and writing rooms, to starboard, the shop. Proceeding forward, the smoking room and on the extreme right, the orchestra floor of the Salle de Spectacle.

Opposite, bottom left: The main floor of the tourist class dining room on Main Deck.

Opposite, bottom right: The after end of Upper Deck, showing the tourist class pool and some cabins.

simple convenience, pioneered aboard *France* but commonplace at sea today, a double bed. The suite's bedroom could accommodate three, a double inboard and single outboard, presumably for parents and their child.

The original October date for *France*'s sea trials was delayed, largely because of the late installation of air-conditioning ductwork, a newbuilding complication never before encountered at Penhoët. Inspection team reports bore the same legends, either *"pratiquement terminés"* (nearly finished) or sometimes a more hopeful *"terminés à 80%."* Those seemingly endless miles of ducts provoked worrying delays and necessitated employment of an additional three hundred *toliers* (sheet metal workers).

Let us momentarily forsake onboard minutiae for a cinematic pull back, absorbing *France*'s single most compelling feature. Having documented steel interiors, we must not neglect steel exterior, the exquisitely wrought shell enrobing them.

From the earliest days of construction on the *cale de lancement*, alongside her fitting-out pier or maneuvered into Forme Joubert, *France*'s graceful hull astounded. So in service, steaming between Havrais breakwaters, being nudged alongside Southampton's Ocean Terminal, or undocking from Pier 88 to slide sternfirst into the North River, its stunning length materialized with the singing flourish of a rapier being withdrawn from its scabbard.

There was not a trace of *Normandie*'s bloated, midship spread. Rather, her sinuous form suggested

In early June 1959, from atop the cement margins of Forme Joubert, one of G19's davits and a sample lifeboat were put through their paces. No *France* lifeboat would ever be launched in peril, only for crew drills or shore excursions. (Chantiers de l'Atlantique/Cliché Ecomusée de Saint-Nazaire)

a slender, muscled thoroughbred. At 1,035 feet (315 meters) overall and a width of 110 feet (33.5 meters), *France*'s length-to-beam ratio was 9.3, reminiscent of the dimensions of Penhoët's pencil-slim, early-twentieth-century tonnage.

Although her winged funnels inevitably attracted first admiration, it was the endless, sculpted perfection of steel below that ultimately transfixed. However her interiors were later

rewrought, the hull containing them retained its original Breton genes. Officers and crew—French or Norwegian, at sea or in port, crossing or cruising—were bewitched.

The only contemporary rivaling those hull lines would be Cunard's *Queen Elizabeth 2*. Since she would not appear for seven years, until then *France*'s breathtaking good looks ruled the transatlantic roost.

Final decision: both wings, top and bottom, have been repainted black. *France* is poised to leave Chantiers de l'Atlantique for her builder's sea trials. (Chantiers de l'Atlantique/Cliché Ecomusée de Saint-Nazaire)

CHAPTER FOUR

INTERIOR DILEMMA

Un bateau n'est pas un musée, il ne saurait avoir la prétention de constituer un résumé des tendances de l'art du moment. Il n'est fait pour l'instruction de ses passagères mais pour leur agrément.

(An ocean liner is not a museum, it has no compunction to present a résumé documenting today's art. It is not made for the instruction of its passengers but for their enjoyment.)

Edmond Lanier, director-general of the French Line

In a year's time, the Cinémathèque Française will be as well known as the Comédie Française.

André Malraux, French minister of cultural affairs

Opposite: *France's* smoking room boasted an outdoor after terrace, sheltered from the wind and offering a bracing view over the stern. (Tee Adams Photo)

Having inspected France's *naked steel, we should consider the decorative clothing to follow.*

But until every deck, bulkhead, and deck head had been plastered, painted, carpeted, curtained, furnished, and lit, that finished look remained terra incognita.

Today's cruise lines have arsenals of projectiles with which they can carpet-bomb the public with images of new ships. None of that digital abracadabra existed half a century ago. Renderings of *France*'s public rooms were devised by fantasists, masters of hyperbolic distortion: ceilings were heightened, perspectives bent, decks attenuated, glitz amplified, and the occupants socially elevated. They told a spurious tale. It must be said: beloved as *France* was, her decor disappointed. Shipwide cohesion remained elusive. Rather than entrust interiors to a single ombudsman, rooms were assigned to individual designers.

Of course, those creating the final look of anything—vessel, terminal, hotel, dwelling, apartment, office—try to bring off a decorative coup that survives the structure's existence. Lone exceptions? Most cathedral builders. Those conceiving Notre

The atrium of Carnival's *Fascination* typifies the splendiferous foyers greeting passengers aboard today's megaships. (Author's collection)

Dame, Salisbury, or Canterbury would clearly not survive completion.

But passenger vessels are notorious short-timers, their life span just three decades. Some exceed the norm. *Queen Elizabeth 2* racked up 6 million miles after forty years, *Aquitania* did almost as well, and *Mauretania* steamed for twenty-eight years. Regardless, all their designers agonized about decorative shelf life. Successful lay (as opposed to naval) architects strove for interiors that would retain topicality for thirty years; what compels in 1962 should still turn heads in 1992.

Cruise ship decorators must churn out ever fresh concepts. In turn, owners hope that the work of their chosen design teams will please and impress passengers. Candidly speaking, those expectations are naive. Passengers are both fickle and stubbornly unobservant. An uncomfortable bed, awkward drawer, bad sight line, brusque steward, slippery deck, indifferent food, or malfunctioning plumbing arouse instant opprobrium, yet evaluation of a vessel's decor is voiced by no more than one or two in a thousand. Passenger attention is directed elsewhere—what's in the shops, why is my cabin so small, when can we go ashore, why are the shows so loud, and, always, when do we eat?

An equivalent inertia plagued French postwar designers. The 1950s, that decade from which they sought inspiration, offered little. Nothing concrete had emerged since the war although, in fact, concrete brutalism dominated postwar reconstruction. The Quai Johannès Couvert, from which French Line tonnage sailed, lay in ruins; Urbain Cassan's art deco tidal tower was rubble. The replacement Gare Maritime was a soulless, pebble-dashed bunker; as I write, it is being torn down.

Just as *Normandie*'s designers had embraced 1925's art deco, *France*'s sought a similarly compelling handle but found nothing. In New York, Lever House and the Seagram Building had inaugurated the International style on Park Avenue but no Gallic equivalent emerged. Anchored to no decorative thrust, *France*'s interiors were adrift. The country's tastemakers were confronted by a disinterested, postmodernist generation embracing alien shibboleths. Film was the new benchmark and an unconvincing celluloid intrusion permeated *France*'s design vacuum. Her interiors revealed a cinematic vernacular, as though dreamed up on a

sound stage at Nice's Victorine studios, the Riviera's Hollywood equivalent.

Artistic choices seemed overwhelmed by mundane practicality. All was antiseptically clean and efficient, every detail burnished with a high-tech patina. Boxed light panels marched overhead and man-made materials clad every surface, whether carpet underfoot or nonflammable bulkheads of metal, glass, and Formica. Fluorescent lighting was endemic and, capping the aluminum intricacy of Raymond Subes's *grand descente*, *France* banisters were prototypically industrial. Extruded black handrails shrouded underlying steel as at Orly airport and postwar railway stations. Clearly, the vessel's decorative antisepsis reflected *France*'s preoccupation with fire safety, understandable from a company that had seen too many ships succumb to flames, *Normandie*, *Paris*, and *Lafayette* to name but a chilling few.

Let us embark. One dated omission aboard *France* was a showy entry, the inevitable "wow" factor to which owners of contemporary megaships subscribe. Ever since 1984, when a two-deck atrium appeared aboard *Royal Princess*, rival owners have striven for taller and more garish atria. Those glittering voids are always sited just inside the shell plating, in order to overwhelm the impressionable with drop-dead decor.

France boasted no such flimflam, offering the very reverse: instead of threshold impact, threshold indifference reigned. Embarkation seemed almost surreptitious, a nonevent, apotheosis replaced by practicality. Clients boarded for a line voyage; hence the term "ocean liner," that gleaming, humming, powerful conveyance that would carry them swiftly across a formidable ocean with no stop save a token, cross-Channel drop-off.

One entered *France* on Pont Principal (Main Deck), through an understated lobby one deck high. Past the traditional bristly doormat, Bastian Spade's mottled blue, gray, and beige walls of anodized steel surrounded maroon carpeting underfoot. Nearly all public rooms were out of sight. Stooping passengers could just see the dining room through glass doors down some imposing stairs.

Cheek by jowl around the embarkation lobby was every convenience required by the newly embarked,

Entering *France* through her understated Embarkation Lobby, passengers embark for the shakedown cruise to the Canaries. (Tee Adams Photo)

A stroll through the vessel's public spaces reveals disparate choices suggesting little more than a random film set. (Compagnie Générale Transatlantique)

stations of the crossing. On the right was the *commissaire principale* (chief purser) and *chef de reception*, or chief steward's office. Opposite was the Salon de Radiotéléphone and the *chef de bagages* (baggage master), cashier's office, and Bureau de Renseignements (Information Desk). Around the portside corner were safe deposit boxes (*France* cabins boasted only locked compartments, not safes) and public telephone booths, patched into Manhattan's Bell Telephone system. In those pre-mobile days, they offered passengers heaven-sent

opportunity to dial and defuse last-minute emergencies.

Piercing *France*'s embarkation lobby was a vertical thoroughfare, first class's main staircase or *grande descente*. Subes had stunningly enriched it with a balustrade made up of repeats of woven aluminum ribbon, bright counterpoint to the muted walls. To either side, Subes had contributed twin stainless steel sculptures, vertical Möbius loops atop tapering, fluted posts, ringed by a table-height marble disc.

Decks, alleyways, and staircases were carpeted with a monochromatic fabric devoid of pattern. Its shade—labeled *couquet Bordeaux*—replicated the funnel color. The man-made fabric trademarked Rilsan was of the glued-down, nap-free variety that seemed poured rather than woven. Stained or disfigured spots could be excised and seamlessly replaced. But its trap was its lack of pattern; every scrap of lint, crumb, or detritus was evident. Throughout *France*, the diligent roar of vacuum cleaners never ceased.

The ocean liner's great public room triad—dining room, main lounge, and smoking room—exists as a circadian carousel of passenger visitation. Not one transatlantic day goes by when all three are not patronized by everyone on board. And since one essential embarkation ritual is selecting a dining table, we should descend first to the dining room.

Its look had been assigned to *decoratrice* Germaine Darbois-Gaudin. She had carpeted the room in rich, hunter green Rilsan. The most numerous tables were eighty-one for two; passengers then as now preferred dining *à deux*. For the more sociably congenial, one table seated eight and half a dozen accommodated six.

Mystifying were their surrounding chairs; they would prove dangerous. Oh, they were comfortable enough, seats and backs upholstered in brown, yellow, orange, or gray (at 152 the most numerous), their arms softened by right-angled leather rests. Of archetypal sixties design, their slightly bloated carapaces were perched atop skinny steel spider legs.

But it was other steel, doubled wraparound brackets encircling the backs, that gave trouble. Their naked corners, projecting at thigh height, could wound the unwary during rough weather. They remained in place throughout *France*'s life. Dining chairs selected for tourist class—smaller so that more fitted within denser surrounds—were more prudently designed.

On the walls, a long mannerist mural predominated. Created by Jean Mandaroux and titled *Les Plaisirs de la Vie* (The Pleasures of Life), it offered an arrangement of primitive stick figures with odd, triangular heads, like interplanetary aliens. They were incised across bronzed aluminum panels, each nearly a meter (3 feet, 4 inches) wide. Glimpsed upon entry, the figures read badly; seen close-up, individual panels seemed overbearing.

The only advantage of that metallic cladding was its indestructibility. Shipboard's dining room walls are notoriously susceptible to dings, scratches, and scars. Unsupervised night cleaners vacuuming crumbs were the worst offenders. But unlike fragile canvas those aluminum panels remained impervious. Given their inviolability, one wishes their decoration appealed more.

The room's third negative was glare. Overhead, the central dome's rim was encircled with a circumference of bronze fluorescent fixtures. It radiated

Bottom left: The view toward the staircase of *France*'s first class dining room. Chairs reveal their lethal steel corners. (Author's collection)

Bottom right: Crowded with passengers during the Canaries' shakedown cruise. The dome, it was discovered, conveyed sotto voce conversations clearly from one side to the other; stewards were instructed to curb their tongues. (Compagnie Générale Transatlantique)

garish levels of light for every staircase descent; at least the faces of late arrivals could be seen clearly. But that punishing glare was not restricted to dome country. Clusters of additional fluorescent fixtures stitched the surrounding ceiling in all directions, overexposing every corner of the room.

Were light levels ramped up to compensate for absent daylight? Passengers were assaulted with the same overpowering luminescence at every meal. Even during dinner, no festive, comforting glow ever appeared. The sun, it has been posited, never set on the British empire; an electrified sun never set in *France*'s first class Salle à Manger.

French sixties designers were in thrall to fluorescent lighting. Its advantages included lack of heat, reduced consumption, longer bulb life, and trouble-free operation. Its downside was that there was no way to dim it. One turned a fluorescent tube on or turned it off. Today, fluorescents can be dimmed but they rarely are; designers have moved on to the more compelling drama of neon.

So a low score for *France*'s first class dining room decor, needlessly flawed by lethal chairs, vapid walls, and abusive lighting. Doubly damaging, that dining room was the passengers' only catering source. Memorable exception to Madame Darbois-Gaudin's shortcomings was *La Louisiane*, the elegant children's dining room just to the left of the staircase, designed by Charriot. Once the last underage passengers had been tucked up, it might be used as a private dining room by their elders.

One down, two to go. Habitual postprandial destination was the Grand Salon, up two flights on Promenade Deck, the responsibility of Maxime Old. Capacious and bright, the space was flooded with daylight from flanking promenades. One entered from the room's forward end through port or starboard glass doors. At the after end was a bandstand behind a beige marble dance floor, replicating the dimensions of an overhead cavern. Swarming within that ceiling depression was yet more fluorescence; not a floor lamp or sconce was in evidence.

Monsieur Old counteracted the room's overriding coolness with six individual tapestries. Those fields of intense color warmed it up beautifully. The longest, on the forward wall, had been designed by Camille Hilaire. *Sous-Bois* (Under Woods) revealed contiguous forest glades, branches festooned with the same turning leaves that so prettily carpeted the forest floor, a polychromatic riot of stylized foliage and sun-dappled vistas.

Behind the bandstand was a triptych of Lucien Coutaud's *Femmes Fleurs I, II,* and *III*. These "women flowers" were representative floral couples, simulacra figures made up of flower petals and leaves; human hands and sometimes legs intruded. The effect was captivating, a charming phantasmagoria of pistils, petals, leaves, vines, and tendrils. Additional tapestries hanging along both sides were the work of Claude Idoux, a Lyonnaise artist. They were made up of variegated, vertical

Bottom left: First class's Grand Salon with empty bandstand against the after wall, its ceiling depression packed with a plethora of fluorescent fixtures. (Compagnie Générale Transatlantique)

Bottom right: From the other direction, looking forward, the tapestry *Sous-Bois* and a glimpse of those impractical, semi-armless chairs. (Compagnie Générale Transatlantique)

white bands, their repetitive span fractured yet interlocked. These abstractions contrasted neatly with florid extravaganza elsewhere.

France's Grand Salon answered multiple social demands around the clock, a passenger arena responding to that chiaroscuro of impulse, encounter, and languor that contributes to mid-ocean's precious limbo. Of *France*'s four hundred first class passengers, half could be seated in their Grand Salon. Were all to assemble at once, two hundred would remain standing. But passenger gridlock was averted by passenger vagaries. Recluses remained determinedly cabinbound, drinkers hunkered down in the smoking room, readers browsed the library, correspondents clogged the writing room, and bridge addicts shuffled, dealt, and fulminated in the Salon de Bridge. Dozens occupied deck chairs, either sheltered or braving open skies aft, and walkers tramped the decks. While others roamed the shops, shipboard hearties exulted in the squash court, sweated in the gymnasium, or splashed in the pool.

Throughout morning, afternoon, and early evening, a two hundred–strong tide of their sedentary fellows flooded and ebbed from the Grand Salon, pursuing sometimes conflicting pastimes: games, puzzles, quizzes, lectures, concerts, knitting, needlepoint, reading, bingo, horse racing, reverie, dancing, and, inevitably, gossip. Successive light refreshments were part of the mix: bouillon, coffee, pre-lunch aperitif, afternoon tea, and finally cocktails.

After dinner, Grand Salon segued into showbiz. No longer entertaining themselves, passengers were entertained by professionals. Just forward, the Salle de Spectacle offered films or concerts but nothing else; Las Vegian production shows lay in the future.

The seating was as unfortunate in its own way as Madame Darbois-Gaudin's dining room choices three decks below. (Did a persistent chair jinx haunt *France*?) Monsieur Old had created conversational encampments of chairs, sofas, and tables. Like all public room furniture each element was substantial. During rough weather, chairs, tables, and sofas must stay put. That immobility can be achieved by either making things sufficiently heavy or tethering them with discreet umbilical cords. Monsieur Old, ignoring umbilicals, opted instead for weighty chairs that stayed put but were not easy for stewards, let alone passengers, to shift or turn.

Coutaud's tapestried triptych served as a warmly detailed backdrop for the orchestra. (Author's collection)

La Salle de Spectacle combined cinema and concert hall but definitely *not* show lounge. (Author's collection)

Rigged for recital, the piano has been elevated from its below-stage lair. (Author's collection)

Of the five he selected, the most numerous were sloping chairs with angled backs, low to the ground, their depth inordinately long, rather like the wood-and-canvas collapsible chairs popular in British gardens. But these were extremely heavy steel with cloth or leather upholstery, with low arms that neither supported the elbow nor cradled the occupant. Moreover, their soporific angle of recline discouraged the attentive posture for which cabaret artistes yearn.

Sofas boasted a generous four places but lacked arms. Many seating groups surrounded metal-framed coffee tables, some heavily tiled and almost immovable. Finally, light cavalry to the rescue: folding chairs and tables were distributed around the room on gala nights, when capacity was always the fullest. So a mixed verdict for *France*'s Grand Salon, cumbersomely furnished but prettily decorated, its exuberant, color-filled tapestries inspired.

While we are forward, we should dwell briefly on the Salle de Spectacle and beyond. Whenever a concert was scheduled instead of a movie, a white Pleyel piano would levitate magically into view. Auditorium seating, yet again ubiquitous Rilsan, were dove gray and underfoot carpeting plum. The walls were enlivened with overlapping arcs of light interspersed by Pansart's gilded, aluminum-oxide panels. The whole decorative ensemble made for a sleek, soft surround, an elegant, private screening room.

To port and forward was the vessel's double-decked barbershop and hairdressing salon. It was under the control of concessionaire Pierre Jacobovici—Jacy for short—who headed a staff of fifteen coiffeurs and beauticians. Though largely French, concessionaires and their subordinates were described as *personnel étrangère* (foreign workers); all occupied passenger rather than crew cabins.

Since the complex straddled the frontier separating *France*'s classes, passengers were admitted for appointments through different entrances. Pursers could trust only that they exited through the same doors. This was, perforce, the vessel's second Checkpoint Charlie.

Just to starboard was the ship's chapel, more modest than *Normandie*'s and inestimably more *moderne*. "We're a long way from the little country church," mused art critic Madeleine Gaume after a Havrais tour. Its interior was executed by Raymond Subes and his altarpiece, with its extended cross and two flanking consoles, prettily evoked *France*'s winged funnels.

Fluorescently backlit, Anne Carlu's stained-glass reredos remained *France*'s most pleasing work of art. Suiting its congregants' midocean vulnerability, she had created a primitive Christ figure, right hand upraised in benison while the left held encroaching waves at bay.

Just forward was the first class children's playroom, about the size of two Volkswagen buses. It

Bottom left: *France*'s chapel, Promenade Deck, starboard side forward. Anne Carlu's peerless reredos survives in a Floridian Norwegian seamen's church. (Author's collection)

Bottom right: The first class children's playroom, an overly precious travesty. (Author's collection)

was devoid of juvenile furnishing save a round table and matching chairs, wheel of fortune and some ninepins. Really a pretentious *bonbouche* to delight parents rather than offspring, it was utterly impractical. In high summer, droves of American children would be among the first class passenger load yet no more than a dozen could be accommodated. Furthermore, any redblooded boy or girl deposited there would have clamored for instant admission to tourist class's roomier facility, tantalizingly visible through glass doors just forward.

So there, on Verandah Deck, a third (and sometimes grudging) Checkpoint Charlie was established. Playroom doors were kept locked so hardpressed attendants had to open them for countless first class intruders. Younger children congregated happily either in the Promenade Deck portion with its rocking-horse trio, sandbox, seesaw, jungle gym, and carousel or ventured into a neighboring playroom where a daily performance of *Grand Guignol en Mer* (Punch & Judy at sea) cheered up everyone. The inboard wall was decorated with a whimsical mural by the artist whose paintings enriched dining room menus: Jean Mercier's mural of *France* as Noah's Ark was peopled with whimsical animal duos.

First class teenagers pressed through to tourist class's portside haunt, an adolescent hangout called the Salle des Jeunes (room of the young).

My four children straddled the ages for both spaces, the two younger happily entertained to starboard while their older siblings spent transatlantic hours—nay, days and evenings!—consumed with *flipper*, foosball or mini-foot, a soda fountain, and newfound shipboard peers.

Their parents were equally attracted to an adult hangout aft on Promenade Deck. The first class smoking room was an exhilarating, double-height space with windows to either side encompassing views of two ascending decks. Enclosed *terrasses* filled lower panes while through the upper Boat Deck passersby could be spied through white Austrian shades.

The room was designed by André Arbus (unrelated to the celebrated American photographer). It was the only public room boasting different levels, because its elevated center accommodated tourist class's Grand Salon raised ceiling cavity below. Gentle, five-step flights at the forward bar achieved descent to the lower level.

Perhaps the room's musical vibes contributed to the seductive shape with which Arbus delineated its levels. Rather than conform to the angularity of ceiling cavity below, he implemented a softer boundary, gracefully curved to duplicate a violin, in plan the cursive purfling of a Stradivarius.

Arbus relied on the decorative enrichment of a single work of art 17 meters (55 feet) wide and 4

The "outdoor/indoor" tourist class playroom spread. Bottom left: On Promenade Deck, slide and rocking horses combined with (*out of sight*) sandbox and carousel kept *France*'s smallest passengers content for hours. Bottom right: Through generous windows can be seen juvenile tables and chairs, Guignol puppet stage, and, along the inboard wall, Jean Mercier's charming mural. (Author's collection)

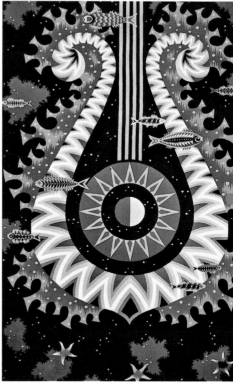

Top (both): The first class smoking room, unquestionably *France*'s most appealing space. One of two vertical bookends of Picart Le Doux's tapestry that defined the bar is shown at right. (Author's collection)

Left: *France*'s portside terrace, among its delights a rattling view of the vessel's four-screwed wake. (Author's collection)

Jean Leleu's handsome library "rotunda." I can still hear the gentle rattle of the bookshelves' curved glazing when seas were restive. (Nelson B. Arnstein, M.D., collection)

meters (13 feet) tall. Jean Picart Le Doux's tapestry clad the smoking room's forward wall and bar, a woolen triptych. Called *Les Phases du Temps* (Time Phases), navy blue, black, white, and gold threads depicted a stylized sunburst; hence, *Le Bar du Soleil* (The Sun Bar). The radiant orb was surrounded by a planetary orbit, along which traveled progressively eclipsing moons.

However his subliminal violin captivated Arbus, it remained unperceived by all save Picart Le Doux. Extending the musical imagery, his tapestry's left and right extremities incorporated representations of either violins, guitars, or lyres, doubling as reefs for schools of fish.

With high center and flanking lows, the three smoking room levels formed a second triptych. Another materialized overhead, where beams and their supporting columns divided the ceiling into longitudinal thirds. Parading down them were bronze, star-shaped electrical fixtures with downlights at their center.

Countering illuminative excess elsewhere, Arbus soft-pedaled fluorescence; wattage was freighted in favor of incandescence: 96 fluorescent tubes were outgunned by 212 conventional bulbs.

Blimp-shaped glass fixtures were mounted on every column and side wall, rheostatically adjustable from cocktail glitter to nightclub glow.

To either side of glass doors giving onto the after *terrasse*, Arbus commissioned two surrealist landscapes by Roger Chapelain-Midy. Each treillaged garden vista, framed by an identical stone arch, was festooned with draped white fabric. Contrasting centerpieces included a flower vase and a fruit arrangement. The starboard canvas also featured a pheasant while, to port, a long-legged heron reigned.

Though *France* had many other public rooms, most boasted less decorative significance. That said, Jean Leleu's first class library was impressive. It existed in two parts, a long reading room coupled with a separate, oval rotunda: encircling walls incorporated ascending bookshelves, enclosed behind beautiful curved glazing.

This chapter concludes by evoking a Far Eastern construction philosophy from the third century B.C. Rich or poor, the Chinese never dig a foundation without summoning a feng shui master. However imposing, a Shanghai office tower with incorrectly applied feng shui will never achieve success or contentment.

Feng shui embodies arcane Confucian tradition to determine in exactly which direction structures should face. Geographical and magnetic harmonies are evaluated. Good Chinese spirits waft in from the south and evil spirits always travel in straight lines. The juxtaposition of doors and windows is crucial to ensure that exits sharing the same axis will not drain the building's luck outdoors.

Feng shui has never concerned naval architects because their dwellings are continually turning and moving. Yet the literal English translation of *feng shui* is "wind and water," suggesting a germane, maritime application. If ever a structure radiated enviable feng shui, it was surely *France/Norway*. For four decades, she remained a finely tuned conveyance combining beauty, practicality, and delight where contentment abounded.

Evaluations like that would only accrue later, however. *France*'s departure from St.-Nazaire preoccupies us now. Largely because of the lagging ductwork, an additional month's delay meant that the vessel missed October's high tides. Not until 19 November 1961, four years since her keel laying, would *France* steam from the port for trials, never to return.

Her departure triggered an emotional adieu. Whenever Penhoët newbuildings enter the world's oceans, they disappear. De Gaulle's launch words haunted every Breton: "France *va épouser la mer*" ("*France* has married the sea").

Just prior to departure, St.-Nazaire seemed *en fête*. Hordes anticipated only during summer months inundated the city. Streets, sidewalks, hotels, and restaurants were jammed. The post office sold thousands of souvenir *France* stamps, and Hubert Chémereau, four years old, clearly remembers an evening concert of Breton favorites played on the Penhoët quay by the Lann Bihouée Bagad (military pipe band).

Preparatory fever gripped all who were sailing. On their final night, a reception was mounted at the Hotel de Ville (town hall) for officers and crew. But few of *France*'s personnel had time for more than a token glass. Their priorities were readying for sea. Officers bid farewell to Breton landladies, wrestled luggage aboard, and turned in rental cars. Crewmen struggling up gangways with their belongings breasted descending files of workers shouldering toolboxes.

Finally in command was commandant Georges Croisile. Retired commandant Le Huédé returned for departure and trials. Representing the company was Gustave Anduze-Faris, Transat's chairman and managing director.

At 2:07 P.M. on 19 November, the sea caisson imprisoning the vessel and her tugs within Forme Joubert slid ponderously aside. It was overcast and cold with only fitful rays of sunlight occasionally piercing the gloom. Throughout downriver passage, port and ship were enveloped in monochromatic gray, sea and sky a ghostly canvas shrouding what seemed a phantom ocean liner moving relentlessly and mysteriously downstream.

Every dock, pier, and cape en route was occupied, the Mindin Pier "*noir de monde,*" black with crowds. Roads downharbor carried unbroken traffic phalanxes paralleling the vessel's course. Shorelines were packed with cars, packed in turn with families sheltering from the weather. Some had slept in their vehicles to retain front-row priority. A spectator fleet crowded the estuary, naval warships, tugs, and pleasure boats, a flotilla of farewell, in Breton patois, *kenavo*. *France*'s whistle boomed repeatedly through the mist, haunting tocsin of departure and regret.

The mood ashore was as bittersweet as the sound. Shipyards must keep their workforce occupied and the dispatch of a completed vessel always triggers unease; what ocean liner would grow next on the ways? It would be the Israeli Zim Lines' much smaller *Shalom*.

One cannot exaggerate the loyalty of the Bretons who repeatedly converged at Chantiers de l'Atlantique. They came first to ogle construction, then to witness G19's launch, and then to surround Forme Joubert when *France*'s propellers were installed. Now they gathered yet again, in their thousands, for a farewell glimpse of their vessel.

Few were prospective passengers. A North Atlantic crossing, even in tourist, lay beyond the reach of France's working class. Yet their involvement was of an intensity deeper than mere fans or hobbyists. They were consumed by an almost religious devotion to Brittany no less than to every vessel that Breton hearts and hands had fashioned for over a century. Breton blood is made up of saltwater and trace elements of oak, canvas, teak, hemp, brass, steel, iron, and bronze.

As *France* vanished, voices choked and tears were shed. Wherever she sailed, whether Le Havre, Southampton, New York, Singapore, Miami, Bergen, or Alang, her imperishable Breton bonds would endure forever.

France committed to the oceans of the world, a canvas by maritime artist Stephen Card. (Author's collection)

CHAPTER FIVE

DEBUT

Le Commandant, seul maître après Dieu . . .

(The captain, save for God, the only master . . .)

Traditional French maritime dictum

This is also a ship of very modern design, and it is to be in service on the Atlantic route. It is expected that this ship will have a high service speed and may win for France the Blue Riband of the Atlantic.

The Shipbuilder & Marine Engine Builder (January 1962)

When the ship goes wop (with a wiggle between) . . .

Rudyard Kipling

Opposite: During the trials, Commandant Croisile and naval architect Jean Coune warm up in the wheelhouse. (Philippe Baudry collection, courtesy Patrick Depelsenaire)

A week before France *departed St.-Nazaire for sea trials, the company's predecessor flagship* Liberté

sailed from New York for the last time. To newsmen, the chief engineer confided, "She's just a tired old lady who soon won't be able to make the grade. She doesn't have the zing in her engine room any more."

A potential west coast reprieve remained unrealized. Seattle's 1962 World's Fair would open the following spring and city boosters had hoped to charter the liner as a moored hotel. But nothing came of the scheme and so on Armistice Day, 11 November 1961, carrying only 550 passengers, *Liberté* slipped her Pier 88 cables for the last time. Past Ambrose Light, she steamed to Southampton and Le Havre. Her passengers disembarked and she was moored at Quai Joannès Couvert's western end, significantly remote from the Gare Maritime's bustle.

France had sailed from St.-Nazaire in late November, bound northward for builder's trial at the Ile de Glénan, the first of two such outings. She underwent a succession of grueling maneuvers, including crash turns to port and starboard, inclination tests, and lowering then retrieving anchors.

Her most demanding ordeal was shifting from full ahead to full astern, a jarring reversal that would almost certainly never occur normally; regardless, it was obligatory. Full of admiration, Croisile later wrote:

Funnel and name board views of *France*. (Author's collection)

With all four propellers driving full ahead at 31 knots, I issued the required test command: "Full astern, all four propellers . . ." I could sense the steam racketing into the astern turbine casings, feel the ship vibrate and shake beneath my feet in reaction to this sudden putting on of the brakes. But she stopped in exactly 4 minutes and 48 seconds, after running 2100 meters (a mile and a third). Perhaps if you're not a sailor that would not seem remarkable. But if you think for a moment, realize that it represents just over seven times her length; you could never do the same thing with your car.

Four days later *France* raced triumphantly up-Channel and, at 12:30 P.M. on 23 November, first steamed into Le Havre. Despite overcast, foggy conditions, spectators crowded the frontage from St.-Addresse to the semaphore tower heralding the port's entrance. Tugs, fishing boats, and yachts escorted her.

Then tugs got lines aboard and as *France* passed moored *Liberté* a figurative torch was passed. Diminished "zing" notwithstanding, the chief had sufficient steam up to add the sonorous boom of *Liberté*'s whistle to the toots and shrieks of small craft, echoed by hundreds of car horns.

Whereas ocean liner whistles sounded at sea have a finite end to each blast, surrounded by the topographical variables of port and hinterland subsidiary reverberations continue long after the captain releases the button. The ricochet of one salute overlaps the next, producing a seemingly continuous, steam-driven paean.

Owner's trials began on 10 December. *France* returned down-Channel to submit to her most demanding task, confirmation that she could achieve contract speed. She proved astonishingly fast, at one point exceeding 35 knots and, according to Croisile, fulfilled the most demanding maneuvers flawlessly.

Of the vibration that had famously plagued *Normandie* there was not a trace. Highlighting the trial's second afternoon, a group of four company officials, Edmond Lanier and Jean Marie, chief engineer Georges Buoey and naval architect Jean Coune, sat on folding chairs around a table on the fantail, as though for an ondeck Mediterranean lunch.

Despite a large Perrier and four glasses, no food appeared. More than gastronomy was on offer. Coune fished a five-franc piece from his pocket and, while *France* rumbled along at 30 knots, placed the coin in the middle of the table, on edge. It remained stunningly vertical. All four men watched for a moment before applauding spontaneously. The Perrier was removed and a bottle of champagne materializing in its place was consumed.

France returned to Le Havre. The ship would be formally handed over on 6 January, on the eve of some maiden voyage preliminaries. Bridge officers, deck gang, and engineers now assumed subsidiary place to *France*'s largest contingent, described by the seamen with the faintly pejorative sobriquet *le civil* (civilians), or hotel department.

Hundreds of Havrais cleaners trooped aboard, mopping, scrubbing, and washing away stubborn Penhoët grime. *Garçons de cabine* and *femmes du chambre* buzzed throughout passenger country like hornets as cabins achieved brochure perfection. Vacuum cleaners roared and brightwork was buffed and shined. Towels, face cloths, bath mats, and shower curtains appeared on bathroom railings.

Within closets, extruded French Line hangers were suspended in rattling rows.

On A Deck, while chef Raymond Grangier's galley staff toiled backstage, stewards uncrated glass, china, and cutlery as carpenters expanded the head table. Maître d'hôtel and purser huddled with Elysée advance men, assigning banquet seats with scrupulous care; ranking government protocol was at stake.

Familiar French Line china was washed before distribution to pantry racks. Glasses and cutlery were put through their own washers, then polished, counted, and consigned to compartmented draw-ers at stewards' stations. Wheeled bins delivered stacks of tablecloths and napkins.

By late afternoon of the fifth, every first class table had been laid with military precision, napkins folded into distinctive starched fans, and place cards positioned. Missing only were table flowers arriving the next morning. After a hasty lunch, the steward teams migrated aft through the galley to work the same housekeeping miracle on both lev-els of the tourist dining room.

The next day—6 January, 1962—was the first of several D-days. Commandant Croisile and his sen-ior officers renounced boiler suits for number one

Successfully executing a crash turn to port, *France*'s stern swings prettily around. (Philippe Baudry collection, courtesy Patrick Depelsenaire)

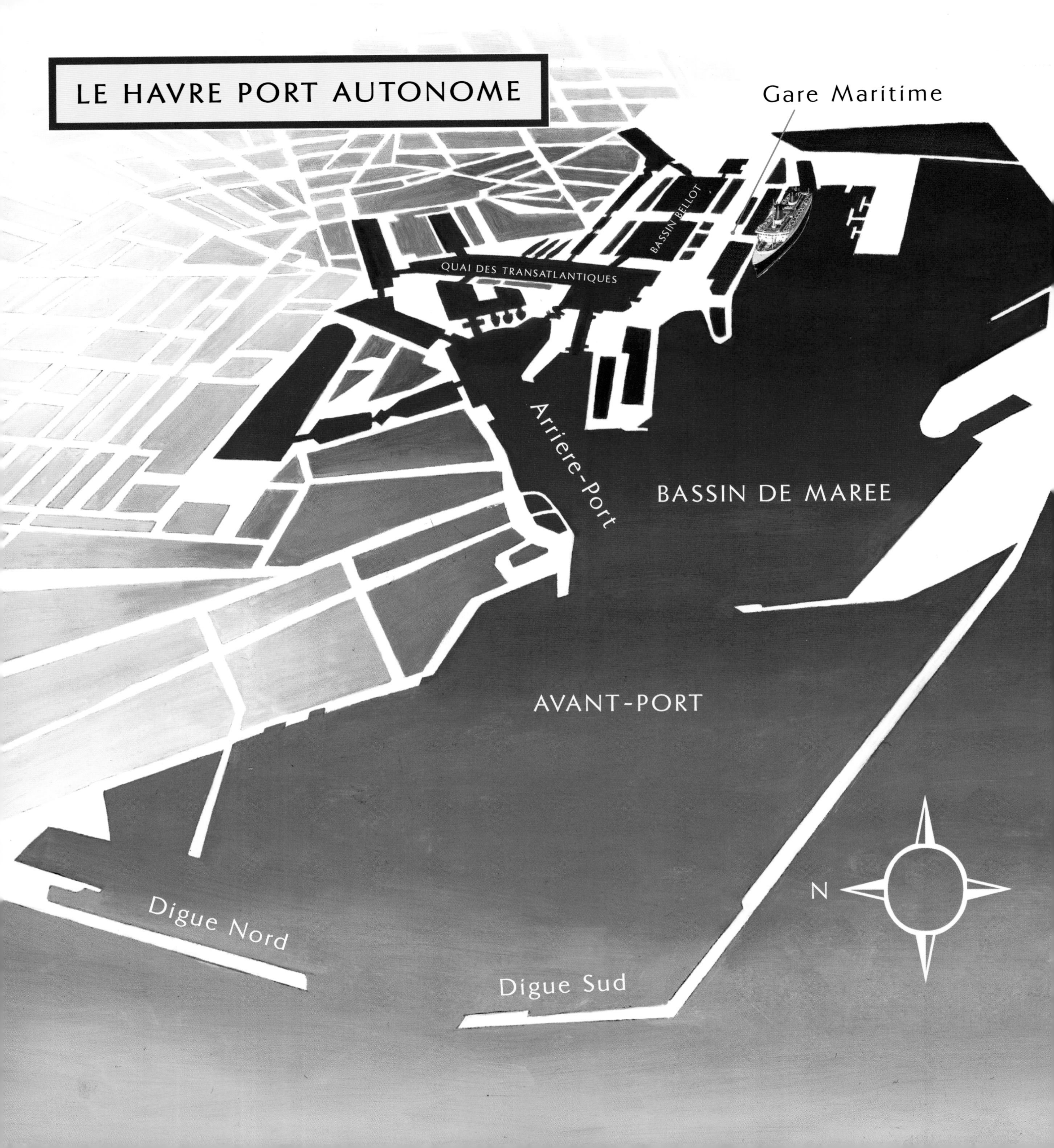

LE HAVRE PORT AUTONOME

Gare Maritime

BASSIN BELLOT

QUAI DES TRANSATLANTIQUES

Arriere-Port

BASSIN DE MAREE

AVANT-PORT

Digue Nord

Digue Sud

N

blues; evening rig was unzipped from protective garment bags. First order of business was the vessel's handover in the Grand Salon. Champagne confirmed that finally, officially, the French Line owned *France*.

In the afternoon, boat trains drew up in the Gare Maritime. Led by president René Coty, four hundred invited guests disembarked. A familiar total: Mrs. Astor's ballroom accommodation of New York's "400," the same number of prestigious passengers who would parade down the staircase that evening for *France*'s first state banquet.

There followed the first of three shakedown cruises. Early the following morning *France* undocked. By the time the previous night's diners descended for breakfast they were halfway to Southampton.

Ostensibly, the company had scheduled that cross-Channel foray to divert their onboard VIPs as well as show the flag in Britain. That maiden call would also ascertain firsthand that a sufficient depth of water obtained in the Ocean Dock, that embarkation and luggage-handling apertures were properly aligned, and that the company's several British *pilotes de choix* (chosen pilots) could start familiarizing themselves with maneuvering *France*.

For the company, Southampton had always been inextricably linked with Le Havre. Throughout many postwar years, *Ile-de-France* and *Liberté* had made contrasting calls at the port, contrasting because of their disparate speeds. Whereas *Ile* required six days to reach New York, *Liberté* had sufficient "zing" to do it in five; so for Southampton calls, the slower *Ile* went docilely upstream like all other inbound tonnage.

Therein lay the rub. What made passage up to the docks so laborious was a vast shoal called the Brambles, the port's notorious navigational disadvantage. Despite a double tide that delivered plentiful depths elsewhere, the Brambles never became sufficiently covered, a muddy bottleneck blocking the entrance to Southampton Water necessitating a circuitous detour around it.

Faster *Liberté* followed *Normandie*'s imperious example, anchoring on Southampton's threshold at the Motherbank, saving six valuable hours and substantial docking fees. Yet however economical, it remained a logistical bore for their passengers. Inbound or out, an hour's tender ride to or from the Motherbank prolonged the ninety-minute London train journey.

Although also a five-day ship, *France* would duplicate *Ile-de-France*'s Southampton routine, offering gangway embarkation to her UK clientele. An additional attraction impelling *France* upstream was the Ocean Terminal, Southampton's great postwar sea station erected on the Ocean Dock's western shore. Conceived in the 1920s, it had been dedicated by Prime Minister Clement Attlee on 31 July, 1950, glittering Phoenix rising above World War II's destruction.

Ocean Terminal was a steel and glass art deco masterpiece, stretching for 1,297 feet (395 meters). Designed like a landlocked superstructure, its seaward facade boasted a glazed, convex bulge topped by a flagged tower. Boat trains from Waterloo snaked through the docks to the terminal's inboard

On the after end, an anxious company group wonders about vibration. (Philippe Baudry collection, courtesy Patrick Depelsenaire)

Coune's coin trick performed on a table right above the propellers resolves all angst. (Jean Coune collection)

platforms, permitting passengers to ascend via escalator into successive levels of convenient splendor that put New York's dreary pier sheds to shame.

First and tourist class reception halls had long counters paralleling comfortable brown leather sofas. Nearby was a W. H. Smith for last-minute newspapers or books as well as a refreshment counter for a first (or final) pint of warm beer or restorative cup of tea. A post office accommodated correspondents and banks of telephone kiosks the more impatient. Passengers embarked or disembarked through enclosed gangways.

The Ocean Terminal remained a welcoming fixture for all Southampton passengers for three decades. But in 1983, after plans for conversion into Southern Television studios were aborted, it was razed, supplanted by the Queen Elizabeth II Terminal farther down the dock peninsular.

For the next quarter century the Ocean Dock handled only freight. One accumulation of scrap metal grew so dangerously high that the dock started collapsing. Then, in April 2009, a new Ocean Terminal was sited along the Ocean Dock's opposite margin, subject to prevailing offshore winds, alas, but initiating a welcome return of pas-

senger traffic within those historic sixteen acres of water, designed originally for *Olympic*-class tonnage in 1910.

Just after midday on 7 January 1962, inbound *France* paused at the Nab pilot station and four pilots clambered up the Jacob's ladder on her starboard side: captains Peter Driver, Jack Holt, Cyril Lintock, and Jack Knight.

France's first Southampton entry proved uneventful. Circumnavigating the Brambles, she was greeted off Hythe Pier by five Alexander Towing Company tugs that would usher her up to the docks.

Since *France* had neither stern- nor bow-thrusters, she needed two tugs forward, two trailing aft, and a fifth "under the shoulder" abaft the bridge. Positioned off the terminal, inboard tugs detached their hawsers and relocated along *France*'s port side, nudging her securely against the dock.

That night, an official welcoming party of Southampton functionaries including British reporters and travel agents was invited to dine. The affair was a glowing success and the press corps rejoiced in print that *France* would become a terminal regular rather than a distant presence at the Motherbank.

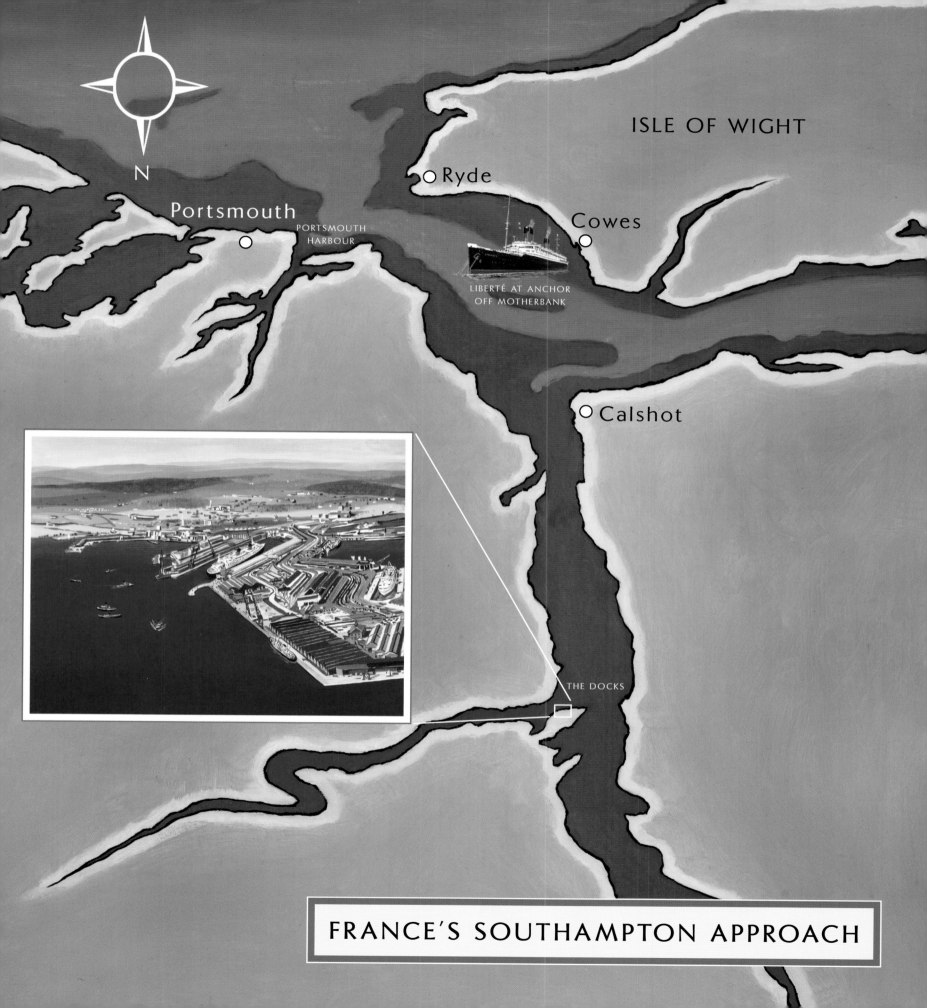

ISLE OF WIGHT

Ryde

Cowes

Portsmouth

PORTSMOUTH
HARBOUR

LIBERTÉ AT ANCHOR
OFF MOTHERBANK

Calshot

THE DOCKS

N

FRANCE'S SOUTHAMPTON APPROACH

The late naval architect Jean Coune poses with his beloved *France*, summer 2008. (Author's collection)

A comparison of the inaugural schedules of the company's last two flagships is interesting, *France*'s in refreshing contrast to *Normandie*'s frantic 1935 ordeal. Far later than expected, *Normandie* did not leave St.-Nazaire for trials until 5 May; regardless, her maiden voyage was scheduled for the twenty-ninth. That truncated month was highly pressured. Cabins and bathrooms were still being completed in Havre, a seamen's strike threatened to muddy the celebratory waters, and the Café-Grill would not open until partway to New York.

By comparison, *France*'s premaiden voyage time line seems positively glacial. Having quit St.-Nazaire on 19 November 1961, she would not sail for New York until 3 February, 1962. Rather than *Normandie*'s hectic twenty-four-day window, *France* had two and a half months at her disposal. There was time for both trials, an initial Southampton call, a Canaries cruise, Le Havre downtime, and a second Southampton visit as well.

On Thursday 11 January, there was a special luncheon, the guest of honor Prime Minister Michel Debré. Among his ministers was then secretary of state for finances Valéry Giscard d'Estaing; as he tucked into his *Fillet de Sole de Dieppe Présidence*, he could never have guessed that, twelve years hence, he would precipitate the vessel's withdrawal.

On 13 January, sandwiched between two droves of continental travel agents that descended to Havre on the twelfth and the fifteenth, there was a gala benefit, the twenty-ninth annual *Bal des Petits Lits Blancs* (Ball of the Little White Beds). Dating from 1921, the ball was a charity for sick children.

The largest overnight contingent to inundate *France* yet, both dining rooms were used. An unprecedented take of 45 million francs enriched the charity's coffers.

Among the fourteen hundred attending was that enviable charity soufflé combining royalty with film star. Patrons included Madame la Baronne Jean Sellière, Princess Paola and Prince Alexander of Yugoslavia, and, clad in a pencil-slim, white satin Givenchy sheath, Audrey Hepburn sat beside Commandant Croisile.

These were not gray government functionaries, raffish reporters, nor rumpled travel agents but quintessentially elegant Parisians. They remained the vessel's *ur*-clientele, the kind that made French Line pursers purr.

It is the summer of 1950, opening day for Southampton's Ocean Terminal. Its seaward end boasts a facade not dissimilar from one of the *Queen*'s bridge screens. (Southampton Libraries' Maritime collection)

The first class embarkation hall was comfortably furnished and outfitted with refreshment counters. Always popular with outbound traffic, they were seldom patronized by inbound passengers hastening to boat trains below. (Associated British Ports)

On the starboard bridge wing, ready for Southampton departure, *pilote de choix* Captain Peter Driver stands between Commandant Christian Pettré and Commandant-Adjoint Jean Nadal, summer 1974. (Author's collection)

unfair competition. That contentious topic headed the conference's December gathering.

A kind of mating dance always preceded final consummation; disputes were resolved by mediators among the membership. Tourist rates went to successful mediation: from Southampton, One-Way Low Season $220, One-Way High Season $246, Half round-trip $198. Embarkation from French ports cost more: One-Way Low Season $225.50, One-Way High Season $251.50, and Half round-trip $ 203.00.

Achieving consensus for first class rates proved thornier. When mediation stalled, Canadian-Pacific was appointed as umpire. That company's (unalterable) decision finally nailed down *France*'s rates: from Britain, One-Way Low Season $412.50, One-Way High Season $432.00, and Half round-trip $371.50. Again, French embarkation rates were higher: One-Way Low Season $423.50, One-Way High Season $443.00, and Half round-trip $381.00.

Those French rates would be put to their first application on 19 January, for *France*'s second shakedown cruise of eight days to the Canaries and back. Four boat trains delivered 1,704 revenue passengers from Paris.

In one sense, their voyage would prove disappointing: midwinter Mediterranean is scarcely subtropical. Regardless, it enabled that exclusively French passenger load to escape Paris's *après*-Christmas slump aboard brand-new *France*. Rewarding for them, the cruise was also a boon for the *civil*. The vessel's systems could be fine-tuned by accommodating, feeding, and entertaining clients at sea rather than tied up tamely alongside.

It was a triumph, dress rehearsal and opening night conjoined. Guests of honor were Madame de Gaulle and her naval officer son, *capitaine de frégate* Pierre de Gaulle. *France* was a very different ship from the one that the president's wife had dispatched into the Loire. Fitted out, finished, and crowded with passengers, she raced southward across heaving Biscay toward Madeira.

Madame de Gaulle proved as enthusiastic a passenger as a *marraine*, anxious to see everything. On her first sea day, *commissaire principale* Joubert gave her a guided tour, starting in the galley. The catering staff never forgot Madame de Gaulle; every Christmas, delicacies from *France*'s *patisserie* would be dispatched to the Elysée Palace. Commandant Croisile welcomed her to the bridge and insisted that she blow the whistle.

Which speaks volumes about the *commissaire principale*. His fiefdom was *France*, his serfs the hardworking *civil*. His all-encompassing eye was ubiquitous and he combined the talents of stage manager, arbiter, chatelain, butler, detective, bailiff, occasional priest, and, always, driven perfectionist. Every square inch of passenger country constituted his bailiwick. And he was never happier than when his public rooms' occupants matched the ambition of the space they adorned.

Yet though the vessel's normal passenger cross section might not be as fastidious, chic, or well bred, they did boast one incontrovertible advantage: revenue. Exactly what passengers would pay to board *France* had been hammered out in a conference room at Paris's Hotel Prince de Galle in early December. Shipboard fares were determined by the Atlantic Conference, a self-governing cooperative of companies established in 1908 to avoid ruinous rate wars.

The French Line's opening salvo had been circulated to conference members by post. Predictably, both Cunard and the United States lines lobbed back fierce objections, branding the estimates too low and insisting they be raised to avoid

She also steered *France* under way, watched anxiously by the quartermaster.

Alongside at Tenerife, the voyage's only *crise* occurred. A first class elevator delivering the de Gaulle party down for disembarkation stopped with a jolt between decks. Worryingly aware of Algerian unrest, the master-at-arms fretted about terrorism. But it was a mechanical glitch, which engineers corrected immediately. Madame de Gaulle returned to Paris highly pleased.

On the morning of 26 January in the Mediterranean, *France* encountered *Liberté* bound for La Spezia's scrapyard. Croisile, a former *Liberté* master, signaled his former command from *France* with three lingering blasts, closing a poignant chapter forever. Along lower decks, *France* crew-men and -women who were *Liberté* veterans wept as the vessel passed.

France's third and final shakedown was another Southampton call, marred by fog. Additional misadventure was the mysterious loss of the starboard anchor, discovered the morning of the Havrais return: fifteen tons of maritime hardware had vanished from the hawse pipe. It would be replaced before *France*'s fourth and most demanding outing, her maiden voyage to New York.

That it took place in early February was unprecedented. Spring or early summer was the norm, to avoid the Scylla of winter storm and Charybdis of summer fog. It was simply bad timing. Had her keel been laid three months later, the maiden voyage would have been pushed more happily into May.

France exits Southampton's Ocean Dock into the River Test on 9 January 1962, the first of two calls at the British port before her shakedown cruise to the Canaries. She gleams like a new pin. (Richard Faber collection)

Top: Archetypal Croisile, immensely proud of a new command, his cap at its customary jaunty angle. (Madame Georges Croisile collection)

Bottom: During her tour of the bridge, Madame de Gaulle was asked by Croisile to sound *France*'s whistle. (Madame Georges Croisile collection)

As though underscoring the seasonal handicap, a chill rain fell in Le Havre as 1,729 passengers trooped aboard on Saturday, 3 February. There were a few Americans among them, including one Marvin Buttles of Great Neck, New York, who had reserved his cabin eight years earlier. A 153-strong contingent of Havrais enthusiasts were sailing only as far as Southampton. Also on board were three first class dogs, two in tourist class, and three canaries of unspecified class.

Despite the downpour, *France* was a brave sight, rainbowed with flags. At the bow flew the *pavillon de partance* (departure flag), what English seamen call the blue peter. Whereas *Normandie*'s had been the Breton banner, *France*'s was a blue/white/red pennant.

Hanging bravely if limply from the starboard yardarm was the company's house flag with its distinctive red ball at the hoist and abbreviated title in the same hue: Cie. Gle. TRANSATLANTIQUE, in full, Compagnie Générale Transatlantique. The ball originated from the red disc on a white field, international flag code for number 1. What better promotional image for a company that prided itself on being the world's number one shipping line?

Saturday departure was a scheduling anomaly because *France*'s first New York turnaround would be longer than usual. An extended stay alongside Pier 88 was on order so that the company could show off the vessel to the customary Manhattan invasion: municipal dignitaries, *amis de maison* (friends of the house), plus a deluge of travel agents who would enjoy an overnight cruise to nowhere.

So, for better or worse, winter rather than spring, wet rather than dry, Saturday rather than Friday, brand-new *France* steamed purposefully past soaked crowds jamming Havre's jetties, disembarked her cross-Channel joy riders, embarked her UK contingent, dropped the pilot at the Nab, and proceeded down-Channel.

One day later she sailed into the teeth of a force-11 gale. On cue, the dread Scylla that a spring departure might have avoided intruded chaotically, dividing the maiden voyage into two disparate halves. Commandant Croisile ordered swimming pools drained and netted, closed all but the after open decks, and reduced speed from 30 to 6 knots, hoping to minimize the discomfort of his fragile human cargo.

Persevering at slow speed into punishing forty-five-foot waves, *France* performed classic, on-coming-storm choreography. Her prow reared high into spindrift-laden air and hung at pitch's apogee for unreal seconds before dropping like a stone atop an oncoming wave with a crash that jarred the entire vessel. *France* seemed to stop, shuddering when her screws emerged from the marbled sea before gathering strength to start that madcap *tour-jeté* all over again.

Bridge occupants were delighted at how the vessel behaved. Only so much can be learned from the artificial turmoil of a testing tank. Now, owners, builders, officers, and naval architects could but admire *France*'s splendid response.

Less admiring were the vessel's occupants. Frivolity was put firmly on hold. What use now evening dresses swaying in cabin closets, pins and bracelets nestled within dressing table compartments, mascara, lipstick, and those imposing beehives teased in the *salon de coiffeur* or deck wear selected in Paris? *France*'s social calendar of westbound twenty-five-hour days was retarded as abruptly as her speed.

But not for all. Some brave souls, exhilarated by rough weather, roamed the public rooms, waltzed along promenade decks, chortled at monstrous waves, and never missed a meal. Indeed, they were on hand when the projecting steel of a dining room chair claimed its first victim. A steward cut on the thigh was evacuated to be stitched up.

For the majority, though, turgid sea motion was a downer: down forks, hunker down, down below, lie down, and, inevitably, down in the dumps. Banging, lurching, slamming, and shuddering, *France* threatened rather than thrilled as public rooms emptied, staircases became defiantly uncooperative, and eating developed into a lost art.

Cabin refuge was not a guaranteed panacea; within that inner below, motion still held sway. Bulkheads creaked, curtains swayed, doors slammed, drawers flew open, trunks toppled, possessions slid off dressing tables, and bottles clattered into tubs. Each time *France* spanked the sea, horizontal cascades of green water darkened every porthole.

The sixties-era grand specific was Dramamine, its inescapable side effect a soporific torpor. Hundreds of *France*'s incapacitated dozed on or in bed. For hardier souls escaping cabin fever, public room sofas sufficed. Those in deck chairs along Promenade Deck, shrouded in tartan rugs, barely watched the fractious sea that was their undoing.

Newly embarked *personnel étrangère*—shop-keepers, hairdressers, librarians, and cabaret artistes—suffered too. Only the most desperately afflicted retreated to their berths; the marginally queasy had to stay on duty. But, to their advantage, *France*'s appalling sea motion of 5 and 6 February was indiscriminately democratic. Every battering jar transmitted equal impact throughout the vessel; no one was immune. So green-faced hairdressers in the Salon de Coiffure had fewer clients; librarians stationed unhappily beside the chattering curved panes covering LeLeu's bookshelves had fewer volumes to sign out; Le Printemps shopkeepers, trying to smile and keep stock from tumbling, found that few browsers entered. Dancers, singers, and jugglers who performed for smaller audiences were applauded more enthusiastically than usual.

After forty-eight hours the low pressure system passed astern. Though headwinds subsided, the seas remained rough. Croisile discreetly ratcheted up propeller revolutions. Slowly, haltingly, passengers recovered equilibrium and mobility.

Public rooms and corridors refilled, shopkeepers started selling, barmen stirred and shook, smoking room stewards were kept hopping, beauty salon dryers hummed, and dining room staircase flow resumed its customary cataract. Indeed, the allure of the table rated high for the reinvigorated. Backlogs of maiden voyage drink and food, including ten thousand bottles of *vin grand cru*, fifteen tons of beef, four tons of chicken, five tons of fish, and three tons of cheese started to be depleted. Though estimates of caviar supplies were not released, hundreds of those gold/blue 14-ounce tins would be opened, cradled in carved ice swans, and dispensed abundantly.

After forty-eight hours of fasting, restored appetites made up for lost time. A roseate glow followed every dining room descent. The opening of those famous doors served as admission into nirvana. Lunches and dinners passed in dazzling review, a cavalcade of lavishly sauced entrées, ever grander, richer, and more splendid: *Foie gras en Croute*, a rich cream of *Petits Pois* Lamballe, Roast Lamb *Appolinaire*, *Ballotine* of Duck, *Terrine de Poularde Angevine* or stuffed squab drenched with truffle sauce. Desserts? Mont Blanc au Marrons, Soufflé Sucré, Pudding *Diplomate*, and, always, *Crêpes Suzette*. And as a finish, those inevitable show stoppers, *specialités* of beribboned baskets heaped with *petits fours*.

Inveterate maiden voyagers Salvador and Gala Dalí were on board though Babou was not. The artist had designed the menu cover for the crossing's *Dîner d'Honneur*. But, in truth, it was almost impossible to distinguish *Dîner d'Honneur* from every other dinner. A nightly captain's table was instituted, full of new faces each time. The only unchanged ones belonged to cohosts Croisile and chairman Anduze-Faris.

Top: Not *bronzé* yet and not likely to be: winter-white Frenchmen try a little *culture physique* in the gymnasium next door to D Deck's pool. **(Compagnie Générale Transatlantique)**

Bottom: Commandant Croisile salutes his former command steaming to the Italian breakers. **(Madame Georges Croisile collection)**

Top left: *France* glitters like a Christmas tree, the last night in her home port before the maiden voyage to New York. (Compagnie Générale Transatlantique)

Top right: *France*'s bridge in calm weather, a contrast from the heaving, wind-battered outpost it became during the first half of the maiden voyage. (Author's collection)

Among their first guests were the French ambassador to the United States and his wife, Monsieur and Madame Hervé Alphand. Gilbert Grandval, secretary-general of the French merchant marine was another. New York passengers of note included Eugenia Sheppard, the *Herald Tribune*'s celebrated feature editor, and Edmond J. Moran, owner of the tugs that would assist *France*'s arrival.

Singing star Juliette Gréco was on board. Her final-night concert in the Salle de Spectacle included her signature rendition of "Valse de l'Au Revoir," received with great acclaim both in the theater as well as at a repeat performance for tourist class.

One cocktail hour in the Grand Salon featured a fashion show; strutting mannequins showed off fabulous Parisian couture while sporting $7 million worth of jewels, rehearsal for a main event scheduled for New York. Dancing was frenzied. Bouncy, indefatigable *chef d'orchestre* René Moos drove his musicians mercilessly; since it was the early 1960s, the twist—"*la danse new-look*"—was all the rage. There was even a twist competition, complete with numbered contestants and distinguished judges. La Barrone Empain won first prize for her performance, dancing captivatingly in bare feet.

The only interruption of almost continuous dancing was a fancy dress parade, including more than one entrant wearing a *France* life ring. Another evening, horse racing was the vogue. One night, stewards covered the dance floor with a canvas rug marked as a chessboard; passengers wearing comic hats were dragooned as chessmen and

women. Appearing on the final gala night were bags full of those zany projectiles called *cotillons*, golf ball–sized white cotton projectiles that could safely be hurled at one's target of choice.

French Line *commissaires* always kept up a relentlessly giddy social pace. When one sensation ended, another must take its place. The moment Juliette Gréco's theater concert ended, *mousses* behind the balcony's last row brought in cylindrical wicker baskets from the bakery filled with baguette-shaped balloons. As the applause died, baskets were upended and multicolored balloons cascaded over the balcony down onto the delighted audience below.

For the commandant, that turbulent maiden voyage was the worst crossing he had experienced in twenty-five years. At night, he later confessed, he lay down rather than slept, concerned about his vessel, her bruised passenger load, and a possibly delayed New York arrival where so many time-sensitive events were on tap.

Thanks to fine seamanship, skill, discipline, and the vessel's reserves of speed, he brought it off. *France* first passed through the Narrows at 10:45 on 8 February 1962, almost on schedule. She anchored at Quarantine off Staten Island's Tompkinsville to embark a contingent of VIPs headed by Richard C. Patterson of the city's Department of Commerce and Public Events. With him were the usual suspects, save for *France*'s ambassador who was already on board: Armand Bérard, France's permanent representative to the United Nations, Guy de

Berc, the French Line's North American manager, Philip Nicholas Jr., commissioner of customs, and Joseph Kelly, collector of the port.

Three hundred reporters and broadcasters packed the deckhouse of the Circle Line's *Miss Liberty*. They could see firsthand evidence of the crossing's ordeal. Hull paint takes months to achieve permanence and the steel plates towering above them were scarred by a rash of rusting primer. Only Nicolas Chatelain, *Le Figaro*'s man in New York, took journalistic note of the damage. Few of the Americans noticed or knew; knowledgeable shipping reporters were already an endangered species. Only the *Herald Tribune* had dispatched its experienced veteran, the renowned Walter Hamshar.

With her expanded shipboard complement on board and lots of new passengers lining either bridge or railings, depending on rank, *France* raised anchor and steamed majestically upharbor with four spouting fireboats as outriders.

Normally, in pilotage waters, captains remain on the bridge in case of an emergency. In a remarkable violation of that protocol, Croisile deserted his post and raced aft to participate in an impromptu press conference in the smoking room. Stewards tried circulating with trays in the midst of a shouting, shoving crowd. Sweating in bulky overcoats, juggling notebooks, pens, pencils, cameras, and champagne, reporters milled impatiently. Photographers clambered shamelessly atop tables. Such was the bedlam as the morning's tipple found its mark that French Line's *président d'honneur* Jean Marie's introduction could scarcely be heard.

When Commandant Croisile stepped to the microphone, photographers shouted for him to turn this way and that. Despite the opportunity to interview the master of a new liner under way, few of the journalists knew what to ask. Predictably, they bawled out clichés.

Croisile fielded every cornball question beautifully. He dwelt initially on the storm, reassuring them that *France* had suffered no damage. In answer to a shouted interruption, he denied that *France* harbored *Ruban Bleu* ambition.

"Even if we had taken it," he temporized diplomatically, "the *United States* with her reserves of speed would just have taken it back. *France*," he concluded, "prefers to keep the record for quality, not *ruban bleu* but *cordon bleu*," a neat epigraph lost on most of his audience.

Left: The worst of the storm behind him, Commandant Croisile descends to dine for one of the maiden voyage's consecutive gala dinners. (Nelson B. Arnstein, M.D., collection)

Overleaf: The end of a rough, cold maiden voyage. *France* steams up New York's North River escorted by four spouting fireboats. (The French Line)

After his encounter with New York's press corps, Croisile bundles up for outdoor docking duty on *France*'s bitterly cold bridge wing. (Madame Georges Croisile collection)

Opposite, top: On 8 February 1962, Moran tugs maneuvered *France* parallel to Pier 88. It was twenty years but one day shy of 9 February 1942 when, on a similarly cold afternoon, a catastrophic fire broke out in *Normandie*'s Grand Salon. (Richard Faber collection)

Opposite, bottom: In service at last: *France* docks on the north side of Pier 88, spring 1962. (Photograph by Walter Lord)

Next clanger? Stowaways. Croisile confessed that one stowaway, a French newsman in love with an American girl, had turned himself in two days out of Le Havre. (Trust Walter Hamshar to ferret out his name—Marc Tessler.) In fact, Tessler had evaded the authorities and disappeared so the presence of a *France* stowaway was never recorded by immigration officials.

Okay, if he were unavailable, *cherchez la femme*: like bloodhounds baying in pursuit, a chorus of "Where's the girl?" arose from a hundred throats. Croisile countered adroitly: "It is difficult enough keeping track of where your own girlfriends are, let alone another girl!"

Then he surrendered the microphone and, donning his cap at its customary angle, saluted his interlocutors and hotfooted it back to the bridge. It was exactly noon and the vessel had already passed the Statue of Liberty. Despite the cold, passengers thronged every open deck, because mountains of their luggage and thirty-five hundred soiled laundry bags obstructed the warmer Promenades.

News helicopters crisscrossed the murky skies and Manhattan's fabled skyline exerted its magic. Waters off the end of Pier 88 were white with brash ice. The docking pilot instituted the start of *France*'s 90-degree turn, which would point her bows eastward into the same slip where poor *Normandie* had come to grief.

A large banner reading WELCOME S/S FRANCE was draped across the pier's apron. Behind it shivered a capacity crowd of New Yorkers. New York's Department of Sanitation band serenaded the vessel's arrival with a (gloved) "La Marseillaise." Moored south at Pier 86, *United States* boomed a welcoming salute, which Croisile, preoccupied with docking, was too busy to acknowledge.

Passengers descended for their final lunch, a perfunctory and distracted farewell. Dining room staff were in a rush to get rid of the passengers and reset tables for four hundred New Yorkers—already in the pier shed—who would embark for lunch.

What price that midwinter debut? *France*'s arrival coincided with New York's worst cold snap. The thermometer fell to 6 degrees Fahrenheit (−14.4° Celsius) and the next day four inches of snow blanketed the suburbs. Flight plans for the thirteen hundred travel agents invited for Sunday's overnight cruise were hurled into disarray.

There was human error to the north. A Nova Scotia trawler inadvertently ruptured the undersea telephone cable connecting France with North America. For a week, no Parisian dispatches could be filed documenting *France*'s reception.

But though France the country might be incommunicado, *France* the ship was not. Thousands swarmed on board. In addition to the privileged four hundred who lunched in the first class restaurant, six thousand more embarked that first day alone, together with another four hundred invited for dinner, Mayor Robert Wagner among them.

They would be joined by twelve hundred afterdinner guests who watched a calmer replay of midocean's fashion show, then danced and drank a great deal. On Saturday night, twenty-five hundred trooped aboard for cocktails but Sunday's overnight cruise was aborted because of inclement weather.

With a full passenger load, *France* departed on the eastbound leg of her maiden voyage on Tuesday, 13 February, at 1:30 P.M. It had been a taxing stay for the hard-pressed *civil*; only deck gang and engineers caroused ashore.

New York took *France* to its collective heart. The only dismaying aftermath was an article on page 14 of 10 February's *New York Times*. Its headline conveyed a frisson of unease: SHIP'S CUISINE IS FOUND NOT IN FRENCH TRADITION.

The review was written by a *Times* man who had lunched aboard the day before. Nothing, he reported, had been quite right. Although preliminary caviar with vodka raised no hackles, a first course of fresh artichoke hearts filled with tomatoes steamed in butter did. The journalist pointed out that there were already tomatoes in his accompanying *Salade Mona Lisa*; that the same vegetable appeared in both disturbed him. He pronounced the *Fillet de Sole Dieppe Présidence*—*France*'s perennial banquet standby—"cold" and the tails of its langoustine garnish "tough," suggesting they had been frozen. Though the *Tournedos de Boeuf Charolais* passed muster, he was annoyed that his stem-free wineglass held half of what he considered a respectable ration of claret. Dessert—an iced parfait garnished with whipped cream and crystallized violets—rated approval but his meal ended with a cheese disappointment: his slice of La Grappa proved to be nothing more than rind studded with a mouthful of grape seeds.

His closing riposte? "Reputedly, the cost of the *France* is $80,000,000. Part of the funds might have been allocated to more than the decor."

One was reminded, ruefully, of Croisile's assurance that *France*'s failure to capture the *ruban bleu* would be offset by *cordon bleu*. Now, writing in America's most influential newspaper, America's most influential foodie delivered a stinging rebuke.

The byline on that slap in *France*'s face was Craig Claiborne. One cannot overestimate the contemporary impact of that name. Claiborne reigned over New York as a well-known if controversial arbiter. He was a dedicated cook who despised iceberg lettuce, loved lemon chicken, and remained at prickly odds with most of his peers. Long before Julia Child urged America to "master the art of French cooking," Claiborne popularized ethnic cooking, changing the way millions of readers approached food.

Had he been younger, one might have dismissed him as enfant terrible; as it was, Craig Claiborne enjoyed the persona of acerbic, articulate snob whose nationwide clout was formidable. Rest assured, he would weigh in again on *France*'s cuisine.

CHAPTER SIX

TWELVE LAVISH YEARS

The French Line's gastronomic tradition was always closer to the Rabelasian concept of overabundance than to the leaner style of the modern cooks.

Joseph Wechsberg

Je peux vous dire qu'on était fiers de notre travail.
On faisait quatorze heures par jour et on était radieux!

(I can tell you that we were proud of our work. We'd put in fourteen-hour days and were radiant!)

René Montier, France maître d'hôtel

Scrambled eggs will never let you down.

Ian Fleming

Opposite: Champagne and cotillons, an irresistible combination
at the height of gala nonsense in the Grand Salon. (Author's collection)

The Maxtone-Grahams' maiden France *embarkation was in December 1968. My first wife, Katrina,*

and I with our four children booked a Christmas/New Year's jaunt to the Caribbean. A cruise as opposed to crossing, it came complete with cruise director, shore excursions, and largely outdoor shipboard, a sea change from gray Atlantic passage.

Still there was gray weather en route. Then, winter Caribbean cruises originated in New York, America's busiest passenger port. Miami and Fort Lauderdale were only the palest carbon copies of the megatermini they would become. Dominating Port Everglades' waterfront that year was retired *Queen Elizabeth*, a failing nightclub, hotel, and curiosity. After a year's Floridian disinterest, Cunard's superannuated flagship was bought by Chinese shipping magnate C. Y. Tung before limping out to Hong Kong and destruction.

France in March 1962 about to depart from Pier 88. (Willis Wright collection)

Conversely, *France* was in her sixth year, blessed with a bountiful servant ratio, incomparable food, and exquisite service. Yet however superb a liner and though marvelously air-conditioned, she proved a makeshift cruise ship. Naval architect Jean Coune had made scant provision for warm-weather deployment. Of the two pools, belowdeck first class's was undeniably indoors. Tourist class's, near the stern, was sited beneath what seemed a retractable Magrodome; in fact, that steel-framed glazing was immovable, sheltering another indoor pool.

Despite those shortcomings, we found our first French Line experience a delight. The six of us were accommodated in three tourist class cabins on Pont Promenade. They were not only roomy enough for all our luggage, including a small trunk of Christmas presents, they also offered views over the bow. Additional advantage was adjacency to portside's Salle des Jeunes for the two older children and starboard side's playroom for the younger.

The French Line's most marvelous perquisite was an extraordinary standard of service, from *commissaire principale* down to the lowliest *mousse* or bellboy. Deferential, deft, and devastatingly efficient, crew skills had been refined to a degree rarely equaled elsewhere. Whether headed south for Martinique or, later, east to Havre, *France* was exemplary.

No finer exemplar greeted us in the dining room than mustachioed Max Lucas, one of five assistant maîtres d'hôtel *de rang* who became our dining room captain of choice. He could recite each day's menu by heart, recommending and advising with judicious aplomb. His skill with a chafing dish was impressive, as were the dispatch and diligence of our *chef de rang* and *commis* waiter whom Lucas galvanized with the loft of an eyebrow. Nothing was impossible: every dish arrived promptly, the food hot or chilled as required, and beluga dispensed, if not with a trowel, with indulgence.

Cruise itineraries periodically disrupt passage with visits ashore. For those inured to North Atlantic's sole embarkation and disembarkation, stepping ashore in mid-passage was novel. *France* would anchor at a Baedeker of destinations, now numbingly familiar but then unknowns. Nowhere could *France* tie up; her hull was too deep and her length too great.

After Nassau, our second call was Martinique. I well remember the utter naïveté with which six Maxtone-Grahams tackled their first port call. Up early, a hasty breakfast, and, encumbered with towels, bathing suits, cameras, and snorkels, we descended for tender embarkation too early and waited more than an hour within the stifling tedium of B Deck's alleyway.

Finally ensconced in an island-based tender, we were treated to an impressive panorama of *France* from sea level, impossible in either New York or Le Havre. There followed a shoreward run into increasing humidity and a landing devoid of welcome. Save for hungry taxi drivers, shopkeepers, or tour operators, locals seemed happiest ignoring us. Lunch was forgettable. I remember queuing up for a bad hamburger while hovering like a Tantalus on the horizon was *France*, aboard which an air-conditioned luncheon, *for which I had already paid*, was being served.

Although a midday buffet was offered along the first class Pont Promenade, discriminating passengers were loath to abandon their civilized dining room. Yet however civilized, jarring informalities obtained. Caps were occasionally worn at table, though not yet backward. Max Lucas and his colleagues learned to accept that sunbathing and swimming passenger loads irrevocably eroded French Line standards. There was no "dress code" aboard *France* and no such rules were ever promulgated; it was simply assumed that passengers would dress appropriately day or night.

France's *mousses* were clad in the same silver-buttoned jackets as their predecessors aboard *Normandie*. For warm weather, red tunics were replaced by white. I admired the extraordinary restraint of the *mousses* manning the glass doors halfway down the staircase entry. Extravagantly dressed lady passengers continually swept past. Never once did either teenager betray, by the slightest flicker, any reaction to that bizarre *paseo*; for ones so young, their discipline was remarkable.

Mousses's epaulettes were color-coded to indicate seniority: black braid adorned every beginner's shoulders, white their senior colleagues'. To improve comprehension, *mousses* had been schooled in conversational English at Le Havre's Ecole des Mousses. Though most were semifluent, French maritime historians Claude Villers and Christian Clères interviewed one retired *mousse* who confessed that he had never mastered more than four English words. Asked any question, he volunteered the same crisp, always effective response: "Two decks down, sir!"

All passengers, French and American alike, spoiled those young shamelessly. They were forever admired, cosseted, and sometimes petted by the indulgent clients they served. *Mousses* were always dragooned as extras for photo shoots and women often posed in their distinctive hats. For Americans, *mousses* recalled a popular image featuring Johnny Rovantini, a 47-inch (119 centimeters) New Yorker Hotel bellhop, perpetually on "Call for Philip Morris!," musically accompanied

Top left: The first class pool with Jean Mayonon's ceramic *Fountain* beside it and a mirrored fixture overhead. (Compagnie Générale Transatlantique)

Top right: *France*'s tourist class pool at the after end of Promenade Deck. Though sheathed with glass, it was still essentially an indoor facility; double doors at the after end were opened for fresh air but the roof was permanent and unmovable. (Norwegian Caribbean Line)

Below: Ballet dancers atop tourist class's pool roof. (Henry Holtz Collection)

Top: A buffet set up along the first class promenade: tempting, but less so than a dining room table. (William Archibald collection)

Bottom: The Maxtone-Grahams enjoy an abstemious deckchair aperitif before lunch. (Author's collection)

room's after terrace. Passenger balconies fatally fragment the passenger corpus and no *France* cabin boasted one. We were all—literally and happily—in the same boat, never more blessedly than at departure time, when *l'heure bleu* (the blue hour) descended.

Leaving a Technicolor smear along the horizon, the sun had vanished. Heat and humidity relented and breezes caressed the open decks. As the turbines' gentle throb started underfoot, retrieved anchors clunked upward, to be hosed off and housed. *France* stood away into the night, and island lights receded astern as, trailing an arc of white wake through semitropical dusk, the pilot boat left our side, saluted by a triple farewell from above.

Aboard ship, movement is all. As passage resumed, suddenly, magically, all was right with our world. Those benevolent twilight episodes set the mood for every night that followed. Contagious, nocturnal giddiness infused every public room.

A different contagion infected our northbound return, painful sting in the cruise's tail. Off Cape Hatteras, gale winds kicked up mountainous seas that jarred *France* badly. Aged forty and more susceptible to ship's motion than today, I found nothing more unpleasant than packing in unruly weather, particularly that far forward. Bending over to transfer clothing from drawer to suitcase became progressively nauseating, toil that finally lapsed in favor of Dramamine-laced, prone therapy. Perhaps a Saint Hatteras should have been nominated as patron saint of Miami and Fort Lauderdale, because sea conditions in the vicinity of that protruding Carolingian coastline plagued too many winter runs into or out of New York.

That jolting finale notwithstanding, *France* hooked us completely. I brought home a souvenir, a gold miniature of the vessel that a jeweler attached to my key chain. The memory of the ship, her crew, and hypnotic onboard ambience ensured that *France* crossings became annual indulgences whenever possible. During the early seventies, the Maxtone-Grahams divided their patronage between *QE2* and *France*.

One coincidental surprise greeting our return was a Craig Claiborne review in the *New York Times* of 2 January, 1969. In stunning contrast to his put-down seven years earlier was utter capitulation. The headline alone was pure gold: "THE FINEST RESTAURANT IN THE WORLD: S.S. FRANCE." Here was a remarkable volte-face, from nitpicking visitor to

by burros' clop-clopping hooves from Ferde Grofé's *Grand Canyon Suite*.

It was those Caribbean evenings aboard *France* that remain in the mind, representing far more than the sum of incomparable food, amusing companions, diverting cabaret, brisk music, and polished service. Perhaps because so many of our cruising days were spent anchored offshore, restorative evenings returning us to sea generated compelling satisfaction.

It seemed that every passenger gathered companionably on deck or crowded the smoking

besotted passenger. Claiborne lionized Henri Le Huédé, *France*'s legendary *chef de cuisine*.

Extravagant accolades for seagoing restaurants are all very well but I find it hard to believe that any galley could seriously compete with a land-based restaurant's daily reprovisioning. Fernand Point's fabled restaurant Pyramide in Vienne, which Claiborne much admired, serves as such a case. Point had at his disposal a rich selection of neighboring markets where the freshest meat, fish, vegetables, cheese, and spices could be selected each day to stock Pyramide's storied larders. How can one equate that cornucopia with spoils from *France*'s cold-storage C-Deck lockers, reprovisioned only every fortnight?

What really prompted Claiborne's accolade was the French Line's enviable catering commitment: throughout every voyage, first class menus were never repeated. Moreover, any passenger requesting a *specialité* was, if humanly possible, accommodated. No request was too special for M. Le Huédé and his driven staff.

One vignette from 1964 reveals the lengths to which *France*'s galley would go. New York academics Allen Hyman and his wife, Valerie, were sailing eastbound for a year's residency at Oxford. On their first night they were handed menus. Despite English translation, neither had the faintest idea what to order.

Then they overheard occupants of an adjoining table. Offered menus, the husband waved them aside and produced some index cards.

"This," he said, handing the captain the top one, "is what we would like tonight. And here"—a second card—"is what we would like for lunch and dinner tomorrow. In fact, for every day of the crossing, if you would be so kind, these are our orders."

Seizing a heaven-sent opportunity, Hyman told his captain: "We'll have what they're having."

And they did. A succession of incredible dishes, not one of them on the menu, was delivered to the two adjacent tables all the way to Le Havre.

It was, then, the provision of those apparently limitless menus, no less than the additional privilege of ordering outside them, that prompted Claiborne's panegyric. Yet despite its extravagant headline, his was not quite an unqualified rave. Two things distressed him. The size of *France*'s wine glasses still upset him and another complaint, matching my own: "The decor of the dining room is not one of the glories of *France*. It is handsome

and comfortable but somehow too cold and bright."

He crossed aboard *France* many times in company with celebrated chef Pierre Franey. On one occasion, only hours before *France*'s Havrais departure, the two were invited onto the pier by Le Huédé to participate in a privileged ritual, a *dégustation* (tasting) that took place at a table for three just inside a warehouse door. For two hours, Claiborne, Franey, and their host sampled freshly opened provender—caviar, foie gras, fruits, hams, and cheeses. After each had been tasted and evaluated, those deemed ac-

Aboard for a crossing, Alfred Hitchcock clowns with a cooperative *mousse*. Having stolen his hat, Hitch throttles the young crewman for good measure. **(The French Line)**

ceptable were entered by an *aide de cuisine* into a black-bound ledger and consigned on board.

On that same crossing, Claiborne and Franey hosted a cooking demonstration starring—who else?—Chef Le Huédé. It was a bravura performance, complete with diagonal sloping mirror suspended above a combined oven and cooking range that was wheeled in and set up before a capacity passenger audience.

Traveling with four children, three double cabins were obligatory. I recall their every detail. There was no single or double bed option; *France* couples slept *à part* in single beds, one below the porthole, the other paralleling the bathroom wall. The outboard bed became a sofa by day but, rigged for sleep, the resultant bed provided a perfect night's rest, its linen of exceptional quality and pillows boasting a superior loft.

Suiting the vessel's stringently nonflammable regime, metal predominated. Paired, four-drawer steel bureaus, nearly 5 feet (1.5 meters) wide, filled the wall between beds, their facades softened by Henri Lancel's exquisitely mottled, blue-gray enameling. There were no knobs, only a segmented vertical bar that opened every drawer easily. They clicked shut thanks to a built-in latch that kept them closed save during the worst turbulence. One top drawer came equipped with a sliding lid that became a cantilevered writing surface. It proved, alas, useless for no cabin chair was the correct height for it.

Bolted in place atop the bureau was a table lamp, its triangular glass base topped by a cylindrical white parchment shade. The (unconcealed) telephone next to it was a standard French instrument with a special chrome clip that kept the handset firmly cradled. A similar bad-weather failsafe protected cabin flower arrangements. *France*'s standard vase was made of trumpet-shaped chrome with a CGT logo on one side. Its secret weapon? A powerful magnet concealed in the base locked it firmly in place on the steel bureau's surface.

There was one oversize, comfortable armchair in the middle of the room and a low table that, quasi-Canterbury, incorporated into one end a vertical rack for storing magazines or newspapers.

Erected atop *France*'s after funnel was a fixed television aerial for shipboard reception. But only *appartements de luxe* were equipped with sets and all their programming originated on board. There were no satellites and neither nonexistent CNN nor ESPN could be beamed aboard in midocean.

Cabin lighting was markedly improved over *Liberté*'s. Late-night readers were accommodated with beautifully masked lamps built into the wall at the head of each berth; light spilled nowhere but onto the page. All lights could be remotely controlled via master switches near each pillow; extinguished, they glowed in waiting. There was one mystery ceiling lamp high above. It seemed a natural were an upper berth to be deployed from the ceiling, but the same fixture hung in accommodations without that overhead berth.

Along the opposite wall was a dressing table backed by a three-way mirror, a full-length oval glass flanked by adjustable winged additions. Its kidney-shaped top had room for makeup, brushes, and combs, and a switch box was studded with three ivory-colored buttons. One, incised with a violin, delivered classical music, its neighbor's saxophone promised lighter fare, and the third broadcast shipboard announcements. Two additional buttons summoned cabin staff, a red one for *garçon de cabine* and a green for *femme du chambre*.

Bracketing the dressing table on one side was a curtained alcove in which several suitcases or a trunk could be strapped. On the other side were closets, either two or three, depending on whether the cabin had an optional upper berth. The great advantage of accommodations catering to a nonexistent third occupant was additional hanging space. All *France* closet rods were made purposely thinner than American ones, so too the diameter of the hooks atop the plastic hangers, extruded undersize to discourage pilferage.

Adjoining bathrooms were white/black, their only color intrusion turquoise-patterned bath mats and hand towels, suspended on rails encircling the sink's overhang. Generous white bath towels hung from steam-heated pipes. Anchored on clips low on the wall was a stainless steel waste basket, elevated handily above floor level for ease of mopping.

Though huge, bathtubs could be filled in a trice because of torrents delivered through a heroic spout. Unlike already dated bathrooms aboard both *Queens*, saltwater faucets had vanished; the French Line no longer offered that traditional ancient saline option.

Beneath the sink's mixing spout was a supplementary outlet dispensing ice water. The medicine cupboard was equipped with fluorescent strips top and bottom for better shaving. A slit cut into the back of the cupboard accepted used double-

Above: Prosaic but practical, *France* standard flower vase with its patented magnetized base. In rough weather, flowers might slop but they never slid or toppled. (Author's collection)

edged razor blades of the period, accumulation of which would never overflow the generous cavity into which they fell. As I write these words, workers tearing *Norway* to pieces must be disinterring caches of rusted blades, detritus from millions of shaves accumulated over the vessel's four decades.

France stewards had an ingenious means of determining when their passengers departed their cabins of a morning. On Cunarders and, indeed, aboard most cruise ships, stewards insert a telltale scrap of paper into their cabins' doorjambs. Once the door opens, the paper falls, ignored by the occupant but indicating a vacated cabin.

France's system was tidier. Out of lead foil from empty wine bottles, stewards cut a piece about 1 inch × ½ inch (2½ × 1¼ centimeters). After folding it in half lengthwise, they wrapped the foil loosely around a pin. Crimped together, its ends became a small revolving flag. The pin's point was inserted into the topmost rubber gasket framing the door and the flag flipped up to lean against the door. Once it opened the flag dropped. The following morning it could be reset and no blizzard littered the alleyway.

Among the most interesting cabins aboard *France* were six insides up on Sun Deck aft of number 1 funnel. They were all singles, that rara avis throughout today's cruising fleets; not one cabin for solo occupant exists aboard *Queen Mary 2*. Happily, NCL's *Norwegian Epic* of 2010 has remedied matters.

None of those *France* singles were necessarily grand but they were *located* in grand country. All might have remained insides save for some ingenious legerdemain that transformed them into putative outsides with no sea view. Jean Coune had gouged a square, central opening in their midst, which he christened the Patio de Provence. All six had access to that central patio, turning them into technical outsides, the view, alas, restricted to their neighbors' windows. I never saw passengers enjoying the Patio de Provence, only seagulls, but at least it upgraded the surrounding accommodations to match their more elegant neighbors.

France's class sandwich complicated the task of the berthing department. In the old days, when classes were accommodated vertically, it was relatively simple to shift class barriers to suit passenger demand. Cabins on either side of the frontier were described as interchangeables, the same word in French or English. An interchangeable could be

Top: Classic first class cabin layout. Though no third bunk can be lowered from the ceiling, that strange lamp hangs mysteriously in place. (Philippe Baudry collection, courtesy Patrick Depelsenaire)

Left: That this is a black-and-white photograph makes sense for, apart from towels and bath mats, interior decor was strictly black and white as well. (Philippe Baudry collection, courtesy Patrick Depelsenaire)

viewed as either an inferior first or upgraded tourist so that expectations of either occupant were met. Sited strategically throughout the vessel were 145 of them.

Their existence permitted a marketing strategy as old as port and starboard. Additional first class space could be provided by moving a barrier one way; if the reverse obtained, the barrier was adjusted in the opposite direction. That elastic rejiggering of capacity was a win/win proposition: tourists assigned to interchangeables enjoyed improved perks while the company increased revenue on the barrier's other side.

Over her dozen years of transatlantic service, France's respective class numbers would change: first class grew and tourist shrank. The following table summarizes how her class allotments morphed.

	First	Tourist	Total	Crew
1962	400	1,600	2,000	1,044
1972	518	1,402	1,920	1,044

The only downside of expanding first class was that two sittings became mandatory in the originally designed one-sitting dining room.

For cruises, all France passengers were united within one class. Amazingly, it would not be until June 1969, after seven years of intermittent New York cruises, that the French Line finally faced reality. Commissaire Paul Hermel, France's purser, told me how innocently the brouhaha had begun.

A lost lady passenger asked a steward for directions to the dining room. Before pointing the way, the man understandably inquired, "First or tourist class?"

The twentieth-century aural equivalent of "the face that launched a thousand ships," his words should never have been uttered aboard a one-class vessel. Meals shipwide were presumed to embrace gastronomic parity; inference that one might be superior was a no-no.

The woman's husband, a Manhattan lawyer, demanded of Hermel how there could be a first class and a tourist class dining room aboard a one-class vessel. With the combined tact and diplomacy for which he was justifiably renowned, Hermel deflected the query, mollifying the couple with some champagne and shipboard souvenirs.

Still, that glaring flaw demanded remedy. The moment France tied up in New York, a crash program of generic public room names was instigated.

First- and tourist class dining rooms were renamed Restaurants Chambord and Versailles. First class's Grand Salon was dubbed Salon Fontainebleau and tourist's Salon Saint-Tropez. The first class smoking room became Salon Riviera and, one deck below, tourist's La Rive Gauche (Left Bank). In the cinema, first class balcony and tourist orchestra were thrown open to all.

Plastic signs bearing the new names—elephant gray on a bronze base—were rushed into production in Paris. Twenty-eight of them pointed left and twenty-eight right. Additional cardboard signs, destined for staircases, had angled arrows indicating up or down.

When France steamed into Havre a week later, cartons of signs were embarked and held in readiness for the next cruise. Daily cruising programs would be amended to reflect the new nomenclature and an urgent ukase was circulated forbidding use of the prefixes "first" or "tourist" whenever France went cruising.

From the very first, I became attracted to the smoking room's evocative reek of Gitanes cigarettes; one could buy them on board for 10 cents a pack, $1 a carton. When I renounced cigarettes in 1972, I still possessed fifteen hundred Gitanes that were summarily discarded.

Because of America's present-day disenchantment with tobacco, it may be hard to convey to contemporary readers the appeal of smoking rooms; more—far more—than the demon nicotine was involved.

Transatlantic smoking rooms had metamorphosed from turn-of-the-century, men-only sancta for smoking, drinking, gambling, and occasional vulgarity into larger, less smoky, and prettier public rooms admitting their wives. Make no mistake, these were substantial, well thought out facilities that bore little resemblance to the token, vestigial cigar lairs for the incurables aboard today's cruise ships.

France's was a bright, double-height venue where I always found that the vessel's most amusing passengers gathered for cocktails, games, tea, conversation, or, thanks to its open-air after terrace, breezy contemplation of sea, sky, and stern.

That outdoor option was another smoking room innovation aboard France. Equally groundbreaking and reinforcing the room's unmistakable unisexual character, dancing was on permanent offer as well. A mosaic dance floor occupied the room's

Opposite: Cabin door ingenuity. Top left, one of France's homemade steward's flags, armed and ready. Top right, door opens, flag drops. Bottom, Norwegian Cruise Line's ne plus ultra cabin indicator on contemporary tonnage. Turning a knurled wheel dials up multiple options, from yellow background WELCOME to red DO NOT DISTURB to blue TURN DOWN CABIN. (Author's collection)

center and a six-piece orchestra set up shop nightly. In *France*'s smoking room, dancing was a first.

Also contributing to the special flavor was that it never served as a performance venue. Easily moved furniture could be and was liberated; chairs faced in every direction. Some surrounded card tables while others were grouped with only coffee tables at their centers. There is no more important characteristic of a successful smoking room than seating impulsively amplified numbers: a table for two must become, instantly and effortlessly, a table for ten. One interesting seating option paralleled the bar just aft of its eight white-leather stools. Upholstered in beige leather, it was an athwart-ship row of interlocking "conversational" sofas, each two seats wide. Occupying couples faced alternately bar or dance floor.

The smoking room was a joyous Innisfree, busy, light-filled, and fun. Its sound track still echoes endearingly in the mind's ear—the rattle of backgammon dice, the song of the shaker, the riffle of shuffled bridge or patience decks, the clatter of dominoes or mah-jongg tiles, in exuberant contrast to the freighted silence of a corner chess game. The space was better patronized than the Grand Salon, offering as it did superior sea views because of its surrounding terraces. I remember reading on the starboard *terrasse* one mid-Atlantic morning when a whale surfaced no more than a stone's throw away before vanishing.

Behind the bar, Raymond Cordier held sway, iron hand coupled with winning smile. Having sailed with the company for thirty years, he would not retire until *France* did. At constant beck and call was his corps of genial stewards. Smoking room billets were highly coveted; there was minimal involvement with food—the bane of every shipboard job—and tips were liberal, sometimes tipsily dispensed and hastily pocketed late at night. That substantial cash flow, added to income produced by anchor and mileage pools that passengers never won, ensured bountiful income. In both classes, save for the maîtres d'hôtel, smoking room stewards were the richest nonpassengers on board.

Mind you, every penny was hard-earned. Their discretion and dispatch added immeasurably to the smoking room mystique. An obliging man was perpetually yet unobtrusively at one's elbow, delivering coffee, bouillon, or drink appropriately while, at the same time, never discommoding obsessive

bridge and backgammon nor disrupting conversational flow.

Perhaps the smoking room's greatest attraction was that it was such a congenial imbibing venue. Drinks throughout *France* were not only plentiful and speedily delivered, they were also, like those Gitanes, inexpensive. Shipping lines had not yet zeroed in on booze as a major revenue source and reasonable bar charges were traditional. Each round was paid for on delivery in American dollars, predating today's stringently cash-free shipboard.

In both dining rooms, though, acceptable *vins*

Still first class but, on cruises, no longer so identified; the emergence of Chambord restaurant. (Author's collection)

ordinaires were gratis; the price for more recherché vintages was similarly inexpensive. A presentable Bordeaux, Château Haut-Brion, for instance, sold for 75 francs ($15). Wines aboard *France* were veritable bargains, substantially less expensive than the equivalent charged ashore.

Because of that shipwide benevolence, the pace within all *France* public rooms was brisk, tempi that intensified after sunset. And robust *France* evenings were different from those aboard today's cruise ships because, I believe, a more independent passenger mind-set prevailed. Despite evening films, an occasional concert in the Salle de Spectacle, or sessions of cabaret or games in the Grand Salon, a persuasive and infectious life force suffused every public room. Long after dinner, sustained if necessary by late-night delicacies from the Cabaret de l'Atlantique, one danced and drank every night away.

Because of passenger enthusiasm and low prices, much alcohol was consumed. One smoking room ceremony I recall every sunset was the de-

fenestration of hundreds of empties—beer, wine, and spirits—that had accumulated in the bar pantry. They filled several dozen tall wicker baskets that, one by one, toiling barmen dragged out onto the starboard terrace and emptied noisily through an opened window into the sea.

The procedure was, alas, typical of those ignorant, carefree days, before ecological prudence took precedence and the sea was no longer perceived as an unfettered dump. I sometimes envision the ocean floor underlying French Line tracks between Le Havre and New York as thickly carpeted with an inert accumulation of bottles.

But *France* passenger life did not revolve exclusively around alcohol. Ship's personnel were forever at pains to enhance every passenger's crossing. In 1970, Dr. Stanley Yachnin, a University of Chicago professor specializing in hematology/oncology, was en route to spend a sabbatical in England. His friend Bob Lapin came down to Pier 88 to see him off aboard *France*. Yachnin had just endured a bitter divorce and was feeling low. Before disembarking, Lapin cornered tourist class's maître d'hôtel, suggesting that Dr. Yachnin needed cheering up.

"*Je comprends complètement*" (I understand perfectly), was his response. That enterprising factotum assigned the Chicagoan to a tableful of single ladies. Suffice to say, Yachnin enjoyed a riotous crossing.

Although he is no longer alive, both his daughter Catherine and his friend Robert Lapin sailed with me aboard *Queen Mary 2* in 2008. Catherine Yachnin, now Braendel, recalled returning home aboard *France* with her father after his sabbatical in July 1971. As they stood at the rail sailing down Southampton water, he suggested some ground rules.

"Catherine, on this crossing, you are free to do as you wish all day. My only stipulation is that, dressed appropriately, you join me promptly each night for dinner. Otherwise, you are totally on your own."

So began, for a delighted eight-year-old, five carefree days, replete with blessed independence. Urban American children, protectively supervised at home, thrive on shipboard freedom. There was another girl her age at the table and the two became inseparable, spending endless, waterlogged hours in tourist class's pool. By night, they roamed the open decks, hanging over the railings to watch the sea race past in *France*'s porthole spill. "I was never bored!" she confessed.

Catherine has twice sailed aboard *Queen Mary 2* with her husband, Addison, and their children. Grown-ups crossing by sea inevitably replicate the parental indulgences so fondly recalled from childhood, perpetuating shipboard's generational continuum to perfection. Their two sons and a daughter flourished under the same freedom she had enjoyed at their age.

Another fellow passenger on that same crossing was also a dedicated *France* veteran, Ligoa Raymond Seligman. Her Greek mother had been Penelope Sekelianos and her American father, Raymond Duncan, was the brother of the celebrated dancer Isadora.

Born in Paris, Ligoa grew up during the German occupation, camping out for much of the day in a revival cinema on the rue des Ecoles, which was warmer than her frigid apartment. From repeatedly screened Fred and Ginger sound tracks, Ligoa taught herself English.

Postwar, sailing westbound to Paris aboard *Liberté*, the master introduced her to the man she would marry, William Benbow Seligman, an Alsatian, *not* a German, as she insisted to her momentarily outraged mother. She and Bill were married in 1956. A year later, Ligoa gave birth to a daughter, Dorée.

The Seligmans became art dealers, establishing the Duncan Art Center in Manhattan. They used to cross twice yearly aboard *France*, concealing French canvases in their personal luggage, a customs violation. Once, a dozen rolled canvases had been consigned inside a wicker trunk of her aunt Isadora's. A suspicious agent plunged a probe repeatedly through the wicker but, fortunately, not a painting was pierced.

Whenever her father Raymond sailed with them, he insisted they travel first class. "Finest restaurant in the world" or no, ruthless vegetarian Raymond ate only porridge and baked potatoes. Sailing on their own, the three Seligmans were content in tourist, always booked in cabin 329 aft on Pont Promenade, adjacent to the pool where Ligoa swam every day before breakfast. She and Bill preferred eating at large tables, on either the main floor or the balcony. Ligoa ate only pasta, bread, and—insatiably—*crêpes suzette*, to which, she freely confessed at age ninety-three, she is still addicted.

MENU

Fruits Rafraîchis aux Liqueurs

Saumon Fumé d'Ecosse
Homard Cocktail
Terrine de Foie Gras de Strasbourg

La Soupe à l'Oignon au Parmesan
Consommé Froid Madrilène

Welsh Rarebit
Œufs Brouillés sur Canapé ·· Œufs Plat au Jambon

Petites Saucisses Grillées ·· Hot Dog

Club Sandwich

Jambon de Bayonne ·· Jambon d'York
Poulet Froid
Glace ·· Petits Fours Secs

≡

Late-night sustenance available from the Cabaret de l'Atlantique. It did a land office business. (Stirling Kenny collection)

Her quest for the perfect crêpe was relentless. On her first *France* crossing, she asked the maître d'hôtel which of his four captains made the best. "All of them are excellent," he assured her. Dissatisfied, Ligoa decided to find out for herself. The first gala evening, carrying plate and fork, she circled both dining room levels, sampling crêpes from four rival pans before selecting her favorite. Its owner would prepare her *crêpes suzette* on every crossing.

A fourth member graced the Seligman party, Chi-chi, a much-adored Chihuahua. He crossed regularly aboard *France* and accompanied his mistress everywhere, perched inside a carryall. Nights were spent with his owners in cabin 329 rather than the ship's kennel. But whenever the ship called at Southampton, Chi-chi had to be confined within a kennel cage because of United Kingdom quarantine regulations. Once, by error, the dog was inadvertently left caged overnight. So annoyed and bereft was he, Ligoa reports, that "for three days, Chi-chi would not speak to us."

A promotional packet of Gitanes; *gitane* means "gypsy," hence the exotic silhouette. The reverse shows that *France* was in league with the manufacturer, endorsing the product with some unmistakable funnels.

(Author's collection)

On one of their last crossings, during a family visit to the bridge, Commandant Pettré let teenager Dorée steer the vessel. That the master should indulge Ligoa was scarcely surprising; she was an indefatigable and infectiously enthusiastic passenger. She often sang from the stage of the Salle de Spectacle, sometimes performing on the same bill as Parisian cellist Maurice Baquet. Her performances were well received; one first class shipmate, impresario Sir Rudolf Bing, praised both her range and her style. After *France* was withdrawn, the Seligmans switched their allegiance, reluctantly, to *Mikhail Lermontov*.

Fortunately, I have never yet missed a sailing, but one of *France*'s most junior and newest crew members did on her first day's employment. Odette Escolier was a young Parisian hairdresser who joined the vessel in Havre on 16 June 1969, together with two other equally green male colleagues. They found their cabins, had a meal in the crew mess, and then, to their delight, realized the ship was making a port call, about which they had been told nothing.

It was Southampton, of course. Odette and her two friends walked ashore in search of postcards. It was already 9 P.M. before they reached the center of town, only to discover that everything had closed. But they finally found a hotel that sold both postcards and stamps, which they wrote and posted before strolling back to the docks. When they spied the Ocean Terminal, those distinctive funnels had disappeared. Then they caught sight of *France* in the distance, sailing down Southampton Water without them.

Fortunately, that desperate trio found a marine superintendent with a radio. He called the vessel, advised the bridge, and, minutes later, a tug appeared alongside the dock. They jumped down onto its after deck and set off in pursuit. Their vessel surged to a position beneath an open port in *France*'s side, from which a Jacob's ladder was flung. Ladies first: after identifying herself, Odette scrambled up the ladder and into the arms of waiting crewmen.

For a newcomer it was nerve-racking. She might have lost her job before it began. But there must be a patron saint who looks after those who miss ships. The castaway trio was spared and Odette stayed on board until 1972. Eleven years after her calamitous Southampton adventure, I would encounter Odette Escolier on the same pier under very different circumstances.

In 1967 *France* was beleaguered by financial storms, sailing at a loss for the first time. As a result, she began crossing less and cruising more, completing a total of ninety-three cruises over her dozen years of service. They varied from short Caribbean outings from New York to Mediterranean circuits originating in Le Havre. Longer cruises were dispatched to St. Helena or the African coast. In February 1963, *France* crossed the equator for the first time, steaming down to Rio de Janeiro from New York and back again.

The pinnacle of the company's cruising ambition were two world cruises, in 1972 and 1974. Those epic, three-month circumnavigations were company firsts *and* lasts: *France* remains the only Transat vessel that ever circled the globe.

Because of her post-Panamax dimensions, she had to toil 'round the Horn. And the extent of that South American time cruncher restricted ensuing Pacific deployment. Steaming no farther north than Hong Kong, not one Japanese call was offered; in the opposite direction no Australasian visits were included either.

That 1972 cruise was marketed with a Jules Vernean rubric: *Around the World in 88 Days*. *France* would travel 45,816 nautical miles, departing Havre on 5 January, arriving back at Cannes on 2 April and New York six days later. Her passengers would troop ashore at twenty-nine ports, twenty of them maiden Pacific calls.

Crossing between Havre, Southampton, and New York was easy. Long-established refueling and reprovisioning points were dovetailed neatly between five-day spans. But once 'round the Horn, familiar checkpoints no longer applied. New refueling ports had to be plotted, reprovisioning outlets located, and mountains of soiled linen, tablecloths, towels, and napkins washed far from customary Havrais and New York laundries

Circumnavigations are the World Series of passenger shipping. History's first took place in 1922, when four steamers were dispatched on global itineraries: *Laconia, Resolute,* and *Empress of France* sailed westbound while contrarian *Samaria* persevered east. Westbound passengers enjoyed a winter of twenty-five-hour days, while eastbound *Samarians* were inflicted with twenty-three-hour alternatives. *France* planners momentarily debated an easterly rotation but understandably changed their minds.

Although most embarking in January 1972 were repeaters, none had ever remained on board for so long. The preponderant nationalities were 397 French and 292 Americans. Of the total of 1,984 passengers, only 364 had booked for the entire voyage. And those full-timers remained, as they do aboard every world cruise vessel, aloof from the part-timers; predictably, they were also the ones who required the most hand-holding.

World cruisers pay more than dollars; a profound emotional investment is made as well. Everyone becomes a temporary member of an exclusive club with hefty dues. *France*'s least expensive cabin cost 28,000 francs ($5,600), the most expensive half a million francs ($100,000). Small wonder that her passengers assumed a proprietary air about their floating clubhouse. Moments after boarding, preliminary excitement too often veered toward uglier entitlement.

As the vessel plodded around the globe, pursers worked hard to discourage ennui. A fawning indulgence was mandatory. In their defense, passengers committed to those floating pressure cookers faced complex social hurdles. Those traveling alone—widows were commonplace—had to be well looked after. A special "chit-chat corner" was established at one end of the Salon St. Tropez, in session every sea-day morning.

Modest loners created less problems than overly ambitious couples. What many of those inveterate social climbers never realized was that everything about them—clothes, conversation, cabin location, table number, maître d'hôtel's greeting, even the position of their deck chair—automatically ranked them.

Private cocktail parties assumed huge, tribal significance and passenger diaries became figurative *Almanachs de Gotha*. Hosts could be cruelly selective about who would or would *not* be invited and their eagerly awaited guest lists created minefields of insecurity. The only payoff for angst-filled vigils awaiting a coveted invitation appearing beneath the cabin door was smugness at having been included.

World cruises segue inevitably into fashion shows, requiring heroic accumulations of clothing. *France*'s luggage deluge in Havre, Southampton, and New York was formidable. Huge plywood hanging crates, rented from specialist firms ashore, temporarily cluttered alleyways on sailing day. Later, ship's joiners would be summoned to install hanging rods in luggage alcoves once adjoining closets had seriously overflowed.

The two great liabilities were boredom and, surprisingly, increasingly strained compatibility between spouses. At home, retired couples were seldom together full-time. Husbands spent mornings on the golf course while their wives played bridge, read, shopped, or saw friends. Visiting children or grandchildren took up the slack.

Together aboard *France*, however, they slept, woke, played, walked, drank, ate, and sat together all the time, always in each other's pockets. Victims of unrelenting proximity, normally congenial couples suddenly chafed. A male pastime designed to separate husbands from wives, for even a portion of the day, became an urgent necessity.

Enter enterprising assistant purser Jean-Paul Giquel. His sailor father had taught him how to build ship models inside bottles. When he mentioned that talent to his superior, Hermel saw it as a heaven-sent distraction to segregate husbands from their distaff half.

Giquel's ship-in-a-bottle class was organized like a military operation. Riviera barman Raymond was instructed to wash and stockpile dozens of empties, clear glass only. The bosun had joiners cut and set aside 7-inch lengths of soft pine and multiple sandpaper grades. The chief housekeeper provided black button thread for rigging and stiff paper was culled from the print shop for sails. Unearthed

Top: Posing for a publicity still, James and Jackie McVicar were among *France*'s most popular entertainers. (James and Jackie McVicar collection)

Bottom: Dressed for a Parisian Apache romp, preoccupied McVicars (*far left*) with some of their competing clients in La Rive Gauche. (James and Jackie McVicar collection)

from the unused children's playroom came paint, modeling clay, and glue. Giquel went ashore to buy dozens of pocketknives.

Instantly oversubscribed, the class assembled for two-hour sessions for a month, co-opting the smoking room's starboard terrace. Permanent bridge tables were set up, their baize shrouded with canvas. Under Giquel's tutelage, with only minimal gashes and splinters, miniature sailing ship hulls were whittled, shaped, sanded, and painted. Sails, spars, and rigging were measured, cut, glued, and assembled.

A triumphant finale concluded weeks of labor. Completed models, their rigging in flattened configuration, were coaxed inside bottles atop blue-painted, clay seas. Once glued in place, trailing threads were tautened and raising masts and sails set into upright configuration. Protruding lines were tied off and trimmed, then bottles were corked and sealed and borne down for inspection by admiring wives. The class was repeated for *France*'s 1974 circumnavigation and did much to alleviate excess couple coalescence.

One unceasing world cruise preoccupation was outstanding entertainment. Two of the company's most talented standouts remained on board full-time.

North Londoners James and Jackie McVicar had met as teenagers and become expert ballroom dancers, selected as Junior Amateur and Professional Champions. A Dutch talent agent spotted them on television and hired them for gigs aboard Holland-American vessels. Then New York shipboard entertainment specialist Eph Abramson booked them for *Queen Elizabeth*'s final crossing, a westbound aboard *United States*, and then *France*.

It was love at first sight. The McVicars took to the French Line and *France* passengers to them. I sailed with them on several crossings. However flawless their dancing, they were equally appealing offstage. James was a fount of amusing shipboard stories while pert blonde Jackie was, by her own admission, "cheeky" enough to cement shipboard friendships instantaneously.

They interacted with passengers more than their fellow entertainers because they gave dance lessons. The first of many was open to all comers, followed by paid private lessons if requested. On crossings and world cruises, they officiated at a "Champagne Hour," a participation game dating

from their Holland-American days. The two would demonstrate a waltz and then ask six couples to come up and partner one of them in a dance of their own choosing. Lucky participants might garner some champagne. (Passengers are manic about winning anything, no matter what the prize.) Sometimes, French competitors tried stumping them with obscure provincial choreography. But from those informal displays remunerative lessons emerged, nicely supplementing the McVicar coffers.

Whatever the occasion, whether Champagne Hour or dance lesson, the McVicars' excelled, their apparently ad-libbed patter endearing. They had absorbed sufficient French to be comprehensible and their cockney accents captivated. Their vaudevillian routines had been refined into installments of a James & Jackie Show, winsome instruction leavened with broad asides and occasional zingers. James played curmudgeon to Jackie's glib *compère*/hostess, each persona perfectly attuned to the other's.

The couple became not only much-loved components of the company's world cruise appeal, but they instigated long-lasting friendships as well. On the 1972 junket, there was an Englishman on board new to cruising called Joe Levy; his wife was one of their most enthusiastic dance clients. One day, he took James aside and asked, "What are all these cocktail parties about?"

James explained carefully, suggesting that Joe choose a date, alert the chief steward, reserve a room, order liquor, ice, setups, and canapés, and send out invitations to friends.

Joe thanked him and drifted off. A week later, having heard nothing further about the party, James asked him how things were progressing.

"Oh, I've organized the date and laid on the drink. That's all done and dusted. But so far I haven't made any friends."

In fact, Levy's party was never consummated but the couple became the McVicars' close shipboard friends. He was, they discovered, a millionaire many times over and had met his talented wife when she was a dancer at London's Windmill Club. Years later, Jackie reminisced: "They both hated people that tried to be something they were not. This is why they liked us as we were the only ordinary couple of the cruise."

She was right. The McVicars' strongest suit was a guileless, down-to-earth ordinariness that set

William Archibald, *France*'s shore excursion manager, with Commandant Pettré on the bridge during the 1974 world cruise. Flying signal flags indicate that the vessel is in port. Only days earlier both men had soundly rebuked the McVicars for apparently disparaging shore excursions. (William Archibald collection)

South Pacific idyll. Off-duty crewmen soak up sun on *France*'s forward hatch cover. (William Archibald collection)

them apart from too many of their jockeying ship-mates. When they returned to London in the spring, the Levys invited them, as a token of their *France* friendship, to enjoy a week's holiday on their own aboard his crewed yacht in the Riviera.

A McVicar episode from the second world cruise was less salubrious. After the vessel had rounded the Horn, she was steaming north through the Chilean fjords. James was at the star-board rail enjoying the scenery when a neighbor-ing passenger friend, Arthur Swift, asked him what he planned to do the following day in Puerto Montt. James told him that he would probably stroll ashore, grab some lunch, and maybe go shop-ping with Jackie. Swift thanked him and James thought no more about it.

They were overheard by another railbird, Bill Archibald, head of the vessel's tour operations. A balding *Caronia* veteran and longtime shore-excursion specialist, Archibald was dedicated. He and his Thomas Cook staff were the "suits" of the ship, dressed in office garb every day. Archibald's mission was the complete dispatch of every pas-senger ashore, booked on one of his excursions— "all but the infirm or incontinent," he once sug-gested crisply.

That evening, James and Jackie were sum-moned to Commandant Pettré's quarters for what they expected to be cocktails with the master. But there were no other guests and no drinks, only a furious shore excursion manager and irritated captain. Archibald paraphrased both Swift's query and James's innocent response. Then Pettré took up the cudgel, advising the McVicars that if they ever again suggested that passengers go ashore in-dependently, they would be fired and flown home. *France* shore excursion revenue was a sa-cred cash cow.

A few weeks later, Archibald got his comeup-pance, though not because of any McVicar reprisal. *France* was scheduled for a stop at Port Moresby on New Guinea's humid south coast. On offer was an expensive excursion, flying passengers up into the relative cool of the Highlands for a feast of pit-baked pig and a sing-sing by colorfully dressed "stone-age" tribesmen.

Many passengers signed up. Archibald cabled ahead to the port agent, advising him that he would need air transport for several hundred into the hin-terlands. The agent corralled every available DC3 in the territory and, on the morning of *France*'s

The image of *France* juxtaposed against Sydney's famous coat-hanger bridge tells us that she did make an Australian call in 1974 if not in 1972.
(William Archibald collection)

landfall, had them parked nose to tail along Port Moresby's airstrip.

Relays of passengers were bused from pier to plane and clambered aboard to fly up into the Highlands. But when the last aircraft departed two score passengers still waited on the tarmac. Archibald was mystified as to why his carefully calculated head count had gone so disastrously wrong.

He found out later. The agent had laid on the correct number of seats, but his "seats" were aluminum benches with dimpled depressions lining both sides of the fuselage. Though easily accommodating New Guinea rumps, *France* passengers' ampler rumps overlapped into adjacent spaces. Hence the shortfall, hence Archibald's disgruntled leftovers stranded in oppressive humidity, awaiting the return of an empty plane.

Back in transatlantic service, a New York couple who loved ships embarked on a westbound crossing from Le Havre in 1965. Arnold Roth, now a *New Yorker* cartoonist, and his painter wife, Caroline, had sailed eastbound in first class aboard *Rotterdam*; one fellow passenger couple they enjoyed was a Baltimore jeweler named Calvin Smythe, traveling with his mother.

In London, the Roths sublet a flat in Earls Court Square and were delighted to be established for the summer in their favorite city. Arnold produced a daily syndicated half-page commission for the *Chicago Tribune*—"Poor Arnold's Almanac"—which not only kept the wolf from the door but also provided a comfortable London standard of living.

They decided to return to New York aboard *France* but, since the *Tribune* syndication was terminated, booked in tourist class. Their Baltimore friends the Smythes were on board in first and sent a message down to the Roths: "All around us, food is going up in flames and we don't know what to order!"

In tourist class, the Roths knew what to order but faced other problems. Rather than fire, their table for two was engulfed by indifference. The just-completed Havrais turnaround had been disrupted by labor unrest; reflecting it, their steward provided only perfunctory service. Worse, their veal arrived practically raw. They, as well as neighboring tablemates, complained. Pointedly, the steward feigned no knowledge of English. Yet he had clearly understood, for the following night every platter of meat was grossly *over*cooked.

An indignant group complaint to the maître d'hôtel sorted things out. The malcontent steward was reassigned and, in turn, the Roths were reassigned to a genial table for eight. Morale improved.

Both Roths enjoyed their *France* crossing enormously. Arnold became a regular at the Rive Gauche's bar while Caroline remained equally delighted with her book and tea tray delivered to her deck chair.

Originally a Philadelphian, Arnold was a fan of the Phillies. The team had done well that summer and he was anxious to know the scores. American sports data were circulated daily on a printed broadsheet but, to Roth's annoyance, the Philadelphia scores were never included.

He pointed out the problem to an assistant purser but, the next day, still no Philadelphia listings; so too the following day. When he approached the desk a third time, the same assistant purser saw him coming. Arnold, in an obviously misguided attempt at humor, raised one knee as though to climb over the desk. Terrified, the purser retired behind a door, which he slammed and locked. For his pains, Arnold had to await New York arrival before catching up with his team.

Instead of fear, another raised passenger knee during a 1968 eastbound aroused an instantaneous, life-saving response. Bob Rubin, his wife, and his mother were having tea in their deck chairs when a middle-aged lady passenger rose from a neighboring seat and made her way to the rail. Once there, she began climbing, hoisting herself up via a vertical stanchion with one hand while her other grasped the railing. Within moments she would have been over the top.

Her movements had been made in surreal, slow motion, so ordinary that no one but the three transfixed New Yorkers took note. Luckily, alert deck stewards did too, seizing the potential suicide by the elbows, lifting her from the railing, and escorting her below to the ship's surgeon.

"Had that woman been successful," mused Rubin, "who knows what our reaction would have been and how would we have felt about making additional crossings?"

From tourist class back to first. Perhaps it is indicative of *France*'s gastronomic renown that so many shipboard anecdotes revolve around food. Though the company prided itself on never repeating menu choices, my favorite *France* dish was, by request, oft-repeated for lunch, a *specialité* that

Max Lucas prepared on demand, *oeufs brouillés* (scrambled eggs).

Atop a serving table, Lucas would gently beat three eggs with a fork in a copper bowl. Then, having anointed his chafing dish with a dab of Norman butter, he decanted the eggs onto it, stirring, cooking, watching, and waiting, occasionally sliding the dish off his flickering twin flames. As they began to cook, he coaxed the eggs into perfect, scrambled consistency before adding cream and another knob of butter, "to stop the cooking," he would mutter conspiratorially.

Then he heaped the concoction onto a heated plate and surrounded it with a singular garnish: four spoonfuls of icy Beluga caviar, set like the compass points in four directions. Max would wipe the plate's rim clean and hand it to the *chef de rang*, who set it before me.

Ian Fleming was right: scrambled eggs, especially *those* scrambled eggs, never let me down.

A 1972 Chambord luncheon: Max Lucas, in black, brass-buttoned jacket, stands nearby. (*Seated, left to right*) Madeleine Jaouen, our au pair, Katrina Maxtone-Graham, and, with back to camera, the author. Serving-table detritus indicates that Lucas's famous scrambled eggs have been dished up. (Ian Maxtone-Graham collection)

CHAPTER SEVEN

DEMISE I

Nous regrettons que votre voyage se termine d'une façon aussi inattendue;
veuillez nous en excuser et comprenez que c'est la seule chance pour nous de voir ce navire
maintenu en service. Nous espérons réussir et avoir la chance de vous accueiller de
nouveau à board. Merci de votre comprehension et de votre collaboration.

(We regret that your voyage on board is being terminated in such an unusual way. Please forgive us and
understand that this is our last and only chance to keep this ship in service. We hope to succeed and to have a
chance to welcome you again in the future on board. Thank you for your understanding and cooperation.)

L'Equipage de "France" (*France*'s crew)

My God! Well, at least there's plenty of food and liquor on board—
the passengers will probably have a ball.

—French Line spokesman on hearing about *France*'s mutiny

Il vaut mieux Norway *libre que* France *enchainé.*

(Better a liberated Norway than an imprisoned France.)

—Retired commandant Georges Croisile

Opposite: Early on the morning of 4 September, 1974, *France* enters a Manhattan slip to tie up
at Pier 88 for the last time. The author stands nearest the camera. (William Jory collection)

Although the jets doomed France, *another factor contributed to her downfall. Just as* Normandie

had been bedeviled by the depression, her postwar successor fell afoul of a worldwide vendetta. In 1960, oil-rich countries allied beneath the acronym OPEC (Organization of Petroleum Exporting Countries) and a second fatal die was cast.

Inevitable ructions followed. In 1977 American drivers faced the first crippling gasoline shortages, leading to unprecedented lines at the pump. But that was only a foretaste of OPEC's increased clout in the first decade of the twenty-first century when the American price per gallon surged past four dollars.

France felt the pinch early on. Her fuel was described in industry parlance as Bunker C crude. This was a residual by-product, the viscous black goo remaining after everything else had been extracted from the original crude. The consistency of molasses, Bunker C crude had to be heated and thinned before ignition. At speed, *France* gobbled a ton a mile. For years, that ton had cost $12; in the seventies, its price escalated to six times its pre-OPEC level.

The visionary de Gaulle might have countenanced that supplementary expense, but his successor, former finance minister Valéry Giscard d'Estaing, chose not to. He saw no reason why French taxpayers should underwrite the expense of transporting largely American passenger loads across the Atlantic. Although a fuel surcharge of $40 was factored into individual ticket prices, the French Line never slowed down *France* although, near 30 knots, ocean liners devour fuel exponentially.

In another attempt to close the gap, *France's* merchant marine minister tried renegotiating *France's* wage scales. But the crew defiantly rejected the proposal. Adversarial positions hardened and the government announced that the vessel would be withdrawn in October 1974. This was a jolting prospect for *France's* crew and passengers, among them the Maxtone-Grahams. Katrina and I and the children were booked for what turned out to be the vessel's last westbound crossing on 30 August, 1974.

The ship was patently at risk. After embarking from Le Havre's Gare Maritime, my son Ian and I returned to the station platform. I asked him to bring his raincoat.

The boat train was still in place. An unforgivable act of thievery followed, which ocean liner collectors among my readers may well condone.

Surreptitiously, we detached one of the enameled French Line plaques from a carriage and tucked it beneath Ian's coat. Then we reembarked, having salvaged at least a vestige of the company's—literal—track record. Had the plaque remained in place, doubtless it would have been junked.

We sailed late from Havre, crossing the Channel overnight to Britain's south coast. Waiting to embark in Southampton was another passenger couple with four children, British ophthalmologist Bill Jory, his wife, Carolyn, and, in descending order from ages ten to three, David, Richard, Virginia, and Clare.

Having spent a fortnight in the UK visiting family, the Jorys were returning to Vancouver. Bill had, in fact, recently read my book *The Only Way to Cross* while recovering from flu in Vancouver. A line from Walter Lord's foreword alarmed him: "The Atlantic liner was taken from us as suddenly as a friend hit by a train."

Before they disappeared, he decided that the Jorys should cross the world's two great oceans. His transatlantic preference was not via "hybrid" *QE2* but pure ocean liner *France*. (Two years later, fulfilling his vow, all six Jorys steamed from Los Angeles to New Zealand aboard *Canberra*.)

They spent their final UK night at Southampton's Dolphin Hotel. Carrying his movie camera, Bill roused his family before dawn and drove them to the Ocean Terminal. The dock gate policeman initially turned them away but Bill persuaded him that this was an historic moment he had to share with his family.

The man waved Bill through and he drove to the pier for some striking footage of inbound *France*. Her illuminated name board confirmed that she was indeed *France* but Bill remembers that the distinctive aroma of Gallic cigarettes wafting across the dock unmistakably betrayed her nationality.

He had booked in tourist class on the starboard side. En route down-Channel, Carolyn had a momentary scare when her two boys disappeared. After a fruitless search of adjacent alleyways, the two miscreants were discovered perched quietly on a porthole ledge, concealed by drawn curtains and enjoying the Cornish coast.

At lunch, Bill and Carolyn were afraid that their brood would deplete the vessel's smoked

A *France* engineer in front of the ignition chamber of a boiler. By 1974 price of the vessel's fuel had become exorbitant. (Compagnie Générale Transatlantique)

salmon supply; it remained their dish of choice for every meal, breakfast included. When they took the children to the playroom, gaining admission from what Bill described as the *gauleiter* at the door, that far forward the motion was unpleasant and the children, by mutual agreement, never returned. Sharp-eyed David had more interesting ploys. He noticed that stewards went into first class by kicking the bottom of a certain pass door; by following suit, he and his siblings managed their own entrée, penetrating first class whenever they wished.

That crossing took place more than three decades ago and its details escape me. I did deliver some lectures because Jory saved his programs and it was after one of them that we met. He thanked me, suggesting tactfully that I had misidentified a Cunarder. I was grateful for the correction and that midocean encounter initiated a long friendship that continues to this day.

The Jorys had embarked in the nick of time. Indeed, hundreds had also decided "to sail on the *France* before it was too late." Jack Sauter, head of an insurance franchise in Manhasset, New York, and his wife, Marianne, boarded for one more *aller/retour*, eastbound from New York on 11 July, coincidentally our eastbound crossing as well.

We reembarked aboard a despondent ship. Though the traditional service patina remained intact, it was offset by a mood of deepest foreboding. Max Lucas's ebullience had dimmed. Betraying his *tristesse* was a vocal tell conveyed by upset Frenchmen, a fricative intake of breath through tightened lips and teeth.

The same malaise infected all the crew, regardless of the fact that their own intransigence had precipitated the crisis. Defiant posturing was over. Their bluff had been called and d'Estaing's hardball response had put jobs and futures in jeopardy.

Maiden voyages are delights. Whereas new ships entering service generate excitement and promise, final voyages, mirror images ending a vessel's life span, are quite different. Compelling for many, they remain less so for me, a reluctance dating, I am convinced, from that uneasy westbound aboard *France* in August 1974.

I wonder about those hundreds of Cunard diehards who, in fall 2008, booked either *QE2*'s last crossings or her final passage to Dubai. What was the lure? Bidding farewell to an old friend, enjoying the cachet of an historic voyage, or draining

The plaque removed from a boat-train carriage at Le Havre on the occasion of *France*'s last westbound crossing to New York. (Katrina Maxtone-Graham collection)

a nearly empty glass? Whatever their reason, reservations had to be made months in advance.

That summer of 1974, though, *France*'s unanticipated last westbound derailed a beloved conveyance. Unwilling extras in a third act crowd scene, none of us had expected that denouement yet. We had no interest in seeing the curtain fall; we all fervently wanted the play to continue.

But there was no reprieve, instead, the very opposite: halfway across, word circulated that negotiations between company and crew had broken down completely and that *France* would be withdrawn, not as announced in October but immediately on her return to Le Havre.

France's penultimate entry into Southampton's Ocean Dock, late August 1974. (William Jory collection)

That time of year, the vessel was packed with home-bound Americans. Many seemed unmoved. I think reaction to that chilling bulletin depended entirely on one's familiarity with the vessel: recidivists were stricken, first-timers indifferent. Maybe they did not realize it was happening. Gossip is the currency of shipboard and there cannot have been a deck chair, dining table, beauty salon, or public room exchange that did not dwell on withdrawal.

How, one wonders, do the condemned cope with imminent mortality? We faced the same dilemma. Long after he disembarked, Jack Sauter summed up what he called "the bits and pieces that made the French Line distinctive." His list encompassed both breakfast's flaky croissants and dinner's crusty rolls, the starched tablecloths and napkins, waiters and captains who "greeted you with a warm smile and performed with the precision of a marine drill team." Like all of us, the Sauters were "trying desperately to burn these images into their memories." But however precious, day-to-day morsels cannot be flash-frozen for later consumption.

A related phenomenon was poignantly documented by Thornton Wilder in *Our Town*. When deceased Emily Gibbs revisits her mother's kitchen in Act III, the minutes tick past as life's drumbeat continues, successive vignettes we neither acknowledge nor savor; only Emily's soul takes anguished note.

Ultimately, we all adopted the same strategy: *carpe diem*, seize the day, and relish what remained as imperturbable *France*, gulping her pricey fuel, thundered westbound to New York. Inevitably, one seized at more than the day. We lingered longer in various public rooms, absorbing the smoking room's special ambience to the max, or sought out special souvenirs. In the Galeries Lafayette, I splurged on a gold *France* money clip, adorned with the final world cruise's logo and its presciently sinister date, 1974. At table, we reordered favorite dishes, danced—how many?—"last dances," and strolled along Sun Deck on successive wind-swept evenings, drinking in the roar of transatlantic night sweeping past those heroic funnels.

Having children in tow helped dictate those final *France* days. I took younger Emily and Guy for daily swims in the pool each morning. Every afternoon, we played as bingo numbers were called or risked a few dollars on those unpredictable, die-driven horses.

Fully-fledged adolescents, Sarah and Ian roamed the vessel at will. Once their Chambord dinner was over, they left the table to dress down for descent to tourist where all the fun was. Sarah recalls that though she had never seen a nightclub in New York, she spent hours in the Cabaret de l'Atlantique where they were reunited with tourist class chums from the Salle des Jeunes. And Ian confessed recently that out on the stern one night,

a beautiful German teenager called Andréa gave him his first French kiss; that it was delivered aboard *France* seems sublimely apropos.

We would always rendezvous for four o'clock tea in our deck chairs. As stewards converged with trays, teapots, sandwiches, and pastry, I agonized about their future. Where would those weather-beaten stalwarts be a month from now? No shore employment would capitalize on their effortless way with tray or glass, their ministrations to the seasick, their ease of rearranging chairs into or out of the sun, and their adjustment of tartan rugs against midocean chill.

These were skills refined by hundreds of crossings. Replacement hotel work ashore would be pedestrian, nine-to-five employment. Moreover, they would cease to be seamen, no longer inhabitants of a unique floating community, within which, either resigned or addicted, they were inextricably enmeshed.

The captain's table against the first class dining room's forward wall is only partially set. That evening, a *dîner de gala* will be offered for a dozen lucky passengers. (Author's collection)

Jack and Marianne Sauter pose with Commandant Pettré. The tapestry behind them, Camille Hilaire's *Sous-Bois*, indicates that they are in the Grand Salon. (Jack Sauter collection)

A farewell photograph of Christian Pettré. (Author's collection)

The awful unspoken truth was that *France*'s end ended the French Line as well, 112 years of impeccable service between Le Havre and New York obliterated. That famous, red-balled company flag would never again—save once—ripple from a transatlantic halyard. Bridge officers, engineers, and deck hands might transfer to freighters and tankers but stewards could not. Their shipboard concomitants were passengers and, without them, they had no maritime future.

On gala night, I am sure we all got a little tighter than usual. Yet again, Commandant Pettré had included us at his table. *France*'s final master had been in command during several prior crossings and we had become good friends; occasionally, we joined him for lunch in his quarters.

Pettré was pure Rabelasian, an occasionally rumbustious creature whose beard and slightly hooded eyes imparted a saturnine mien, the very model of a Mideastern potentate. His pear shape matched perfectly the crew's traditional captain's cognomen *Pascha*. Pettré made the perfect pasha, in love with good food, drink, and conversation. A strict disciplinarian, he remained, for passengers, an entertaining and essentially benign host.

An episode from his cargo-carrying days indicates the kind of master he would become. Postwar, the French Line operated ex-Liberty ships renamed after Norman ports. Jacques Cachot was *commandant–adjoint* of *Avranche* and a companion vessel was under the command of a younger, slimmer, and clean-shaven Christian Pettré.

Those vessels carried French-made cars; once Peugeots and Renaults had been off-loaded in Port Newark, the ships repositioned south to take on eastbound cargoes of coal. Along Hampton Roads' grimy foreshore, they moored beneath towering chutes that, gravity powered, filled their open holds with deafening cascades of coal, inundating everything in a pall of black dust.

Once, their cargo loaded, *Avranche*'s master had invited Pettré for lunch. He arrived and consumed an indifferent meal, the decks, corridors, and wardroom still gritty with coal. On their next Norfolk turnaround, it was Pettré's return invitation that Cachot remembered. Jacques and his American wife, Ethel, were welcomed aboard by a host clad in spotless whites. The interiors were equally spotless and a parade of rich courses appeared, each accompanied by a noble vintage. It duplicated, the Cachots agreed, the kind of banquet expected aboard *Liberté*.

Every master creates his own shipboard style and that was Christian Pettré's. He relished the finer things of life, indulging himself and his guests wherever he sailed. No more suitable *France* avatar ever existed.

The dinner at his table that last gala night was as first rate as ever. The evening began in the Salon Debussy, just forward of the Grand Salon. There, at eight sharp, would assemble a fortunate dozen passengers for cocktails with the commandant. Half an hour later maître d'hôtel Louis Pellegrin would enter to advise Pettré that dinner was served. He and we would rise and be ushered into one of two co-opted elevators for uninterrupted descent.

We paraded down the staircase in languid procession and threaded our way between lesser tables to our assigned places at the captain's, set along the forward wall. Correct dinner party protocol was observed: husbands and wives were mixed and conversation flowed. First order of business was a group photograph, the second, as caviar was dispensed, a preview of the meal to come. *Commis* waiters displayed to each end of the table a splendid platter of fish, followed by an equally splendid platter laden with a roast.

At dinner's end we were escorted up to the Salon Fontainebleau and the commandant's *table de gala*. We played the same silly games and hurled more than our customary handfuls of *cotillons* at each other. It was a bittersweet evening, doubly so because we would never experience it again.

The following night, I retired early because Pettré had invited me to the bridge for entry into New York. I was on hand at five, just before Ambrose. Sandy Hook's *pilote de choix* entered the wheelhouse moments later, an old Pettré friend who delivered his obligatory *Daily News* and a jovial greeting.

An hour later, *France* slipped beneath rush-hour traffic buzzing across Verrazano's bridge, the intrusive, abrasive, New York bustle that dispels every crossing's languor. On that cool September morning, the sun ascended into a cloudless sky over Brooklyn. The World Trade Center towers, Manhattan sentinels that had been welcoming incoming ships for three years, now gleamed in the sunlight.

We clattered out of the wheelhouse atop those legged, mahogany grid sections that, since day one, had surfaced both bridge wings. Commandant,

commandant-adjoint, officers, and guests emerged, first to port during passage past Lady Liberty and then to starboard, for docking. After the Chelsea piers, our docking pilot breezed in, greeted Pettré, and, taking the con, retarded *France* preparatory to implementing the starboard pivot that would swing her prow through 90 degrees for eastbound plunge into the slip.

After the vessel was alongside, Pettré and I shook hands, wishing each other *au revoir* rather than *adieu*. I never saw him again save on news-reels.

Then I hastened down for breakfast. Katrina and the children were already at table and many of the stewards, ours included, were weeping unashamedly. I think Manhattan landfall had triggered the tears. New York arrival marked their voyage's halfway point and every ensuing eastbound mile hastened their Havrais homecoming. Now, perhaps, they realized that they would never reach Manhattan by sea again.

We had already distributed our tip envelopes the night before so, apart from ordering breakfast, there was little to say. Emily and Guy told me how a woman at a neighboring table had complained loudly to Max Lucas about a coffee stain on her tablecloth. Exhibiting superhuman punctiliousness, Lucas asked her steward to change it.

At meal's end, we shook hands solemnly with both our stewards and their captain. Max Lucas's parting words were a melancholy "*Bon débarquement.*" Then we climbed the staircase and deposited the younger children in the cinema where nonstop cartoons were always screened during long disembarkation waits.

Two hours later, after corralling the older two, we picked up Emily and Guy and disembarked. En route to the gangway, a steward whom Sarah knew rebuked her lachrymose departure: "Why are you crying? For you, life goes on. For me, I am losing my job."

On the pier there was nothing left but to find our luggage, clear it through customs, and go home to East 78th Street.

Some of our fellow passengers dawdled. David Jory hung back as his family trooped out onto Pier 88. He was intent on qualifying as *France*'s final disembarking westbound passenger; he did.

Over the weeks that followed, it was Guy who hatched his own salvation plot. "If we all saved our pennies and sent them to the French Line, then

DINNER

Green Olives - Ripe Olives - Celery in Branch
Normandy Butter
Grapefruit, Pineapple, Tomato Juices
Smoked Salmon
American Salad - Antipasto à la Sarde
Veal and Ham Pâté in Crust
Fruits Cocktail in Cup with Liquors

Vegetable Cream Nivernaise
Double Consomme with Japan Pearls

Stuffed Eggs Verdier

Sole Poêlée Alphonse - XIII

Roast Rib of Prime Beef Florian

Braised Heart of Fresh Celery Demi-Glace
Green Peas Bayonnaise
Risotto Valenciennes
Baked Idaho Potatoes - Boiled Potatoes
Potatoes Saratoga - Potatoes Sautées Allemande

Lazagnes Palermitaine

Broiled Double Saddle of Lamb on Charcoal

Duckling with Canadian Apples

English Ham - Mountain Ham
Glazed Virginia Ham with Honey
Slice of Beef Bourgeoise - Sirloin with Variantes
Rack of Lamb with Mint - Smoked Tongue à l'Ecarlate
Farmer Chicken Sauce Tartare

Salad Aïda
Mixed Salad with Sweet Pimentoes

Assorted
Cheese

Iced Cup Eugénie
Neapolitan Ice Cream - Lemon Custard
Religieuse with Coffee - Rocher Nélusko
Frivolités Gourmandes

Assorted Stewed Fruits

Basket of Fruits

———————

French Coffee - American Coffee - Maxwell Instant Coffee
Nescafé without Caffeine - Sanka Coffee - Medaglia d'Oro Coffee
Nescafé - French Coffee without Caffeine
China Tea - Ceylon Tea
Vervain - Linden Tea - Mint - Camomille

White Wine - Red Wine "France"

*Besides these wines - included in the meal - a complete
WINE LIST may be obtained from the wine Steward.*

Little though they realize it, Stirling and Clare Kenny are descending to dine for one of their final *France* dinners. (W. Stirling Kenny collection)

Menu for the vessel's final gala dinner on 1 September, 1974, the first to be disrupted by a mutiny.
(W. Stirling Kenny collection)

Top: Bound for shore, the Kennys' final view of *France* taken from the Thoreson ferry *Viking III*. Mutineers on the forepeak wave cheerfully. (W. Stirling Kenny collection)

Bottom: *France* moored at *le quai de l'oubli*. An accumulation of rust is already disfiguring white paint on the starboard side as her long layup begins. (Norwegian Caribbean Line)

France could still sail," he insisted. Finally, I told him that *France* would never enter New York again, little realizing that when it did, six years later as *Norway*, I would be on board.

Sarah said that before we disembarked she had spied some crewmen brandishing crudely lettered placards though I did not. At the end of the vessel's last Manhattan turnaround, she sailed late, at 8:15 P.M. instead of the advertised 6:45 P.M., the delay produced by militant crewmen plotting their next move.

Twelve hundred had embarked, among them a young Canadian lawyer, Stirling Kenny, and his wife, Clare, from Stratford, Ontario. Originally booked for an October crossing, they had advanced their sailing to 5 September, the day after we had disembarked.

For the Kennys it was a dream come true. They had met at the Sorbonne as students in 1963 and their *France* crossing lived up to their fondest Gallic expectations—"truly an excursion into paradise," Stirling recalled.

At 1:30 on 11 September, the vessel tied up in Southampton. Once the London-bound contingent had disembarked, *France* undocked and continued up-Channel. Since Havre arrival time would be midnight, passengers would spend their final night alongside.

That night, half an hour into Chambord's second sitting, the mutineers struck. If Pettré had been inadvertently cast as Captain Bligh, his Fletcher Christian was a ruthless ex-soldier named Marcel Raulin. A veteran of World War II's Italian campaign, he favored militaristic terminology: the mutiny was code-named Opération Amenez les Oranges (operation bring the oranges) and "L'heure H" (H hour) was six minutes past nine P.M. Once in control, his coded signal to fellow unionists in Havre read: *"T'as le bonjour d'Alfred"* (greetings from Alfred).

When Raulin entered the bridge, he carried in his pocket some pepper with which he planned to blind the commandant should he be armed. But unarmed Pettré succumbed without a struggle; there were, he later explained, too many *mutins* crowding the bridge.

Then Raulin ordered him to inform the passengers. Pettré delivered a brief announcement, first in French and then in English, words never before articulated aboard a French Line vessel. *France*, he explained, was in the hands of mutinous crewmen and he was a prisoner in his quarters. Later, he would be ordered to anchor *France* so that she blocked the Havrais channel.

Once his announcement finished, outbursts of conversation united formerly disparate tables into an incredulous babble. The cadre of *maîtres d'hôtel*, *chefs de rang*, *commis* waiters, and *sommeliers*, putative mutineers all, continued as though nothing had happened.

Only after leaving the dining room and walking aft for a nightcap in the smoking room did the Kennys absorb the mutiny's impact; paradise was degenerating into a purgatory. Salon Riviera was closed, its bandstand deserted, the Bar du Soleil shuttered, and neither barman nor steward in evidence. At that moment, the crew had been summoned by Raulin to a meeting in tourist class's Versailles restaurant.

Stirling and Clare ventured outdoors onto the after terrace. The vessel was anchored and the lights of Le Havre glittered off the port rather than starboard side.

Unwilling to relinquish the nostalgic mystique of their last night, Stirling and Clare decided on a strike of their own. To fellow passengers they proposed a "mutiny party" in the Salon Fontainebleau.

Their idea excited vociferous agreement. Since striking waiters had locked the bar pantries, partygoers retrieved bottles and glasses from their cabins. A passenger pianist opened the keyboard and started playing. Another amateur musician appeared with a saxophone and a third took over the drums. Music filled the room and spirited dancing and singing ensued.

The mutiny party was such a noisy success that it attracted the strikers' attention. Their Versailles meeting adjourned, and curious waiters peered in through the room's after doors, goggle-eyed at the spectacle of passenger high jinks emanating from a public room with neither waiters nor musicians present. "It wasn't a *France* gala," recalls Kenny, "but it was truly a first!"

While they caroused, mutineers co-opted the print shop to run off hundreds of copies of the bilingual apologia/manifesto that serves as this chapter's first epigraph. A copy was at every passenger place for breakfast, which was, incidentally, served the following morning with business-as-usual formality.

Later that day, passengers were transferred to the Thorenson ferry *Viking III*, tied up along *France*'s after port quarter. Once all were on board, many shouted a chorus of "Auld Lang Syne" to waving mutineers before the ferry cast off to enter Le Havre.

Passengers disembarked with difficulty: *Viking III*'s freeboard did not match Quai Joannès Couvert's so rigging a gangway proved problematical. The pier was deserted; no French Line officials or longshoremen were in sight.

Two hours later three tugs appeared, laden with passenger luggage. It was off-loaded in nets and dumped unceremoniously in 18-foot (5½ meters)

stacks, first and tourist jumbled together. Retrieving the correct suitcase was no less shambolic than transporting it down to the boat train platform. This predated wheeled suitcases and the fact that tourist class's boat train departure time was suddenly advanced only added to passenger angst. But at least they had their belongings; those with hold luggage or cars parked in *France*'s garage would not see either for weeks.

The first class boat trains departed last at 6:00 P.M. A derailment up the line stalled them for an hour. Since no explanatory announcement was forthcoming, Kenny and several others disembarked, walking forward to the locomotive to quiz the engineer. But the train suddenly jolted into movement and there was a fearful scramble to reboard before being stranded in the Norman countryside.

It was midnight before they drew up in Paris's Gare St.-Lazare. Platform 24 was also devoid of company representatives and customs inspectors. *France*'s final passenger load felt contaminated, given a wide berth like lepers.

Taxi drivers proposed outrageous fares to carry the exhausted castaways to hotels. The Kennys had reservations at the Intercontinental and managed to find rooms for several others. In the lobby, they encountered groups of westbound *France* passengers prepared to take the boat train to Havre on the morrow; the inbound refugees clued them in. So ended *France*'s final crossing.

The crew stayed defiantly on board for four more weeks. Mutiny, however benign, is still mutiny but, to my knowledge, not one mutineer was ever punished or penalized. Once they had abandoned the vessel, Pettré resumed command as tugs maneuvered her into the backwaters of Havre through the Tancarville Canal. She was finally moored along a desolate shore with cattle grazing in adjacent fields. The press would christen that makeshift berth *le quai de l'oubli* (the pier of the forgotten).

Though isolated, *France* was not forgotten. In addition to her maritime strikers, restive labor unions of every persuasion employed the idled liner as a symbolic touchstone of defiance. Striking printers from one of the capital's newspapers, *Parisian Libéré*, gathered noisily but fruitlessly up around the funnels. But regardless who rallied or postured, it proved pointless. *France* was finished, the French Line was out of business, and the public was disinterested.

A *France* maiden voyage medallion (top) and a rare miniature (center). Although engravers at Paris's Hôtel de la Monnaie would not be pleased to hear it, their funnel wings are not quite right. The reverse of another medallion (bottom) commemorates two October 1974 farewell cruises that never took place. (Author's collection)

Her crew dispersed, some back to Brittany but many more in or around Le Havre. Pasha Pettré disembarked just before Christmas and went home to Neuilly. *Chef de patisserie* Léon Tardy-Panit was a Havrais, a soft-spoken, gentle man whom I had come to know well. He would join *Queen Elizabeth 2* as assistant confectioner, a comedown from his seniority aboard *France* but at least continuation of his maritime trade. He told me during a subsequent Cunard crossing that, from a balcony of his house, he could see laid-up *France*. But the sight so upset him that he never set foot out there.

A thirty-five-man skeleton crew rattled about the deserted vessel, keeping her as shipshape as possible. But there was neither budget nor manpower for exterior maintenance and, over five Norman winters, rust and corrosion took their toll. One Channel storm sundered her moorings and tugs were summoned to resecure her. Later, she was dry docked to have her underwater hull and propellers scaled.

Two potential reprieves materialized, the first from Saudi Arabian petro mogul Akram Ojjeh. In 1977 he bought *France* for $24 million with the announced intention of converting her into a gambling hell anchored off Fort Lauderdale. His alternate dream was to berth *France* permanently in Montreal and refurnish her public rooms with antiques from New York's Wildenstein Galleries. Nothing came of either scheme.

The second reprieve arose from the 1960s' only positive passenger shipping news, the emergence of a buoyant, Miami-based cruise industry. At the same time that most North Atlantic liners were fading, purpose-built cruise ships started coining money in the Caribbean.

Two Scandinavian owners would thrive, Norwegian Caribbean Line and Royal Caribbean Cruise Line. The former was the brainchild of an Oslo shipping man named Knut Utstein Kloster Jr. His grandfather Lauritz had founded Klosters Rederi A/S in 1905, which grew into an extremely profitable fleet of tankers and cargo vessels.

After attending MIT, Knut succeeded as head of the company on his father's death. Remunerative tankers notwithstanding, it was the potential of cruising that intrigued Klosters Rederi's new chief. In 1963 he contacted the Danish firm of Knud E. Hansen, designers of innumerable Baltic ferries. Tage (pronounced *tah-gay*) Wandborg, the com-

pany's senior naval architect, drew up specifications for Kloster's experimental vessel. A construction contract was signed with the Bergen yard Bergens Mekaniske Verksteder. Kloster recalled, "It was so simple in those days, you know. A general arrangement plan and a slim outline specification." Costing 43.75 million Norwegian kroner ($6,250,000), she was the largest vessel ever built in Norway.

She emerged as an 8,666-ton car ferry, with capacious lower decks for vehicles topped by air-conditioned cabins and public rooms. Dominating her blue-trimmed superstructure were two ultra-modern funnels, flaring rakishly outboard. Sine qua non for cruising tonnage, an ondeck pool had pride of place and a sunburst logo adorned both sides of the white hull. Kloster call her *Sunward*, establishing an identifying *-ward* company suffix that would link her with three subsequent consorts: *Skyward*, *Starward*, and *Southward*, nicknamed the "White Fleet."

Sunward's initial deployment was embarking British tourists on weekly itineraries between Southampton and Vigo, ending the cruise at Gibraltar. The only fly in the ointment was inescapable passage across the notoriously unsettled Bay of Biscay.

Over the summer of 1966 business was encouraging. But, that fall, a catastrophic fly in the ointment: Franco prohibited access through the border town of La Linea, effectively sealing access to Spain from Gibraltar. Hoping to reclaim the rock, the generalissimo's strategy proved unsuccessful; all he achieved was scuttling Kloster's itinerary.

Sunward returned to Bergen for temporary layup. Kloster debated substituting Málaga for Gibraltar but foresaw difficulties in maintaining schedule. Final unfortunate capper were newly imposed travel restrictions limiting British tourists' overseas allowance to a paltry £50 ($142.50) apiece. Clearly, *Sunward*'s Gibraltar initiative was finished.

Then a prescient proposal landed in Kloster's lap, an unexpected telephone call from an Israeli engineer in Miami named Ted Arison. His only vessel, the liner *Nili*, had just been seized by the Israeli government to settle a delinquent partner's debts; Arison had personnel and a catering operation but no vessel. *Sunward*, he pointed out, was idle. Might its Norwegian owner consider a joint Caribbean venture?

Kloster and operations chief Kjell Nielsen flew to Miami, to be met at the airport by Arison. The three toured the port. Its existing cruise fleet were dated steamers from the past. But a new facility, Dodge Island, was under construction, made from spoil dredged from Government Cut, Miami's entrance channel. Even though the island was unfinished, bounded by marginal quays with only the framework of a cruise terminal, Kloster stipulated that, were he to relocate *Sunward* to Miami, she had to be berthed there rather than parked among Miami's antiquated fleet on the mainland.

Arison and Kloster signed a formal agreement that fall and *Sunward* was dispatched to Miami on 6 December 1966. Since, by agreement, Arison was providing the hotel staff, her existing cooks and stewards were laid off prior to departure. En route to Florida she carried only deck and engine personnel.

One Norwegian cook remained aboard, a sous chef who had sailed with the vessel since day one. His name was Rolf Harry Skjong-Nielsen, originally from Stavanger. Skjong-Nielsen (pronounced *shong*) had applied for work at Klosters

Opposite: Five consecutive Norman winters left their mark along *France*'s normally pristine open decks. (Norwegian Caribbean Line)

Below: One of *France*'s rare outings from *le quai de l'oubli*, into dry dock for maintenance of the hull's underside. Prospective buyers were expected and it was time to dress up the merchandise. (Norwegian Caribbean Line)

Knut Utstein Kloster and his pioneering *Southnward.* (Norwegian Caribbean Line)

Rederi on 27 March, 1966, and signed on as a sous chef. Save for a brief Stavanger hiatus in 1976, he remained with the company for thirty-two years, rising to director of hotel operations.

Sunward, identified now as Klosters Rederi d.b.a. Norwegian Caribbean Line, sailed up Government Cut the week before Christmas 1966. From the moment she tied up at Dodge Island, as promised, not a moment was wasted. The vessel was provisioned, Arison's staff embarked to reactivate the galley, and onboard receptions introduced the novel ship to Miami's maritime and municipal establishment. On 19 December, *Sunward* sailed on her maiden four-day cruise, from Miami to Nassau and back. The car decks remained profitably in place so that *Sunward* could carry passengers and containers between Jamaica and Florida.

That first voyage sold out, as did every one to follow; *Sunward* was an instant hit. Knut Kloster's prototypical vessel inaugurated south Florida's modern-day cruise industry, providing impressive returns for the Kloster/Arison partnership. Within ten years Miami would become the world's premier passenger port.

Small wonder. The United States is ideally situated for mass-market cruising, each corner encompassing an irresistible market. To the southeast, Florida's peninsula dangles on the threshold of a warm, year-round playground; to the northwest, Alaskan fjords and mountains beckon—when fall tints New England, foliage cruises to Canada are popular; in the southwest, vessels have sundrenched access to Mexico's Riviera; for a final geographical bonus, westbound across the Pacific lies verdant Hawaii.

Those unparalleled opportunities surpass anything in the old world. Northern Europeans are awkwardly remote from warm-weather sailings. No continental or British port duplicates Miami's year-round immediacy to idyllic, maritime pleasure. Winsome islands are only hours away, their subtropical shores lapped year-round by an invariably placid Caribbean. Though sometimes hurricanes appear in the fall, blue skies, green islands, white beaches, and turquoise waters are the norm.

Americans flocked aboard *Sunward*, embracing the delights of Kloster's novel shipboard. Sundrenched seven- or fourteen-day itineraries were enriched by reasonable prices, comfortable cabins, frequent meals, well-trained stewards, and nightly entertainment. Norwegian Caribbean Line offered a sunny, swimming, eating, dancing, drinking, and partying ethos delivering exceptional value.

Kloster's earliest slogan touched all the right bases: "Norwegians for their seamanship, Caribbean for the fun of it." He was not alone in capitalizing on Norway's seafaring heritage. Ed Stephan, who together with Oslovian shipping men would create rival Royal Caribbean Cruise Line in 1970, espoused the same Nordic resonances. NCL and RCCL advertisements offered identical imagery: spotless white ships, bronzed Nordic officers, Norway's mail pennant at the hoist, enviable Norwegian expertise, and unfailingly smooth seas.

Kloster was a shipping man like no other. Although faced with all the logistical headaches of running a fleet, he boasted a sometimes naive but heartfelt idealism, staunch ethics, visionary zeal, transparent honesty, and a dedicated sense of fair play. Repeatedly, Kloster dreamed the right dream and then acted on it. Conceiving and building *Sunward* was his first; transferring her to the Caribbean his second; and, as it turned out, buying *France* the third.

Only four years after joining forces, Kloster and Arison parted company in a bitter wrangle over shared ticket advances, a dispute that would finally be resolved in the courts. Though Kloster was dismayed by the breakup, Arison seemed indifferent and went on to found the immensely successful Carnival Cruise Line.

Also immensely successful, Kloster's White Fleet was sailing out of Miami at over 100 percent capacity. By 1979, after thirteen profitable years, expansion was essential. Kloster could either build a fifth vessel or buy an existing one. Whereas building would consume three years, buying would take one.

He went shopping, visiting Genoa to examine idled *Michelangelo* and *Raffaelo*. But he found their interiors disappointing. Then, at the bottom of a list of twenty laid-up hulls circulated by an Oslovian ship broker, he spied the name *France*. Intrigued, he had NCL executive Bruce Nierenberg join him in Le Havre in February 1979. They rendezvoused on board with Tage Wandborg, *Sunward*'s naval architect.

The moment Kloster alerted him Tage was intrigued. *France* was tailor-made for him. The world's leading conversion specialist, Tage Wandborg had 160 such commissions to his credit; *France* would be his 161st and, unquestionably, the most ambitious.

Though an Elsinore resident, no melancholy Dane he. With his thatch of silver hair, sometimes whimsical demeanor, and overscale round eyeglasses imparting a look of owlish wisdom, Tage radiated the persona of a bemused academic, not dissimilar from that of Charles Nelson Reilly. But his ready smile and sometimes boisterous humor belied devastating shipbuilding savvy.

The giant black hull that greeted the visitors offered promise and challenge. Seen from the rutted approach track, it was obvious that five years of crewless neglect had left their mark. *France*'s hull was streaked and her superstructure speckled with encroaching rust.

The Embarkation Lobby, high above on Pont Principal, was sealed. Visitors and crew alike were announced via a land-based sentry who telephoned the vessel's interior. Moments later, the

Left: On a bleak winter morning, Tage Wandborg and NCL staff tramp around *France*'s open decks. (Norwegian Caribbean Line)

Right: Library furniture shrouded in linen covers. (Norwegian Caribbean Line)

hydraulically operated shell door was opened and the party embarked. They entered on B Deck, using the same entrance through which, in happier days, *chef de cuisine* Le Huédé and Claiborne had dispatched the approved fruits of their pier-side *dégustation*.

Welcoming them was the commandant-adjoint Jean Nadal and the chief engineer Jean Allaire. They commanded a skeleton crew occupying moribund *France*. Save for ceaseless fire patrols, life on board was restricted largely to the echoing, steel corridors of crew country. They took indifferent meals in B Deck's crew mess and were berthed in adjacent cabins. Commandant Pettré was long gone; Nadal and Allaire occupied their original quarters aft of the bridge.

After a briefing, the visitors descended for inspection of the engine spaces. Part of the vessel's weekly routine was activating turning gear for an hour, revolving all turbine rotors and propeller shafts. Then they tramped up the main staircase to the Embarkation Hall. Frayed passenger deck plans in hand, they spent a long afternoon on an exhaustive, exploratory walkabout.

France's interiors conveyed a curious ambivalence, impressive but neglected. Well illuminated via electrical mains from shore, 'tween decks were glacially cold. Light through grimy windows revealed dust everywhere. Chairs and tables were shrouded in protective linen covers. There was no camphor reek because Rilsan carpeting was invulnerable to moths. But whiffs of drains assaulted them, a smell extremely familiar to conversion specialist Tage. Scores of cabin vacuum cleaners were parked surreally along the starboard promenade, as though drawn up in review.

Conditioned to White Fleet dimensions, the visitors were swallowed up in that taller, grander shipboard. Repeatedly consulting deck plans to double-check their location, they plodded up and down staircases, through public rooms, suites, and cabins, exploring every vista to its sometimes remote end.

Those NCL visitors could not suppress their admiration. Despite her abandonment *France* still compelled. Hers was a remarkable infrastructure, the solidity and workmanship of every element only too apparent, a one-of-a-kind survivor from an extraordinary transatlantic league.

Tage later confessed to being both overwhelmed and exhilarated. "Space, space, space,

Tage Wandborg poses next to a *France* model. (Norwegian Caribbean Line)

length, width, height," he recalls. That evening, he wandered across adjacent fields, drinking in *France*'s image from afar. Though not prone to fantasy, he sensed that the vessel was calling to him: "Take me and give me a new life." To a Copenhagen colleague, he later confided succinctly, "She smelled good."

Before any final decision was taken, sixty more specialists—corporate staff, engineers, designers, decorators, housekeepers, hotel and entertainment personnel—made the same Havrais pilgrimage. One summer visit, Kloster was joined by his wife, Katrine, as well as Skjong-Nielsen, staff captain Torbjorn Hauge, and marine superintendent Svenn Dahl.

The number and enthusiasm of those overseas visitors did not escape notice. At the Havrais hotel to which they returned each evening, the bartender announced in Kloster's (unknown) presence that "a crazy Norwegian shipowner is going to buy *France*."

The ship seduced them all. Skjong-Nielsen, whose honest Norwegian face belies a sometimes fey imagination, was bewitched. He told me that he too had clearly heard *France* speak: "Please release me from these chains and let me sail."

Back in Oslo, naval architect and owner discussed possible conversion strategy. *France*'s bulk would forbid entry into Caribbean ports; tendering would be inevitable. Only half her extravagant transatlantic power plant would be needed for placid interisland itineraries. Though the vessel's present capacity was three times greater than any contemporary cruise ship, Tage confided to Knut, "I see a possibility to build more staterooms on board."

As Tage's panegyric wound down, the prospective owner brought him down to earth.

"We have an option to buy her for thirty days. How much time do you need to say yes or no? And can the vessel be converted into a successful cruise liner?"

Tage pondered no more than an instant. Adapting instantly to Kloster's deadline, he replied, "Give me three weeks."

Kloster smiled. "Okay. But in case you say yes, then also inform me about the estimated cost involved."

Their simple exchange neither acknowledged nor dwelt on the vastness of their concept. Millions of dollars and hundreds of tons of steel fabrication lay ahead, yet the conversational tenor between owner and naval architect remained as casual as it was cool.

Wandborg and a Copenhagen team—draftsman, estimator, and specification writer—flew back to Havre and set up shop in *France*'s engineers' mess. For three weeks, Tage and his team breathed, lived, explored, and dreamed *France*, toiling at one remove: the vision preoccupying them was not *France* but her subtropical doppelgänger to come.

From *France*'s log, Tage ascertained the number of tugs required in Havre and New York; in the Caribbean, bow- and stern thrusters would replace them. How would her twenty-four hundred passengers get ashore? Tage already had a prototype in existence, a converted U.S. Navy landing craft adapted to ferry White Fleet passengers from ship to beach at NCL's private Bahamian out island. The industry's first, its creation had been prompted by a simple passenger query overheard by Bruce Nierenberg: "Why can't we go ashore straight to a beach?" For *Norway*, Tage would need oversized tenders hoisted aboard.

France's afterdecks needed work. "She must be opened up, like a flower in the sun," Tage insisted. A large outdoor pool surrounded by expanded deck space was mandatory. Was one pool sufficient or should there be another?

What about food? Prowling the afterdecks, Tage zeroed in on a perfect alternate dining space, a facility denied *France* but crucial for the Caribbean. Simplifying Tage's task was *France*'s two-class, spatial largesse. Further deliberation inspired an interesting rework of the promenade decks.

Successful conversion plans combine existing reality with future fabrication. Tage and his teammates researched, debated, and improvised. Although their task could have been pursued in Copenhagen, working in situ offered unparalleled advantages. Wrestling with a challenge, Tage could be at the location in minutes, eyeballing the curve of a railing, pacing out a teak span, or ascertaining correct clearance between bulkhead and proposed restructure.

At the end of his allotted three weeks, the imperturbable Dane arrived back in Oslo laden with drawings.

"Yes," he reported, "it can be done—sixty million dollars." Kloster agreed to his naval architect's recommendations and his estimate. Then he dispatched him back to Le Havre to prepare specific

Naval architect and owner inspect actual *France* at Havre. (Norwegian Caribbean Line)

conversion details. Tage's on-site team grew to nine, including four steel draftsmen.

Buoyed by the pace of developments, Knut and Katrine returned to *France* as well. During one visit, an accompanying French photographer posed Knut at various shipboard locations. On the bridge, he self-consciously grasped the wheel; in Tage's paper-strewn engineers' mess he seemed in conference; in the Chambord dining room, he and Katrine perched wistfully amidst a clutter of shrouded chairs. On their last day, "the crazy Norwegian" brought with him champagne and two glasses. Husband and wife toasted each other and the ship in the same field from which Tage had heard *France* speak.

Knut Kloster is exactly my age; we were both born in 1929. So, in 1979, he was fifty, already exuding the same stubborn sincerity that had propelled his career so successfully. Though he confesses that he had been prepared to buy *France* from the beginning, he awaited the verdict of his Miami colleagues. Their final, unanimous consensus was that the project was eminently doable; *France* would make an admirable if overscale Caribbean cruise ship.

Knut and Katrine Kloster visit *France* at Le Havre, posing for the photographer in Restaurant Chambord, on the bridge, and, with champagne, in a neighboring field. (Norwegian Caribbean Line)

Two Miami regulars, NCL executive Greg Tighe and Lorraine Evering, were in love. They asked Wandborg if they could be married in *France*'s chapel. Love always finds a way. The Reverend Agnar Holme, a Havrais Norwegian seamen's priest, officiated. To Tage, that touching ceremony perfectly symbolized *France*'s renaissance.

News of Kloster's decision aroused astonished disbelief. Shipping club members worldwide did double takes. Reaction throughout Miami was mixed. That Kloster proposed allying a giant ocean liner with a quartet of smaller consorts seemed either foolish or impractical, or both; more than once "apples and oranges" were cited.

Kloster was too busy to pay attention. Akram Ojjeh, *France*'s owner of record since 1977, refused to sell the vessel to the Norwegian until the two had met. Kloster flew to Paris; a car met him at Le Bourget and drove him to the Saudi Arabian's office.

There, the Norwegian cooled his heels for some time before finally being summoned upstairs into Ojjeh's presence. Presumably, Knut passed muster. In a signed agreement dated 25 June, 1979, the ship was his for a bargain $18 million; the Saudi Arabian took a $6 million loss on the deal.

Next complication: Kloster had to obtain the government's permission before removing the vessel from French waters. He was also presented with two conditional caveats: *France* could never return to her country of origin and no representation of the vessel in French livery was to appear in NCL publicity.

Kloster agreed to both stipulations but, before signing, as a matter of curiosity, he asked how much it had cost to build *France*. No one, he recalls, could or would tell him.

His only Norwegian hurdle was obtaining permission from the palace to rechristen the vessel *Norway*. His Majesty King Olav V granted the request but word of the proposed name change was purposely withheld. Though Tage had prepared drawings for NORWAY letters and indicated their correct placement, the vessel would leave Le Havre ostensibly as *France*.

Finding a shipyard to implement the conversion was not difficult. Chantiers de l'Atlantique would not take it on. Worried about image, it set the price too high and suggested its order book was too crowded.

So Kloster approached Hapag-Lloyd Werft in Bremerhaven, the same yard that had built his *Sky-*

ward and *Starward*. It not only had the time and space but its price was competitive. Most important, the yard guaranteed delivery within ten months. A contract was signed.

Back in Le Havre, accumulated silt was dredged alongside *le quai de l'oubli*. When Norwegian engineers fired up a boiler, clouds of black smoke emerged once again from those distinctive stacks. But the first onboard steam raised in five years was only for provision of service electricity. *France* would get to Bremerhaven at the end of a 1100 meter (3,600-foot) cable, connecting via a towing bridle behind a seagoing tug called *Abeille-Provence* (bee of Provence).

As sailing day—19 August, 1979—approached, Kloster heard menacing rumors that hard-core elements among the Havrais dockers might try to prevent *France*'s departure. A detachment of French paratroopers in combat gear was mustered pierside and Captain Torbjorn Hauge—newly promoted—was assigned four bodyguards. Though thousands of inhabitants and former crewmen came out to watch, there was no untoward incident.

Still flying the tricolor from her truck, *France* was maneuvered slowly, majestically, silently toward the port's entry. There was no whistled salute for crowds ashore; Hauge had been instructed to keep as low a profile as possible. The only sound heard was the tolling bell of Havre's l'Eglise de Saint-Joseph and one tortured cry from a packed jetty as the vessel passed: "France *ne nous abandonne pas!*" (*France*, don't leave us.)

Kloster did not sail with the vessel but flew to Bremerhaven to await her arrival. Out in the Channel, after the pilot had disembarked, rather than turn to port for Southampton and New York the vessel's bows were swung up-Channel. Only then did Hauge order the tricolor lowered and Norway's flag sent aloft.

After years of neglect and imprisonment, ocean liner *France* was to become cruise ship *Norway*. It would be the largest conversion since the 1920s, when William Francis Gibbs had wrought troopship *Leviathan*-ex-*Vaterland* into a full-blown American ocean liner.

But in this event, complications abounded. Tricky nationalistic boundaries had to be negotiated, converting a French liner at a German yard into a Norwegian cruise ship managed by and catering largely to Americans.

Away from Havre and out in the Channel, France's tricolor is gone and the Norwegian postal banner flutters atop the vessel. (Norwegian Caribbean Line)

CHAPTER EIGHT

FRANCO/NORDIC CONVERSION

Those who own the boat should give it a name.

Ancient Norwegian proverb

The vessel has two classes, first and tourist, completely separated from each other. The only place the two are together is in the lifeboats.

Tage Wandborg, *Norway's* naval architect

When we left Oslo, after the unbelievable reception there, I was up on the bridge thinking about what to say to the passengers, when I welcomed them onboard. Given the whole special situation, and knowing how important it was to make the passengers feel appreciated and comfortable, I announced on the loudspeaker system that all the bars onboard would serve them "on the house," so to speak, free of charge all the way to New York. I knew it was a somewhat daring decision but it went very well.

Letter from Knut Kloster (2009)

Opposite: *Norway's* successful funnel livery, photographed in the Caribbean from the crow's nest. (Nelson B. Arnstein, M.D., collection)

Awaiting Norway's arrival in Bremerhaven, Kloster was tipped off that militant French unionists

were importuning their German colleagues to sabotage her conversion. His response was archetypal Kloster. He telephoned the headquarters of the Norsk Sjømannsforbund (Norwegian seamen's union), alerting them to the threat. Their members among *Norway*'s crew, he pointed out, would be put out of work if tactics of that kind were initiated at Lloyd Werft. The Norwegian union chief immediately telephoned his opposite number in Havre and called the Frenchman's bluff. Shipyard labor unrest never happened.

Buoyed by resolution of that unpleasant possibility, Kloster watched his new acquisition approach Bremerhaven's cobbled pier, standing with enthusiastic townspeople. Her conversion was a huge contract for yard and port alike, work that would start the following day.

Less than twenty-four hours later, the assault began. A welter of hose, cable, and piping inundated the ship's side, infamous "snake garden" tangles that would befoul staircases and alleyways for months. Strings of electric cable festooned with bulb-filled yellow plastic buckets provided illumination, looking like giant Christmas garlands. Ship's speakers broadcast relentless rock and roll and chill North Sea gales probed every corridor.

Her first open-sea tow concluded, *Norway* arrives in Bremerhaven.

(Norwegian Caribbean Line)

May's deadline already loomed, goading everyone on board—Tage Wandborg and his staff, Captain Hauge and the crew, gathering subcontractors, and Lloyd Werft's workforce. Whether days or months, every shipyard visit precipitates an identical struggle against the clock.

Formalizing the Nordic takeover, replacement nomenclature arrived from Miami, combining Norwegian with Floridian resonances. All passenger decks were renamed: *France*'s Sun Deck became *Norway*'s Fjord Deck and Upper Deck morphed into Viking Deck. The list reveals a democratic thrust as prestigious Gallic references were supplanted by the nautical and Norwegian, a fresh, populist appeal.

Those new names were essentially paper changes. More challenging were Wandborg's steel changes instigated at the same time. Two demolitions started the ball rolling. Fjord Deck's squash court was removed; in its place, Tage planned eight large suites, four per side bracketing a central alleyway. Forward on the same deck, twenty-four new minisuites would take shape. Four decks down, the fixed steel-and-glass roof protecting tourist class's pool was cut free, lifted off, and discarded. Those two preliminaries paved the way for Tage's bold transformation of the ends of three descending

Norway levels—Oslo, International, and Pool decks—opening *Norway* "like a flower to the sun."

That cliché of incompatibility—square pegs in round holes—describes his conversion to perfection. Think of the arc, in plan, of *France*'s stern as a "round hole." That graceful parabola would be almost obliterated beneath what Tage described as his carrier decks, three "square pegs" transcending the hull's original soft line. Only by amplifying her superstructure thus could Wandborg successfully adapt *Norway* for cruising. Extending over either side, the lowest of those three broadened deck ends accommodated an open-air pool and generous teak lido where hundreds could gather.

Wandborg pools frequently boast underwater portholes. The two gracing its forward end revealed his ingenious recycling of *France*'s tourist class pool. Welders filled it with steel framing, electricians added infinite lighting effects, and carpenters topped it with Plexiglas slabs that become the dance floor of Dazzles discotheque. Gyrating as though atop the pool's frozen surface, dancing couples could spy their swimming fellows through the new pool's portholes.

Below expanded Pool Deck's squared end protruded the fantail, relegated now to sunning space

Top left: Less than a week later, the tourist class pool's roof has been removed and the serious business of reworking *Norway*'s stern begins. (Norwegian Caribbean Line)

Top right: A snake garden penetrates the hull. (Tom Graboski collection)

France Decks	Norway Decks	France Public Rooms	Norway Public Rooms	New
Observation Deck	Sun Deck	*First Class*		The Great Outdoor Restaurant
Sun Deck	Fjord Deck	Chambord Restaurant	Windward Restaurant	Lido Bar
Boat Deck	Oslo Deck	Salle de Spectacle	Saga Theatre	Dazzles Discotheque
Verandah Deck	International Deck	Salon Fontainebleau	Checkers Cabaret	Windjammer Bar
Promenade Deck	Pool Deck	Salon Riviera	Club Internationale	Multiple Boutiques
Upper Deck	Viking Deck	Galeries Lafayette	Upstairs at the Downstairs	Sunspot Bar
Main Deck	Norway Deck	Bibliotheque	Ibsen Library	
A Deck	Atlantic Deck			
B Deck	Biscayne Deck*	*Tourist Class*		
C Deck	Caribbean Deck†	Versailles Restaurant	Leeward Restaurant	
D Deck	Dolphin Deck‡	Salon St.-Tropez	North Cape Lounge	
		La Rive Gauche	Monte Carlo Room	

*Passenger cabins to port, crew cabins to starboard
†All crew cabins
‡Little Crew Village

Crew Area

Automobile Garage   Crew Gymnasium

for off-duty crew. The stern's jack staff was raised a level and remounted on Pool Deck's railing.

Sited forward of the lido was an enclosed, air-conditioned Lido Bar. Directly above it, the expanded overhang of International Deck—our second "square peg"—accommodated The Great Outdoor Restaurant. Tage's alternate dining venue filled a lamentable French void with a Norwegian essential.

Most *Norway* clientele would spend sea days swimming and sunbathing. They would prefer lunching bathing-suited on deck rather than dressing for dining room descent. Hence those umbrella-shaded tables one short flight up. Four buffet lines laid fore and aft were approachable from either side, catering to peak feeding demand. They were shaded beneath the overhang of Oslo Deck's basketball court, the third and final "square peg."

One casualty of The Great Outdoor Restaurant was the athwart-ship terrace formerly gracing the smoking room's after end. The back wall of the Club Internationale—or Club I, to employ its popular diminutive—was closed up. Though port and starboard terraces remained, Club I's after view

and access were co-opted by pantries. When the restaurant filled, overflow passengers could either repair down one level to tables along Pool Deck's margins or carry trays forward to Club I's flanking terraces.

The promenade deck's entire length had been transformed by Wandborgian sleight of hand. Where *France* passengers surveyed the sea from deck chairs, their *Norway* replacements strolled along a deck covered with asphalt-colored tiles without a deck chair in sight. Wicker chairs and sofas lined what can only be described as a seagoing boulevard. Effecting a Yankee/Gallic interface, Tage renamed port side Fifth Avenue and starboard Champs Elysées. Every shop or bar along the way was provided with an exterior door affording instant access from outdoors to in.

Circuit the ship along the starboard "French" side. Just beyond Club I, one could enter a double-decked shop called Upstairs at the Downstairs. (Public Television's *Masterpiece Theatre* was popular at the time.) This replaced both *France*'s vanished Cabaret de l'Atlantique and her midocean branch of Galeries Lafayette.

No better view conveys the ingenuity of Tage Wandborg's Caribbean makeover of *Norway*'s afterdecks. On the left, The Great Outdoor Restaurant and, on the right, *France*'s stern, "round hole" protruding from beneath "square peg." (Norwegian Caribbean Line)

Farther along was the Café de Paris, an "outdoor" sidewalk café. Forward was a Chinese boutique followed by a narrow West Indian handicrafts shop nestled into the interior curve of Saga Theatre's balcony. Next, a portrait artist worked at his easel and, beyond, a children's boutique occupied *France*'s unlamented first class playroom. Final starboard destination was Sven's Ice Cream Parlor. Though the youngest children's playroom forward had been retained, Salle des Jeunes had metamorphosed into yet another shop.

Heading back aft along port side's Fifth Avenue, consecutive destinations included a West Indian bar and the music-filled Windjammer Bar. Then another convenient inspiration: pursers and shore excursion desks occupied counters along that busy

thoroughfare. Farther aft, one could drop into Checkers for a lecture, browse Ibsen Library shelves, or wander into the card room for a game. Near the restaurant, white wrought-iron tables and chairs were positioned.

Traditional shipboard promenades were always deserted after dark and would pay no Caribbean dividends. Transforming their prime acreage into a circumnavigable street of dreams, along which passengers could find entertainment, shops, bars, food, or friends, was ideal. Tage's adventurous street retained—indeed, *amplified!*—shipboard's two essential I's: the impulsive and the impromptu, perfectly evoking *Norway*'s subtropical raison d'être.

If first class's promenade had segued into a mall, what about its tourist class equivalent below?

Delivering on his promise to Kloster, Tage created additional accommodations, leaving in place a narrow access alleyway for thirty-four interesting cabins, seventeen a side. Boasting lavish fenestration, each was illuminated not by porthole or window but three—count 'em, *three!*—generous expanses of Promenade Deck plate glass. Occupants breakfasting in bed were rewarded with a virtually Cinemascopic panorama.

The only downside were the cramped, prefabricated bathrooms parked in their inboard corners. Experienced passenger/readers are familiar with shipboard's spatial tradeoff: smaller bathrooms mean larger cabins. Delivered to Lloyd Werft as compact sealed units, those new bathrooms were lined up in position before surrounding cabin walls enclosed them.

Norway's final passenger count, with every berth occupied, rose from *France*'s 2,254 to over 2,400. Fjord Deck's eight new suites and twenty-four semisuites added sixty-four berths; that enlargement, together with Pool Deck's thirty-four cabins, made for a total of 132 additional berths.

However spacious his after pool, Tage wanted another amidships. Tailor-made as a site was *France*'s Patio de Provence. He designed a prefabricated pool with signature portholes piercing all four sides of it; it was delivered by crane, resembling a dirigible's gondola. In position, the pool rested on Fjord Deck. Since it did not entirely fill the patio, occupants of the surrounding cabins could walk around it, perusing the depths.

France's funnels were reevaluated. Tage had a model made of what he called his Kempinski funnel, conceived after spending a night in Berlin's hotel of the same name. His logic ran as follows: since only two inboard propellers would exist for *Norway*, the forward engine room would become moribund, perhaps necessitating a new single funnel aft.

He and Kloster booked Berlin Technical University's wind tunnel to check the Kempinski funnel's performance. Though it rated well, after comparing it with the original 1958 French tests from Poitier they found the existing funnels' performance scored higher. Moreover, garbage incinerators and/or service electricity generators might well need to vent through their own forward funnel.

So both men agreed that retaining *France*'s existing stacks made sense. Their only change was cosmetic, a vast improvement over the French Line's black/red scheme. Cap and wings were overpainted

Diversions along International Deck include public room entrances plus plentiful shopping, seating, food, and drink. The North Atlantic's standard Promenade has disappeared. The starboard-side way station, the Café de Paris (bottom), is dubbed the Shelf. (Norwegian Caribbean Line and Tom Graboski collection)

A model of Tage Wandborg's Kempinski funnel. (Author's collection)

ing Caribbean waters. International Paints prepared a royal blue mix and, deploying surely the world's largest paint chip, tested it on a Lloyd Werft warehouse. Knut and Tage agreed that it seemed odd beneath Bremerhaven's wintry overcast but would doubtless improve in Caribbean sunlight. The hull was sandblasted down to steel, primed, and given successive coats. Just as Parisian couturier Jeanne Lanvin had created Lanvin blue and Velazquez green, Tage and Kloster devised *Norway* blue.

The most noticeable forward additions to the vessel were two passenger tenders designed by Tage. They were large landing craft with catamaran hulls and easily lowered bow ramps, permitting beach or pier landings. Inside the enclosed wheelhouse, operators controlled two Schottels, 360-degree azimuthing propellers, obviating the need for rudders. Displacing 35 tons, each tender was 90 feet (27.5 meters) overall and 26 feet (8 meters) in the beam. Capacity was four hundred and fifty passengers, seated, like bullfight aficionados, half in sun, half shaded below. Two round-trips by the pair would convey most of *Norway*'s passenger load ashore.

Tage ordered them from Norway's Fiskestrand Shipyard consortium in Alesund. To expedite

navy blue and, forward, a narrowing dark blue band tapered down the front of the white shaft, paralleled by supplementary stripes of cornflower blue on either side.

Kloster's restrictive contract with the French prohibited not only mention of *France* but also replication of the funnels' French Line livery. But their continued prominence, even repainted, conveyed a powerful subliminal message: *Norway* had indeed been wrought from the classic liner.

Though NCL hulls were white, Tage felt that duplicating the color for *Norway*'s might "destroy its grace and sheer." He favored a shade approximat-

Over white primer, a preliminary coat of *Norway* blue is sprayed on. Right, the upper deck overhang is in place, the outboard propellers have been detached, and the weld detritus of *France* is about to disappear. (Norwegian Caribbean Line and Tom Graboski collection)

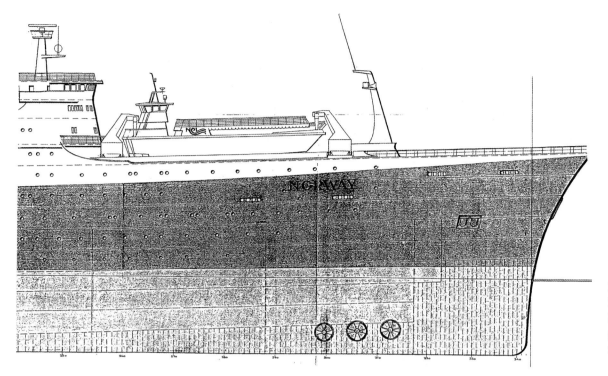

From Tage's original drawing, the starboard tender profile. Tender and davits had to be contained within exactly 90 feet (27.5 meters) of space, not a millimeter more. (Jeff Macklin collection)

construction, the work was divided between three subcontractors, each given responsibility for a third of the tender's length. Welded together, they would be ready for sea trials eight months later. Qualifying as legitimate vessels, each required individual certificates and inspections.

They were christened *Little Norway I* and *Little Norway II* after the RAF's Norwegian pilots' training station in Canada during World War II. Among those following their construction was a cadet at Alesund's Maritime Academy named Svein Sleipnes, who little realized that, nineteen years later, he would serve as *Norway*'s staff captain and then NCL's marine superintendent.

Tage originally hoped to store his tenders in compartments from which they would emerge via telescopic crane. But internal structural complications forbade that jack-in-the-box approach so he parked them in plain sight below the bridge. To lower them, huge, Dutch-built "superdavits" were installed. Astonishing about *Norway*'s tenders was their natural concealment; painted the same white as their surrounds they were effectively camouflaged and, to distant observers, largely invisible.

NCL's management felt that *Norway*'s public rooms and cabins should be revamped and agonized about the choice of designer. As it happened, a new Omni hotel had just opened near company headquarters; NCL executives lunched there frequently. One of them suggested to his tablemates: "Whoever designed this place should do *Norway*."

The fortuitous "whoever" was Angelo Donghia, a talented Italian-American interior decorator. Born in 1935 and raised in Vandergrift, Pennsylvania, he was the son of a tailor. Not surprisingly, New York beckoned. After graduating from Parsons School of Design, he opened his first retail venture in 1968 and called it Vice Versa; it would later segue into Donghia Textiles. Subsequently, Donghia Furniture was established. He realized early on that to have well-designed components at his disposal for enriching commissions, he should—and did—enter the home furnishings market.

Single-handedly, Donghia went on to become an internationally acclaimed design guru. His touch was inimitable, classic American decoration. The timeless freshness of his textile designs no less than the quality and finish of his furniture remained unparalleled—upscale, durable, and

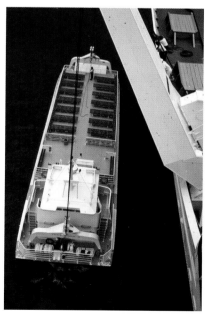

Off St. Thomas, *Little Norway I* is lowered to the water. (Author's collection)

Top left: Newly arrived in Le Havre to assess *France*'s interiors, jet-lagged but chipper Angelo Donghia poses in front of her number 1 funnel. (Donghia, Inc.)

Top right: Daunting commission— Angelo in front of a wall of his public room renderings a year later.

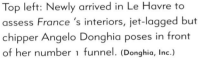

(Ian Maxtone-Graham collection)

devastatingly fashionable. Their excellence established the name Donghia in the firmament of Manhattan's design universe. Important people were entranced and a who's who of celebrated names besieged his studio, among them the Trumps, Liza Minnelli, Calvin Klein, Ralph Lauren, and, more notorious now than then, the Bernard Madoffs.

Two years before the Omni commission that brought him to NCL's attention, Angelo Donghia was inducted into the International Hall of Fame, an extraordinary honor for one just turned forty-two. In sum, everything Donghia touched turned to gold, including *Norway*.

The New York Times asked me to write a piece about *Norway* for its Sunday magazine, timed to coincide with *Norway*'s Manhattan arrival. Eager to chat with Donghia, I tracked him down at his Key West house.

Mary and I arrived on his doorstep the morning after an overnight gale. Angelo greeted us effusively—slim, intense, knowledgeable, and charming, perfect host and fount of information. In the midst of total immersion Italian lessons, the lunch he cooked was focaccia and pasta primavera.

Appropriately, we ate atop a Waring & Gillow table rescued from laid-up *Caronia*.

From the moment his *Norway* commission had been announced, what struck everyone—New York's design community, the *Times*, myself—was whether Angelo's refinement would be squandered fashioning surroundings for, if not necessarily downmarket, at least mass-market passengers; inferences to silk purse and sow's ear were endemic.

Angelo dismissed the thought out of hand. He never had, he insisted, nor never would design down to anyone. "Good taste," he spelled out, "exists in everyone. And that inherent taste will respond to whatever I create." Underlying his enthusiasm was a roguish sense of humor. Recalling his first sight of *Norway*'s scaffolding-shrouded funnels, he confessed never before having seen "a ship up in curlers." *France*'s existing interiors he likened airily to "a dirty suit."

Angelo's decorative sensibility endorsed the soft, forgiving texture of chenille, his upholstery of choice for most *Norway* furniture. If passengers were to sit wearing a bathing suit or shorts, he wanted the material encountering their skin to be, as Italians suggest, *simpatico*.

Crystal-garlanded Neptune coming in for a landing and (right) mounted safely in his niche, portside aft, Club Internationale. (Author's collection)

All Angelo's color choices were zoologically suggestive: gray/brown corridor carpeting he described as elephant, camel-brown distinguished the dining room carpet, panther black stalked Checkers Cabaret, ostrich-egg walls adorned the Lido bar, and antelope walls decorated Club Internationale.

We discussed his Club I renovations. He had retained its star-shaped chandeliers but toned down the bar, juxtaposing it against a white, latticed wall and shifting the focus aft. Chapelain-Midy's avian still lifes were replaced by more than life-sized representations of Triton and Neptune—giddy, crystal-garlanded sea gods from London—recessed within newly created alcoves and flanked by shell-shaped electric sconces. His *Norway* armchairs, upholstered in mottled tweed, surrounded small, brass-girt marble tables. A lamp was affixed atop each, a low-wattage bulb glowing through pinpricks piercing a conical brass shade.

He rewrought *France*'s chilly Salon Fontainebleau into vibrantly warm Checkers Cabaret—"checkers" because of its checked black-and-white marble dance floor. The rest of the room was carpeted in smaller black/red checks. Four chrome palm trees, inspired by the Regency's Brighton Pavilion, cornered the dance floor. The room's dominant colors—panther black and blood red, reminiscent of *The Shining* to come—flooded upholstery, walls, and carpeting. Had he lived to see it, I think NCL's subsequent installation of a giant bar across the back wall would have distressed Donghia acutely.

In fact, Angelo's Checkers formula was symptomatic of his entire, onboard achievement. *France*'s overlit, metallic interiors were enriched yet softened, a shipwide chenillean touch that spread beguiling warmth throughout.

Cooperation between interior decorator Donghia and naval architect Wandborg was seamless; the two got on famously. Angelo renamed only one public room: Tage had wanted to call the discotheque Volcano but Angelo preferred Dazzles.

All *Norway* passengers would travel in one class—"One Class, First Class" the company crowed—which meant that Leeward dining room's capacity could be decreased and Windward's amplified. *France*'s tourist class dining room was also brought up to decorative parity with first's. Tage connected its two levels with its own *grande descente*, a gently curving staircase, while Donghia

enriched the ceiling with a chrome chandelier and new carpeting underfoot.

Windward's wall murals were retained. Though Angelo had never sailed aboard *France*, the naked steel corners sullying Chambord's chairs appalled him. He replaced them with ampler seating, chrome framed and upholstered with chenille. He also uprooted the green Rilsan, substituting a patterned black-and-brown (camel) carpeting. One of his staff later told me what a challenge it had been retaining the pattern's continuity up the treads and risers of the curving, narrowing staircase. Windward's chronic glare was reduced, in one regard, excessively. Overhead circuits lighting the staircase doors were inexplicably extinguished. Until the day *Norway* stopped sailing twenty-three years later, Windward's focal descent was fatally eclipsed; entering faces disappeared.

All *Norway* bed linen would be washed aboard rather than off-loaded to laundries. Much as he admired the richness of the French cabin linen, Angelo accepted that *Norway*'s washing machinery could not handle it. Cabin berths were made up with less luxurious cotton sheets; many of those rumpled compromises were imprinted with Angelo's distinctive windowpane pattern.

Karl Woraschk, on the staff of a Sino/German firm called Jue Man Hing, designed the layout and supervised installation of machinery in the laundry compartment aft on Dolphin Deck. The largest piece of equipment he ordered was a giant, three-roll ironer, into which thousands of sheets, tablecloths, and napkins would be fed over and around heated, rotating drums each day. It was Karl who first advised me *never* to refold a shipboard napkin; if I did, a laundryman would only have to unfold it before committing it to the washer.

Installation of Tage's bow- and stern thrusters meant that when she arrived weekly in Miami *Norway* would spin on a dime in the turning basin, reversing course seaward and mooring alongside two adjacent Dodge Island terminals. Because of those terminal configurations, *France*'s midship embarkation lobby was abandoned. Instead, passengers embarked in two divergent streams, one through the tourist class's forward entrance, the other near the stern. To orient those arrivals, alleyway carpeting was color-coded with standard gender indicators: baby blue forward, pink aft. Reinforcing that fore-or-aft protocol, ticketing materials bore the same identifying colors.

Top and center: The Donghia effect. Two views of Checkers Cabaret, complete with chenille upholstery, table lamps, Brighton Pavilion palms, and signature red/black checked carpet. (Norwegian Caribbean Line)

Bottom: Devoid of counters, now that the purser's desk has been relocated up to Champs Elysées, France's embarkation lobby is now merely a waiting area before meals in the Windward dining room. In the foreground, holdover French chairs from the Grand Salon have been temporarily dragooned into *Norway* service. (Author's collection)

Color-coded carpeting was only a preliminary traffic assist. Needed in addition were new signs for every deck, staircase, public room, and cabin door. Miami graphic designer and signage expert Tom Graboski would make it all happen.

He conducted a two-week Bremerhaven survey and, on his return, pitched a complete signage proposal that was accepted. Tom signed a two-page letter of agreement in lieu of a contract that never appeared and began staffing for the job. On 2 February, he returned to Bremerhaven for an anticipated fortnight; he would not come home until after *Norway* tied up at New York's Pier 88 in May.

He and his group took over *France's* second lavish suite, *Ile de France*; Tage was already ensconced in *Normandie* across the way. Tom scrounged plywood for trestle tables and appropriated whatever chairs he could find. Working conditions were frigid, and he and his colleagues routinely wore sweaters and parkas. A single space heater, borrowed from the yard, was never unplugged until 29 April, the day *Norway* sailed for Kristiansand.

When signs started arriving Graboski requested crew help to install them. First officer Lars Hagroup reported that no ship's personnel were available, so Graboski's people would have to do the job themselves.

More staff—to a total of sixteen—were summoned from the States. They worked relentlessly. There were no weekends, merely weeks of twelve-hour days. Tom did find time to make Tage an

Easter present, a *Norway* profile painted onto an egg. Slowly, methodically, and accurately, his work appeared throughout the vessel, including new numbers affixed to 1,115 cabin doors.

When Graboski moved aboard on the day of departure, he appropriated an empty Biscayne Deck cabin and, for bedding, used tablecloths as sheets. As the ship sailed, berthing teams surveyed every potentially empty cabin, including his *Ile de France* office. They were hoping to find space for crew, some of whom were camping out on chaise longues in the public rooms.

The availability of working cabins would become critical. Knut Kloster had already decided to carry paying passengers to New York. This meant that, immediately after trials, the vessel would have to be in working passenger mode with catering, laundering, entertainment, and shipboard services on line.

I sense that, for Kloster, a proper maiden crossing after a visit to Oslo would prove irresistible. Immensely proud of having affixed his country's name to the world's longest liner, he wanted to show her off to the widest audience. His decision, however heroic, involved risk. Most owners deadhead new vessels westbound, with only crew and shipyard personnel aboard. Moreover, converted ships are special. Whereas a newbuilding's operating systems are consistently new, conversions' combine new components with old, a sometimes uneasy mélange of the untried with the not necessarily true.

Bottom left: Tom Graboski in his splendid office. (Tom Graboski collection)

Bottom right: Rippling signage for *Norway's* al fresco breakfast/lunch option. (Tom Graboski collection)

Graboski's less splendid, co-opted cabin, its lower bunk made up with tablecloth "sheets." (Tom Graboski collection)

Opposite, top: *Norway's* marching band musters on the after end of Oslo Deck, a regular feature of the run to St. Thomas. (Jeff Macklin collection)

Opposite, bottom left: Indefatigable and talented Jean Ann Ryan, Norwegian Cruise Line's reigning impresaria to the present. (Jean Ann Ryan Productions, Inc.)

Opposite, bottom right: Technical turmoil—hanging scenery for *Sea Legs* on Saga Theatre's newly expanded stage. (Jean Ann Ryan Productions, Inc.)

In fact, Kloster perceived *Norway's* crossing as more shakedown cruise than maiden voyage. He wrote:

The yard in Bremerhaven had done a magnificent conversion job but, to put it bluntly, there was no way to make all the toilets and showers work without starting to use them. The whole sewage system had been out of function for so long that flushing many of the toilets was a problem. By having passengers in the staterooms, using toilets and showers, the problems could be located and resolved during the transatlantic voyage.

Both decisions—the Oslo visit as well as the marketed crossing—intensified NCL's preparatory pressure. Steelwork, renovation, and signage were one thing, but shipboard essentials like music and entertainment assumed equal importance.

Dozens of additional musicians were required. Their recruitment was assigned to a former trombonist named Chip Hoehler.

Chip was working for NCL aboard *Southward.* When Kloster bought *France*, NCL's director of entertainment Peter Compton and music director Larry Topall appointed Hoehler *Norway's* music director, dispatching him on a nationwide tour.

Throughout February 1980, he auditioned some twenty-five hundred musicians in twenty-one cities. The forty-six he selected flew from Miami to Bremerhaven at the beginning of April. They would have a three-week rehearsal period on board before the vessel sailed.

That forty-six musicians were recruited for one vessel was unprecedented; even today it remains remarkable. But it came with the territory. Everything about *Norway* was outsize—tenders, hull, signage, crew, musical aggregation, street performers, stars, and musicals—bigger and more lavish than any predecessor's. Chip would conduct a seventeen-piece big band (favored orchestral fare for most middle Americans) as well as a marching band numbering thirty-five.

Entertainment? In a word, overwhelming, thanks to a Cincinnati dancer/choreographer named Jean Ann Ryan. Though her father worked for IBM, her mother, not surprisingly, had been a dancer. Jean Ann followed in her footsteps, choreographing at the Cincinnati Conservatory of Music and, in 1973, joining a road tour as a dancer in *My Fair Lady.* Back in New York she worked with the John Kenley Players and, later in Florida, met

NCL's Peter Compton. He hired Jean Ann to put on industrial shows for White Fleet charters. Subsequently, Ric Widmer asked her to mount passenger shows as well, one of which she called *Sea Legs*.

As the company's entertainment arbiter, Jean Ann Ryan was responsible for *Norway*'s ambitious showbiz regime. In Bremerhaven over the winter of 1979–80, she rehearsed three productions: a mixed-media version of *Sea Legs*, a full-scale production of *Hello, Dolly!*, and, for the North Cape Lounge, a revue called *Everything's Coming Up Broadway*.

However catchy the name, Saga Theatre was more cinema than theater. There was zero wing space; one exited, recalls Jean Ann, "into steel." Prior to Jean Ann's Bremerhaven arrival, performing space had been enlarged by a fellow Cincinnatian, architect Paul Short, whom Jean Ann had recommended for the task. His improved proscenium, seventeen feet downstage of the original, created invaluable additional stage room on a three-degree rake. Two elevated side stages added enviable flexibility.

Backstage dimensions were restricted, because the back wall was an engine room casing. The main dressing room occupied *France*'s chapel, also used for wardrobe preparation and storage; a smaller, supplementary dressing room was located stage right and one small bathroom stage left. Quick changes took place in the wings.

Even the simplest backstage maneuvers required care. Leaving stage for the dressing room (chapel), performers had to run along Pool Deck's corridor and then dash up one flight of Stairtower 2 to International Deck. Passengers strolling nocturnally always wondered why they encountered so many costumed boys and girls tearing around the corridor.

Playing Eliza Doolittle in *My Fair Lady*, Neva Powers once left the dressing room for her entrance but forgot to descend a flight. Instead, she hurried along International Deck to Stairtower 3 and burst into Saga Theatre's occupied balcony. Professional that she was, Ms. Powers found some light and delivered her number from there.

Seating capacity of Paul Short's redesigned auditorium had been reduced to 578. It would not be until a 1987 refit that a major enlargement of the theater balcony would increase capacity to nine hundred.

Jean Ann wrought her theatrical magic again. After weeks of punishing, drafty, scattershot rehearsals, plagued by noise and intrusion, the auditorium echoed with Jerry Herman's infectious melodies as *Hello, Dolly!* was readied for final dress rehearsal. Productions to follow *Norway*'s landmark opening night would be *Barnum*, *My Fair Lady*, *42nd Street*, *Will Rogers Follies*, *Crazy for You*, *Meet Me in St. Louis*, and *Guys and Dolls*, all stamped with Ryan's unmistakable and polished imprimatur.

I spent some fascinating days at Lloyd Werft in March 1980. Donning coveralls and hard hat, I interviewed Wandborg, Graboski, Peter Compton, and Captain Hauge. It was eerie to be wandering around those familiar yet unfamiliar interiors as they underwent strenuous renovation.

That shipboard plumbing might prove a problem was brought home one morning in just decorated Checkers Cabaret. As I watched, a water pipe ruptured, deluging new carpeting and furniture with torrents of water. Wet wool carpeting shrinks as it dries, wrenching apart carefully allied seams. That flood was a sobering foretaste of others to come. A sewage pipe snaking across Windward's flat ceiling—not the dome—sprang a small leak at one point.

Right: In March 1980 a joyous steam plume indicates that one of *Norway*'s boilers is back on line. (Author's collection)

Opposite: Tugs usher *Norway* out of Hapag-Lloyd Werft Yard for sea trials. Captain Hauge wrote me: "We are not bored on board, all the time is filled with work. The only thing that makes you think you are on a cruise is the weather. So far only sunshine, no winds and that makes all the test programs easier." (Hapag-Lloyd, Jeff Macklin collections)

Night delivery. Plucked from the water and delivered across the bow via crane, *Little Norway II* is lowered to its berth.

(Tom Graboski collection)

Yet there were exhilarating pluses. While I stood out on Sun Deck one morning a plume of steam vented noisily from the working funnel; boilers were back on line. Illuminated NORWAY letters were in place and so too were Tage's "superdavits" on the bow, awaiting the tenders. I watched installation of teak decking around the new pool, joiners protected from North Sea winds by orange tarpaulins. I roamed throughout the vessel, from the emergency tiller flat aft to the bridge, where electronic ganglia spilled from gaping consoles. How, one wondered, would the vessel be finished on time?

On the starboard bridge wing next afternoon, at the same spot where, five years earlier, I had bid Christian Pettré farewell, I saw a pile of refuse that workers were about to load into a crib descending that instant from the jib of a crane. *Norway*'s staff captain, normally phlegmatic, pipe-smoking Hartvig von Harling, was distraught because, among the rubbish, he spotted *France*'s propeller indicators. Those two steel boxes, their four working dials showing miniature propellers rotating, had been wrenched from above both bridge doors and discarded.

Acting as one, Hartvig and I rescued them in the nick of time. Today, one is in Bremerhaven's Deutsches Schiffahrtsmuseum and the other at South Street Seaport in New York. It was a happy coincidence that two determined preservationists were on hand at that moment.

No more than a cursory inspection of the engine room revealed that one omitted conversion option was replacing *France*'s turbines with diesels. The company had decided to defer rather than dismiss the possibility. Also arguing against it was the probability of delay: ordering, designing, building, bench testing, delivering, and installing the requisite machinery might have imperiled *Norway*'s schedule. The additional cost was also a consideration, despite the fact that cheaper diesel fuel would offer economies in the long run. Unrealized at the time, deterioration of *Norway*'s boilers after the millennium would have been obviated. Circa 1979, however, turbines were retained. *Norway* would steam rather than chug around the Caribbean, continuing to flaunt the increasingly rare initialed prefix S.S. for "steam ship."

Norway departed Lloyd Werft for a long weekend of sea trials. The vessel's outboard propellers had been deactivated, rendering the forward engine room moribund and a source of spare parts. Quadruple-screwed *France* had segued into twin-screwed *Norway*. Replacement five-bladed propellers produced 25 knots on trials, in excess of *Norway*'s projected 16-knot service speed. Bow- and stern thrusters were tested successfully. To install the latter, Wandborg had thickened *Norway*'s skeg, her projecting after keel.

The tenders had persevered south from Alesund and were in port when *Norway* returned. Tied up with their mother ship's port flank alongside, *Little Norway I* was hoisted conventionally aboard by davits. But *Little Norway II* had to be lifted at night via crane, lofted aerially over the bow, and lowered into place.

On 29 April 1980, *Norway* sailed from Bremerhaven near midnight. On board were crew, subcontractors, musicians, dancers, singers, Haitian engine cleaners, Jamaican stewards, and some three hundred Lloyd Werft workers, a few accompanied by illicit girlfriends.

Towed into port, *Norway* had been confined to Lloyd Werft for a week over eight months. She departed under power. Officers on the bridge, no less than everyone crowding her decks, teared up as

Left: Knut Kloster hosts a Bremerhaven press conference aft on Pool Deck. A present from the shipyard, a model of a square-rigged ship, would decorate the Windjammer. (Norwegian Caribbean Line)

Below: Fresh from the yard, *Norway* awaits the press contingent at anchor in Kristiansand's harbor (Norwegian Caribbean Line)

Norway's allotment of delivered chaise longues. They had to be spread out on every deck in haste one night before the aerial photographer arrived the following day. (Tom Graboski collection)

Top: Like a great blue Pied Piper, *Norway* attracts an exultant following en route up Oslofjord. (Norwegian Caribbean Line)

Bottom: Torbjorn Hauge maneuvers his thrusters to coax *Norway* alongside. (Tom Graboski collection)

the great blue ship slipped out past winking channel markers into a nocturnally calm North Sea.

Her first destination, the Oslofjord, lay 500 miles (805 kilometers) due north. En route, it had been planned to embark a four-hundred-strong press contingent at Gothenburg. But a Swedish general strike, instigated the day prior to *Norway*'s call, shut down airport, port, and the entire country. So rather than bear to starboard for Gothenburg, *Norway* maintained course to Norway's Kristiansand, where there was no general strike but also no pier.

Under way, shipyard work continued. Newly arrived teams toiled below deck. All alleyways were cluttered with furniture and maritime inspectors told the crew that they should be cleared for safety reasons. Unsupervised teams worked with a will, opening port doors and hurling cabin furnishings overboard, including hundreds of new television sets.

When the press group landed at Kristiansand's airport, *Norway* had just anchored. Reporters, commentators, broadcasters, feature writers, and two Maxtone-Grahams embarked via two local tenders. As we drew close to the vessel, worrisome harbingers of disarray appeared. Rolls of carpet and stacks of cartons were stuffed beneath every companionway. After we boarded, the illicit Bremherhaven ladies were disembarked.

After clambering aboard through an after port door, we wrestled suitcases up Tage's new stairtower to International Deck. Assigned a Fjord Deck cabin, we struggled higher, only to find it occupied. Back at the purser's desk, we were redirected to another cabin. It too had a prior occupant. Third time lucky, for we entered an inside that we immediately adopted. Inside or out was unimportant: availability was all that mattered.

Charged with public relations for the maiden voyage was Henrik "Henk" Nissen-Lie, a tall debonair yachtsman. His right hand was a young Norwegian from Son, at the mouth of Oslofjord, named Oivind Mathiesen; he currently edits New York's *Cruise Industry News*.

Norway departed Kristiansand, heading northeast toward Oslofjord. Satellites were nonexistent in those days, of course, so Oivind and Henk had marshaled a dozen VHF telephones and converted Fjord Deck's dog kennel into a press room. All day and night, jostling reporters queued up for a turn to shout bulletins to their editors.

Early the following morning we made a predawn stop off Son—Oivind's hometown—to embark several dozen members of the K.N.S. (Kongelig Norsk Seilforening, the Royal Norwegian Yacht Club), invited as special guests for the Oslo approach. Kloster had hoped that King Olav, a keen member, might board with them. But it was not only too early for His Majesty, he was also

Waiting Akershus, its ramparts full of cheering Oslovians. (Tom Graboski collection)

149

The portrait of His Majesty King Olav V hanging in Club I. Americans invariably assumed that the subject was *Norway*'s first master. (Author's collection)

scrupulous about not favoring one shipowner over another.

Carbon copies of Henk Nissen-Lie congregated around the vessel, clad in yachting rig: blue topsider moccasins, blue corduroys, and blazers with the club's burgee adorning breast pockets. The weather could not have been finer. For four days, unrelenting sunshine was the norm; too often soaking or at least overcast, Oslo had turned radiantly Mediterranean—or perhaps Caribbean?

Norway's progression attracted an ever growing armada. The country's oldest steamboat, coal-fired *Børøysund*, joined the parade, raucously sounding her penetrating steam whistle. Close to the capital, tugs hurled red, white, and blue plumes up into the sunshine. Three engineers found a marvelous box seat for the spectacle, the open end of number 1 funnel's starboard wing.

The stage set onto which starring *Norway* made her entrance was the Akershus, Oslo's thirteenth-century royal palace; directly beneath it lay our pier. No European capital boasts a more compelling mis-en-scène. Palace terraces, walls, and greenswards were packed. Norway has more brass bands per capita than any country in the world and my guess is that most of them crowded the ramparts that day, facing the world's largest podium. From Sun Deck, a bandmaster later led them in a massed concert.

Knut showed off *Norway* to every fellow countryman, from King Olav to Prime Minister Odvar Nordli to thousands of Oslovians invited on board for tours. Both monarch and prime minister would attend a private luncheon that day with Knut and Captain Hauge.

The Klosters had delivered to Tage's office a portrait of the king, gilt-framed and topped with a crown. The morning of 3 May, beneath the Akershus, Tage, his wife, Ingrid, and their children, Peter, Ann, and Tina, walked down Fifth Avenue toward Club I. The girls carried the portrait, Peter a hammer and nail.

I happened to be there when they arrived and Tage asked me where I thought it should be hung. Above the bandstand? Tage agreed. In stocking feet, Peter clambered atop the piano and pounded a nail into the wall. Then Tage had his daughters juggle the frame to level it.

As though on cue, from Champs Elysées in walked the king, escorted by Kloster, Hauge, and hotel manager Wright. The latter took immediate umbrage. "Out, out from here, immediately!" he barked at the children.

"No!" retorted Tage firmly. "Stay where you are and hold on to the king!"

His Majesty chimed in: "Right you are, hold on to the king!"

The gathering dissolved in laughter. Luncheon for the king and premier would be served in Hauge's cabin. At that moment, joiners were extending the table, hence that impromptu royal tour, killing time until lunch was ready. The portrait hung in place for twenty-three years.

The VIP lunch was congenial. Seated on the king's left was Jamaican Wesley Samuels, NCL's senior steward. Near meal's end, Prime Minister Nordli had to leave for an afternoon appointment and Kloster asked Nissen-Lie to escort him ashore. Henk and Ardli descended in the pilot's elevator. But Henk, alas, disembarked from it too early and got hopelessly lost before finding the crew gangway.

The royal family officiated that afternoon for the rechristening ceremony impossible in Le Havre. Wesley Samuels raised the United Nations flag. Kloster had obtained unique permission for *Norway* to fly it from Secretary-General Kurt Waldheim, a tribute to the fifty nationalities comprising his ship's company.

That evening, Mary and I dined with friends in Aas, an hour away by train. When we returned near midnight, "Maxtone-Graham" was echoing ominously over the vessel's loudspeakers. In the press room, I was told by a harried Oivind that we had to disembark on the morrow.

At an earlier meeting, Kloster, Hauge, and Henk had decided that, to free up cabins for Kloster's invited Norwegians, the press had to go. "Keep the goodwill, promise them anything," Kloster insisted, "but get them ashore. We need their cabins."

Sole exceptions were Associated Press, United Press, and Norsk Telegram BYRA; smaller fry were banished. I tried changing hats from *New York Times* reporter to shipboard lecturer to no avail; Oivind was adamant.

Next morning we relocated to Oslo's Grand Hotel as *Norway* steamed down Oslofjord without us, bound for Southampton. We flew to Heathrow, spent a night in London, and, with my lecturer's hat in place, repaired to Waterloo Station. An eighteen-car boat train, with *Norway* stickers plastering every window, lay at Platform 11, awaiting flights of passengers arriving from the States. At the barrier, the same NCL London staffers who had miraculously let Mary and myself board the train presented everyone else with thick envelopes containing London hotel reservations, return air tickets, and vouchers for a future *Norway* cruise.

"Sorry, there aren't enough cabins," those jet-lagged clients were advised. Among the rejected were Californians Larry and Diana Midland who had taken their children out of school for a UK blitz, climaxed by a *Norway* crossing home.

Mary and I departed Waterloo. Ninety minutes later, we descended from our private train at the Ocean Terminal. Because very few were boarding, embarkation took place on the pier. A few Norwegians, the remains of the press corps, and some French Line bigwigs disembarked.

Fretting at the gangway was a French woman, Odette Escolier, former *France* hairdresser, clutching a bouquet of red, white, and blue flowers with which she wanted to *fleuri* (flower) *Norway*. But she had neither boarding pass nor any hope of finding one. Touched by her plight I gave her mine. Tearfully grateful, she scampered up the gangway. I would not see her again for twenty-eight years.

With neither boarding pass nor ticket, I had unwittingly put myself in her position but, fortunately, encountered a ship's officer who spirited us aboard. En route, I fulfilled a sentimental commission. I had written Tardy-Panit that I was crossing aboard *Norway*. He wrote, asking if I would "pat her hull and tell her that he still loved her." As Mary and I negotiated the crew gangway I did just that.

Only two rounds of musical cabins saw us accommodated in an inside just aft of the embarkation lobby, formerly #63 Pont Principal, now Norway Deck #101. Inside or outside was immaterial; important was that the bathroom boasted a huge tub with faucets that actually dispensed water. New York novelist and friend Justin Scott, author of *The Shipkiller* and *Normandie Triangle*, was on board with his wife, Gloria.

Unbeknownst to passengers, *Norway*'s crossing was in jeopardy, following a bleak confrontation in Captain Hauge's office. He and Kloster were advised by Southampton's American Bureau of Shipping surveyor that, though his German colleague had permitted *Norway*'s Bremerhaven departure, he was rescinding the decision. His bilge inspection had revealed an accumulation of Bunker C

Drinks in the Windjammer: (left to right) the author, Mary Maxtone-Graham, Peter Duke ("of Donghia"), Gloria and Justin Scott. (Author's collection)

crude spillage the consistency of asphalt. *Norway*, he announced, was unseaworthy.

A distraught Kloster, who had cleared so many seemingly insuperable hurdles, appealed to Tage and the engineers. Chief Rolf Hille took it all in stride. Carboys of acetone were ordered from a Southampton chandler and a waste barge appeared alongside. A corps of fifty Haitians cleared the bilges and, with pilot Captain Peter Driver ushering us out of Southampton, *Norway* sailed for New York.

How incredible that Mary and I had subverted our banishment, how remarkable that former *France* was back on the Atlantic, and how exhilarating to be part of *Norway*'s maiden crossing. Though the ship was not full, the predominantly Norwegian passenger load exhibited a high degree of sophistication and savvy, re-creating the civilized patina of *France* days. Spontaneously, everyone insisted on dressing for dinner every night, doubtless a distaff decision: ambitious wardrobes must be showed off. Both dining rooms glittered. The galley and its chef rose to the occasion, and though many Jamaican waiters had never experienced mid-Atlantic seas they coped heroically.

Ostensible shakedown cruise became festive maiden voyage and the same Norwegian pride evinced in Oslo remained exuberantly in place. The presence of almost all of NCL's corporate structure was remarkable: owner Knut Kloster, his wife, Katrine, brother Einar, and son Knut, company president Helge Narstad and his wife, Nini, Henk Nissen-Lie, his wife, Uirstin, and son Axel, sales and marketing VP Ric Widmer, and entertainment director Compton. Upper echelon corporate types almost never embark for a complete maiden.

Adding to the fun were some street performers laid on by Compton. There was a mime in whiteface who wandered through the public rooms, aping passenger walks and attitudes, as well as a man riding a unicycle who would pedal into an elevator and exit a deck higher. Eddie Cotts, stage name Edwin Cotteleer, was a skilled magician and gentle soul. He roamed Club I, performing close-up card tricks or putting his hat on the table and materializing a bowl complete with goldfish beneath it.

Inevitably, there were problems. One man confessed that, from Oslo to New York, he shaved with Perrier by choice; abandoning his comfortable but plumbing-deprived cabin was not an option. But as

Tage and Ingrid Wandborg on deck as *Norway* approaches Manhattan, *Christian Radich* escorting. (Author's collection)

Inbound *Queen Elizabeth 2* has displaced *Norway* from her Manhattan berth. Cunard officers throng their port bridge wing to wish her bon voyage. (Cunard Line)

aboard every vessel bound everywhere, hard-core litigious Americans surfaced. Hear Henk Nissen-Lie on how those agitators were magically defused: "Knut had expected problems, sea lawyers brandishing subpoenas and summonses and threatening lawsuits. But nothing happened. Knut was so genial, apologetic, and placating that he disarmed every potential adversary. A typical Kloster performance."

Henk also shared a retrospective observation about *Norway*'s open bars. There are some Norwegians for whom shipboard—for which read overnight Baltic ferries—serves as kneejerk excuse for calamitous overindulgence. Astonishingly, several notorious Norwegian drinkers aboard *Norway* exhibited unusual restraint. One announced at crossing's end that he had never enjoyed a voyage more. Large amounts of sherry, Food & Beverage reported, were consumed.

Three days out, an inverted orange raft was spotted on the horizon. That it might possibly contain a shipwrecked sailor necessitated further investigation. The Scotts and I surmised that Hauge was

delighted to maneuver *Norway* neatly alongside deploying his new thrusters.

The raft proved empty, having probably fallen from a cargo vessel and automatically self-inflated. Hauge ordered it hoisted aboard and destroyed. Carried away by news of that midocean encounter, Oslo newspapers reported jubilantly that the raft's "rescued mariners" were being nursed back to health in *Norway*'s hospital.

The most persistent crossing conundrums were the numbers on board. Musical cabins continued after Southampton as passengers changed quarters repeatedly. Pursers had no idea who occupied which cabin nor even the total passenger count, a figure United States Immigration would demand in New York.

To solve the mystery, Helge and Nini Narstadt formed a task force to conduct a cabin census. One encounter led to a glorious incident of mistaken identity. Although Angelo Donghia himself was not on board, a young employee called Peter Duke served as his representative. Extremely personable, he shared our Windward table.

Same mast, different flags: *France*'s panoply (top) for her 1974 Southampton exit and *Norway*'s (bottom) for her 1980 New York entrance. (Author's collection)

Peter told us he had just stepped out of the shower when a census team pounded on the door. A shouted colloquy ensued.

"Sorry to disturb you but we must know your name and who is sharing the cabin with you."

"I'm alone and I'm Duke, of Donghia," Peter answered.

After a moment's baffled silence: "Thank you, your grace. Sorry for the disturbance."

No ducal Donghia exists but that Helge's team dutifully recorded his presence conveys the exotics who might have comprised the passenger load.

Outside an engine room door, other census takers found oily footprints on the new carpet and decided to follow them. They led down the alleyway, around a corner, and into a cabin. A passkey was produced and on the ceiling inside were the final two footprints. Perhaps, the team concluded, not all those illicit Bremerhaven ladies had disembarked.

Another cabin interloper appeared only after midnight. A fellow lecturer, the late Jimmy Kirkwood, A Chorus Line playwright, was aroused in the small hours by someone opening his door. Others had been disturbed by obviously the same intruder who, never responding, always ran off.

Finally apprehended, the prowler turned out to be an Oslovian stowaway. Having stolen an orange Hapag-Lloyd Werft boiler suit, he mingled with shipyard workers and, as a chronic alcoholic, Kloster's open-bar policy delighted him. Every night he hunted for a berth. Only after capture was he awarded one, confined within an empty cabin.

When Norway sailed into New York Harbor on the morning of 15 May, it was late in the day, just as it had been for the vessel's maiden arrival eighteen years earlier. Fleet Week had started and one appropriate participant was Norway's tall ship Christian Radich. In command was orlogskaptein (commander) Jan Fjeld-Hansen of the Royal Norwegian Navy; his vessel's sails were spread as, below the Verrazano Bridge, she awaited the inbound liner. Jan wrote me recently from his Texas home how "BIG" she seemed.

Nineteen-eighty was Jan's BIG year—he retired from the navy and joined the cruise industry, sailing first with Royal Viking. Later, by fortuitous coincidence, he became master of the ship he had welcomed into New York that unforgettable spring morning.

Every Norway passenger was brandishing a Norwegian flag but I had other flags in mind. Glancing up from Sun Deck, I contemplated Norway's radar mast. I had photographed it during France's 1974 Southampton departure, flying the French Line's company flag and Britain's red duster.

Now, a different array fluttered overhead: the entwined LK cypher of Lauritz Kloster, Norway's postal banner, the United Nations flag, the stars and stripes, and the pilot's red/white signal flag H. Score one for my son Guy; just as he had predicted Norway-ex-France was reentering New York.

After we tied up at Pier 88, disembarkation ground to a halt. Someone—no one ever found out who—had liberated the stowaway and, until he was apprehended, Norway could not be cleared. Despite chronic inebriation, he had all his wits about him, standing on the seat of a public bathroom stall so his feet would not give him away. Hours passed before he was unearthed. He mumbled to his captors that he had to get home because he was expected at a party. Back in Oslo, he became a celebrity spokesman for Norway, recommending her to both fellow countrymen and potential stowaways.

There was an Olympics benefit on the night of the sixteenth but, the following morning, Norway vacated Pier 88 in favor of inbound Queen Elizabeth 2. The two former rivals, which had frequently passed in midocean, passed again in the opalescent dawn of New York's Lower Bay. Cunard officers thronged their port bridge wing as the masters exchanged whistled salutes. QE2 remained on the North Atlantic while Norway would inaugurate the cruising service for which she had been converted.

At 0700 hours on 20 May, she arrived outside Miami in gale conditions so severe that she remained offshore until evening. Then she steamed up recently dredged Government Cut. Charles Whited, a Miami Herald feature writer, commemorated her long-awaited appearance.

She came in like a moving cliff, blue with gleaming white superstructure, twin stacks towering and gull-winged, dwarfing like water-bugs the shepherding tugboats, an Empire State Building on its side.

Norway's first seven-day cruise would depart on 1 June. Nine months and $120 million (twice Tage's original estimate) after her Le Havre departure, the Caribbean's latest, largest, and most extraordinary cruise ship was on station.

Norway's departure from Miami for St. Thomas, the first of hundreds to follow.
(Norwegian Caribbean Line, Jeff Macklin collection)

CHAPTER NINE

THE FIRST CARIBBEAN MEGASHIP

A great and kindly ship.

The late Captain Carl Netherland-Brown, Biscayne Bay pilot and ship's master

Norway was NCL for many years.

Jeff Macklin, former executive with Miami's Tropic Oil Company

My God, such a wealth untapped!

Ted Arison, about the Caribbean

Opposite: *Norway* departing Miami, not for St. Thomas but for Wilmington, North Carolina. (Norwegian Caribbean Line, Jeff Macklin collection)

On Sunday afternoon, 1 June, 1980, Miami pilot Captain Helge Krarup walked onto Norway's

starboard bridge wing and shook hands with Captain Hauge and Staff Captain von Harling. Having returned that morning from a cruise to nowhere, the vessel was ready for her first revenue voyage. A week of press and travel agents' receptions was over. Though the Klosters were not aboard, Knut recalls that there had been some semiserious banter between rival owners about advancing their ships' departure times so that *Norway* sailed last. Then, if she grounded in Government Cut, no one would be bottled up.

Passengers filed across divergent embarkation ramps. Below them, forklifts were still loading suitcase cribs. Between that outbound deluge, the same vehicles thrust pallets of shrink-wrapped supplies—everything from mops to mushrooms—inside the hull.

Port doors were closed and hydraulic mechanisms snugged them outboard, dogging them in place. Telltale monitors on the bridge winked out.

Lifeboat drill was over and *Norway* was ready to depart. Hawsers were singled up. Hanging near the waterline was a cable, fail-safe device if *Norway* needed moving from a possible pier fire. Already, a passenger gallery thronged Sun Deck's monkey island, sporting shorts, T-shirts, caps, sun visors, and flip-flops.

At Hauge's command, von Harling muttered into his handheld radio: *"La gaa alle trosser,"* then, in English, "Let go all." At each end of Norway Deck, mooring officers signaled to longshoremen. *Norway*'s final restraints were relinquished and hawser loops were shrugged off bollards and dropped. Capstans growled and hawsers withdrew toward their mother ship, snaking upward and disappearing.

Duties concluded, Miami's longshoremen normally departed. But that afternoon, players in an historic event, they watched *Norway*'s maiden departure. A light breeze blew up Government Cut.

At the central console, having already called for hard right rudder to minimize lateral drag, Hauge nudged five thruster controls to port. *Norway* moved ponderously sideways. In the resulting gap, scavenging gulls swooped for edibles roiled to the surface. Clear of the dock, Hauge ordered rudder amidships, returned thruster handles to neutral, and called, "Slow ahead."

The vessel began her stately progression to sea, longer, larger, and more lavish than anything

within thousands of miles. Longshoremen's perspective changed, from overwhelming cliff to classic profile, her counter prettily delineated by afternoon sun. As predicted, *Norway* blue proved picture perfect.

As she glided past Royal Caribbean and Carnival rivals, some saluted; Hauge answered with three majestic reverberations. Tooting drivers whizzing along MacArthur Causeway were convinced that *Norway* was responding to them. Dodge Island segued from passenger to cargo terminal.

There was no grounding. Serene, implacable, majestic, the giant ship maintained eight knots, gliding past the Coast Guard pier as a Fisher Island ferry scuttled beneath her stern.

She slowed at the sea buoy. As the pilot boat came alongside, pitching atop its overtaking wake, a Jacob's ladder dropped from Biscayne Deck. The pilot clambered down and grasped the boat's railing. As it swept him back to Miami he waved farewell up to von Harling on the bridge.

Propeller revolutions increased, doubled watches stood down, and sea routine began. Through a roseate dusk, *Norway* began her initial two-day plod toward St. Thomas—in Miami parlance, the milk run.

Outside the twelve-mile limit, passengers stormed the shops. They were soon kitted out in *Norway* T-shirts, *Norway* sweatshirts, and *Norway* caps. Caribbean beginners crave logo'd wear; sporting it brands them indubitably as having been aboard.

Though *France* had made fortnightly crossings between Le Havre and New York, *Norway* embraced repetitive cruise weeks with two stops: St. Thomas and the company's Bahamian out island, Little San Salvador.

St. Thomas is every cruise itinerary's near obligatory port. Daily, year-round, at least six ships disembark acquisitive hordes who overrun the shops before reboarding with loot.

With her deep draft, *Norway* anchored out and deployed her tenders. Unseen, they had triggered controversy. Disembarking *Norway* passengers downtown, the taxi driver union's chief insisted, would create a traffic hazard. They should instead off-load at the West Indian docks like everyone else. Unsaid, they would taxi around the harbor edge, creating additional traffic but lining his members' pockets.

A new name board and funnel livery convey an exuberant message: *Norway* is conquering the Caribbean! (Author's collection)

Cruise ships are seldom seen in Miami after dark. But at the end of May 1980, Norway's first Floridian week, she stayed moored at Dodge Island. Save for one overnight cruise there were onboard receptions and dinners alongside every night. (Norwegian Caribbean Line, Jeff Macklin collection)

Tage responded that he would prefabricate a collapsible pedestrian overpass to offset the "hazard." Nothing happened and, for twenty-three years, *Little Norways* off-loaded passengers for instant access to downtown.

At Little San Salvador two days later, another tender crisis. The previous summer, Captain Hauge had walked out from shore until the water reached his nose; several damp tries later he had pinpointed the optimal landing site.

But that June, when *Little Norway II* reached his position, she grounded. Winter storms had reconfigured the bottom. As passengers fumed, a new approach was selected. After sounding and maneuvering, *Little Norway II* surged toward the beach and lowered her ramp. There was a reek of grilling hamburgers and hot dogs.

Like assaulting marines, 450 passengers poured ashore. Subsequent waves of tendered passengers hit the same beach, carrying snorkels, flippers, towels, and sun-tan lotion. Since Little San Salvador was vulnerable to winter weather, NCL relocated operations to nearby Great Stirrup Cay.

The tenders inspired one scam. A year later, a *Norway* comment card complained about being charged extra for tendering. Investigation revealed that an enterprising crewman had stationed himself at the head of Biscayne Deck's queue, collecting a dollar-a-head "tender fee." He pocketed hundreds before NCL exposed and fired him.

At the end of every cruise, twenty-five hundred *Norway* passengers disembarked, replaced by twenty-five hundred replacements bused from the airport. Aircraft that doomed North Atlantic liners had become cruise ships' allies. In August of 1980 Mary and I found ourselves among those outbound thousands after flying from New York to sample our first *Norway* cruise.

It was truncated by a catastrophic engine failure. Late Monday night *Norway* lost power. A switchboard fire had disabled the Pielstick generator and engineers would consume a stifling day and night to repair things.

For thirty hours, air-conditioning, illumination, refrigeration, and water stopped. Sealed portholes could not admit whatever breezes ruffled Cuban waters. Ingenious passenger Brian Carter, a Princess Cruises manager, opened his porthole by undoing its lugs with a fire ax and had fresh air.

Though bars dispensed complimentary wine, beer, and soft drinks, "Black Tuesday" proved increasingly distressing. Stopped passengers are like subway riders stalled in a tunnel, impatient for their journey's resumption. But blackouts have,

Author's first view of *Norway* at Dodge
Island, 17 August 1980. (Author's collection)

alas, no predictable conclusion; neither Hauge nor
his exhausted engineers knew when it would end.
During those dragging hours, while Mary and I
played solitaire in the card room's dimmed lighting, we encountered Larry and Diana Midland.
They had suffered a double *Norway* whammy—
disruption of the cruise selected to replace their
aborted westbound maiden from Waterloo.

Power was restored early Wednesday morning.
Many passengers, confined within humid cabins
for one night, had slept outdoors for the second.
Sun Deck became a campground, littered with
mattresses, pillows, blankets, and chaise longues.
People awakened at 0300 by inextinguishable deck
lights shrouded them with towels so they could
sleep on.

Hauge proposed Nassau as compensation for
lost St. Thomas. His engineers were exhausted and
he dared not risk a second blackout. Sea lawyers
immediately circulated petitions, threatening legal action if denied their duty-free liquor; Nassau,
they insisted, was unacceptable.

Presented with their written ultimatum, Hauge
responded in kind, canceling Nassau for immedi-

ate Miami return. Far too early, *Norway* limped
into port. Reporters waited to interview disembarking passengers. Meanwhile, NCL shore staff
set up a refund operation in, of all places, Checkers—apropos venue for dispensing reimbursement
checks?—plus a half-price cruise to come.

Not everyone was pleased. A representative
from an uneasy male group advised the purser sotto
voce that, since they had not "officially" (their
word) boarded, refund checks were impossible.
Others confessed that their traveling companions
were not "officially" their wives. The solution?
Cash refunds. Only after news cameras had been
stowed did the "unofficials" slink ashore.

Norway not only attracted record numbers of
passengers, she also bewitched prospective crew.
Norwegian officers clamored for a *Norway* transfer.
The late Geir (pronounced *gear*) Lokøen relished
his years on board.

"I spent more time with her than with my wife
and children. It has become a personal thing between she and me," he recounted.

All his fellow Norwegians felt similarly. In 1982
Svein Sleipnes, who had watched the Alesund

The vessel's upper deck three days later: the blackout ended early that morning and passengers are either awake or still dozing on deck. (Author's collection)

tender construction, sailed with the White Fleet. Four years later he was appointed *Norway*'s chief officer for security and maintenance. Sleipnes confesses that he was initially overwhelmed by the vessel and a year passed before he felt fully comfortable. At the same time, he articulated a familiar refrain: "The great lines in her hull always amazed me. I was really in love with this ship."

In July 1981 Hans Meeg was master of *Tropical Land*, a fruit carrier headed for New York off the Floridian coast. Norwegian voices came over the radio. It was *Norway*. Meeg called Captain Kjell Haugen (Hauge's relief), querying "if it was okay for my ship to approach at a safe distance, make a turn around his stern, and come up on a parallel course for a bit."

Kjell agreed and alerted his passengers. Seven *Tropical Land* officers, all Norwegian, crowded the bridge; Liberian registry notwithstanding, they hoisted their country's flag.

Norway was on the radar, Meeg recalls, "a big blip" (the biggest, in fact!). Then *Norway* herself appeared, steaming at 17 knots. "What a sight coming upon her!" Meeg marveled. "I'll never forget it."

Before breaking off, the vessels exchanged salutes.

Tropical Land carried a dozen passengers. At dinner, they asked the Norwegians if they would sail aboard *Norway*. All of them, the master included, said no. Cargo/passenger life suited them, so informal that they seldom wore uniforms. Meeg had trouble getting his chief engineer to even dine with passengers. But he wrote me recently, "Ten years later, I was at the helm of *Norway*." No Norwegian officer was immune.

Passengers were similarly transfixed. Experienced cruisers David and Joanne Rose from Orillia, Ontario, had often admired the vessel off St. Thomas. David's parents, Edna and Wilfred, had never been anywhere save once, to Mexico; after contracting dysentery, both swore never to leave Canada again. In August 2000, Wilfred was diagnosed with an inoperable brain tumor. He implored his son: "When I go, please do something for Mother. Take her on a trip, I never did." After realizing a $5,000 residue from the estate, the Roses agreed that a *Norway* cruise made the ideal ninetieth birthday present for recently widowed Edna. Having never sailed, she was overwhelmed by the grandeur depicted in NCL's brochure. But she bought no new clothing, merely packed judicious elements from her existing wardrobe, elegant scarves, heels, and silk dresses predominating.

All three shared a Fjord Deck cabin, not for reasons of economy but because the younger Roses feared Edna might get lost. Never lost, it turned out, only dazzled. What for her son and his wife were familiar cruise perks struck her as unbelievable: *Norway*'s size, the variety of shops, tea in Club I, nightly entertainment, and their Windward table for six. One tablemate, a roguish Manhattan septuagenarian, admired Edna enormously and, only half in jest, offered to take her home. He told David that he thought she was seventy-five.

Edna's wardrobe was the sensation of the ship, always impeccably dressed, from morning strolls until afternoon tea and first-sitting dinner. Passengers and crew were charmed. In St. Thomas she paddled in the waters of Meghan's Bay.

Everything delighted Edna. "I cannot believe," she confessed wistfully, "that people live this way." Headed home, during a Miami Airport snow delay, she mused primly, "Everything on the ship was so well run. Why do we have to wait now?"

Addicted *Norway* recidivists were two women from Appleton, Wisconsin, Betty West and her daughter Betsy. Though Betsy was confined to a wheelchair, they raised cocker spaniels at Cinnabar Kennels. Throughout the 1980s and early '90s, mother and daughter returned repeatedly to *Norway*, booking three consecutive cruises and always accommodated in Norway Deck's cabin 88. Though plenty of wheelchair accessible cabins existed on board, Norway 88 was not one of them; moreover, it was inside. But the Wests liked its layout and location. Moreover, Betsy could negotiate her wheelchair around it with ease.

They enjoyed many captain's dinners as well as private meals in his quarters. Hans Meeg entertained them several times. Hotel director Bjorn-Erik Julseth, also a great admirer, once inadvertently neglected to include them at the captain's table.

"If we forgot to invite them," he remembers ruefully, "all hell broke loose, in their own quiet way." We sailed with both Wests several times.

Once, when a Norwegian film crew was on board, Meeg recommended that the director film them, aboard for their 148th cruise. He completed

In Caribbean harness, *Norway* anchored off St. Thomas, her tenders dispatched. (Author's collection)

a long interview. When the program was aired, Norway 88 prompted several viewers to book it for their cruise.

Betsy's disease was cumulatively wasting. Each successive visit, she seemed increasingly disabled and is apparently no longer alive; neither the Wests nor Cinnabar Kennels is listed with Appleton information. Betsy was a radiant creature, and however restrictive her condition it restricted neither high spirits nor enjoyment. In love with *Norway*, she was universally loved in return. For her two hundredth cruise, NCL's president Hans Golteus ordered a commemorative plaque affixed to Norway 88's door.

Contrasting passengers from those incurable repeaters were shipboard neophytes Chuck Replogle and his younger brother Rob from Phillipsburg, Pennsylvania, who enjoyed consecutive *Norway* cruises in 2001 and 2002.

Chuck worked in catering at Penn State University, delivering food for Joe Paterno's Nittany Lions. His brother Rob was a hairdresser. "You can make pretty good money in the hair business and Rob was born to do hair," Chuck suggested.

Both had always been hooked on the *Titanic* and asked their travel agent to recommend some-

thing comparable; without question, she recommended *Norway*. Before their first cruise, Rob went to the bank and took out a loan, his reasoning as follows: "We were booking the best ship and decided to book the best cabin as well." They chose one of *France*'s *appartements de grand luxe*, originally *Normandie*, then Tage's office, and finally *Norway*'s Viking 139, the President Suite. Though one of its two bedrooms had become a neighboring double, the remaining spread was impressive—living room, bedroom, dining room, pantry, and two bathrooms.

The Replogles' cabin tariff was a stiff $5,000 apiece. Onboard expenses and round-trip air added more. Nevertheless, for both *Norway* cruises, they insisted on Cabin 139. They rejoiced in dressing for dinner and showing off their cabin. "It was great fun pretending we were famous," said Chuck. "People thought we owned a gold mine like Molly Brown or something." He sighed wistfully. "*Norway* spoiled you for anything else."

The vessel's crew commitment was also legendary and turnover extraordinarily low. Bandmaster Chip Hoehler established himself in a former sous chef's cabin forward on Norway Deck, a

Tage's triumph. The rendering comes to life as continual sun, swimming, and food enliven *Norway*'s afterdecks.
(Norwegian Caribbean Line)

two-room inside replete with every conceivable (and illicit) cooking device. Dubliner Anne Slevin, the charming redhead he married, joined him. Her first job was working a follow-spot in Saga Theatre. But when Jean Ann Ryan heard that she was a Grafton Fashion Institute graduate, she was transferred backstage, abandoning follow-spot for costumes and serving as *Norway*'s wardrobe mistress for five years, occasionally appearing on-stage.

Her employment shuffle was as nothing compared to Missourian David MacFarland, who holds the record for multiple shipboard posts. He joined *Norway* in Bremerhaven as a hairdresser and used to strum the piano outside the Club I. One hearing convinced Chip to offer him a musician's slot. But David honored his original contract, remaining in the hair salon for a year before accepting Chip's offer. Among the passengers who enjoyed his music were Knut and Katrine Kloster.

Then shipboard politics intruded. His boss informed the cruise director that David was soliciting tips for playing and the cruise director locked the piano and forbade any more MacFarland performances.

A month later Kloster ran into David. When asked why he was no longer playing, he explained. Later, in the Windjammer, Staff Captain von Harling approached him.

"Are you David MacFarland?"

David, afraid he was being disciplined for sitting at the bar, identified himself.

"You will be given a key to all the pianos on the ship and will be allowed to play any of them, any time. This comes from Mr. Kloster."

So the hairdresser played on, first voluntarily and then on the payroll, career number two. He stayed aboard until 1983 before being hired to play at Paris's Crillon Hotel. After six years, proficient in French, he returned to *Norway* in a third guise, assistant purser. A re-created *France* cruise was in the offing and French speakers were needed.

In 1989 he boarded *Seaward* as a sales assistant in the shops, career four. Nowadays, back to his first love, MacFarland tinkles the ivories aboard *Vision of the Seas* but still misses *Norway*.

Another Norwegian officer drawn to *Norway* was engineer Per Odd Sopp. Working for Chevron, Sopp sailed aboard company vessels until 1974 before supervising tanker construction at Nagasaki's Mitsubishi yard. Asked in 1981 to sign on for additional newbuildings he refused, already seduced by a familiar siren song, footage of *Norway* steaming up Oslofjord. He was hooked. "I have to be part of this," he decided, signing on as *Norway*'s first engineer in 1981. He remained with NCL for eighteen years.

During the early eighties *Norway* suffered repeated power outages and fires. Though Floridian newspapers obviously took note, the news was seldom disseminated nationwide and thousands of passengers still clamored to embark. Regardless, the vessel's breakdown rota is sobering.

Our Black Tuesday of August 1980 was followed

From top to pop: contrasting ashtrays from the two vessels tell their own tale. For sale in the shop, the pedestrian *Norway* image is a comedown from *France*'s chic blue glass and jazzy gold profile. (Author's collection)

by a Black Thursday and Friday in April of the following year. Marsha Johnson, her parents, husband, Bill, and two-year-old daughter Kirby occupied two adjacent inside cabins. Late Thursday night the cessation of air-conditioning indicated that power was out. The Johnsons spent their next two nights camped out under the stars, after corralling four chaise longues and two chairs as a makeshift crib. They survived several showers, enjoyed melting ice cream and wilting salads, watched the crew fish over the side, and played too many card and board games.

On Saturday, two White Fleet vessels, having discharged their passengers in Miami, were racing toward *Norway* to take off her passengers. But at the last moment one turbine was nursed to life and the flagship limped home, arriving at Dodge Island on Monday morning.

That same year, 1 May, 1981, the vessel's power was crippled by adulteration of boiler water. Engineers on a previous watch noted an increase in the production of distilled boiler water, indicator that a boiler must be leaking. Engineering officer Steinar Hammervold went to make sure that a supplementary supply of distilled water could be produced if necessary.

At 0400, suddenly, all three working boilers "tripped"—shut themselves down—because their water was too low. Some water tubes had fractured but luckily the fourth boiler was still functioning. By robbing the laundry tank for additional water, *Norway* steamed back to Miami. Bremerhaven personnel were flown in to replace the tubes and *Norway* was sidelined for a week.

In mid-December an engine room fire broke out, an all-too-familiar shipboard scenario: a watertight door's hydraulic valve fractured, spraying hydraulic fluid onto hot steam piping. The fire damage was extensive, destroying much of the space's electrical systems. Not until January 1982 would passenger service resume.

Six weeks later, in the afternoon of 17 March, 1982, *Norway* was leaving Nassau when another engine room fire broke out: oil spurting from a turbine-driven generator hit a hot steam pipe and ignited. Sopp, just off duty, heard the alarm from his cabin and spied smoke in the alleyway. Although the sealed-off space had been flooded with flame-suppressant Halon, it still burned fiercely.

Donning smoke-diver's gear, first engineer Hammervold entered the compartment and dis-

Norwegian revenge: first class playroom becomes video game room.
(Author's collection)

covered that a broken gasket on a pump was feeding compressed air to the blaze. Only after he shut it down could the fire be extinguished.

A shipwide fire alarm had been sounded. With life-jacketed passengers at muster stations, Hauge ordered lifeboats lowered to embarkation level and both tenders into the water. The weather stayed as calm as the passenger load. Unbidden, stewards carried wheelchair occupants safely up pitch-dark staircases to International Deck. Just after 5 P.M. electrical power was restored. Those *Norway* clients missed their out island experience but they disembarked on schedule in Miami without injury.

But devastating damage had afflicted *Norway*'s boiler room, necessitating yet another return to Bremerhaven. Contributing to her recurring blackouts was the lack of backup diesel generators whenever boilers failed. So during that yard visit, an idle French boiler—750 tons and three decks high—was cut up and off-loaded; three diesel generators occupied the vacated space, installations that negated *Norway*'s blackout vulnerability.

During that German visit, two significant things happened to Per. His first glimpse of *Norway* in dry dock bowled him over: "Her lines were absolutely beautiful. I could be down in the dock and look up

Norway anchored near her Bahamian out island. (Nelson B. Arnstein, M.D., collection)

at her forever." Second was an offer to become *Norway*'s superintending port engineer, an appointment requiring Miami residency. He accepted instantly.

"This is not a simple lady to handle," he explained to his wife, Alexsandra. "She needs special attention." Just as she had for Geir Lokøen, *Norway* became, for all Norwegians, the other woman.

Sunday mornings, from their bedroom on the nineteenth floor of Brickell Bay Drive, Per could see *Norway* dock and, through binoculars, tell who was on the bridge. *Norway*'s new superintending port engineer boarded every Sunday to coordinate technical issues and sailed on every sixth cruise. "Other people came and went," Per remembers. "I was the only one that was there all those years. *Norway* was my whole life."

One whose life *Norway* ceased to be was magician Eddie Cotts. In 1983, mortally ill, he gave up his job but not before Sue Carper, NCL's entertainment manager, organized a farewell tribute in

Saga Theatre. He was eulogized before a packed house and presented with a commemorative plaque. Eddie never ceased marveling about that special evening.

Sopp embarked for the vessel's first Atlantic revenue crossings over the summer of 1984. Just as Kloster could not resist taking *Norway* up Oslofjord in 1980, four years later he shared her with the entire country. He had a legitimate excuse: the vessel was due at Hamburg's Blohm & Voss yard that summer so buttressing that rendezvous with passenger crossings in July and September made sense. Since most Europeans were unfamiliar with mass-market cruising, parading *Norway* around northern Europe made for irresistible public relations. After Southampton arrival, an Amsterdam call was factored in before passage to the North Cape and the fjords.

Miami was the golden revenue source, feeding trough for millions of cruising's bottom feeders throughout the United States and Canada. NCL hated letting *Norway* leave. To sell the vessel effectively, she should have remained on station year-round. Whenever Advance Sales switchboards lit up, it invariably presaged *Norway* cabin requests, and rather than "try again in the fall" balked clients instead called Royal Caribbean or Carnival, dutiful Dodge Island stay-at-homes.

Overseas deployment also upset crew training. Stewards learn best via fixed routine. That notorious scheduling bromide—"If it's Tuesday, this must be Belgium"—characterized *Norway*'s immutable week: two sea days, the captain's handshake, St. Thomas, two more sea days, out island, comment cards, luggage tags, customs forms, and disembarkation. Just as *Norway* was a unique Caribbean player, her overseas deployments were unique as well; she became a victim of her own distinction, throwing marketing prudence to the winds.

However disappointed cruise aficionados, crossing advocates hailed *Norway*'s North Atlantic return. Both crossings sold briskly. Peter Compton asked me to lecture, so too pollster George Gallup, commentators Irving R. Levine and Edwin Newman, and also Chicago movie critic Roger Ebert.

Symptomatic of *Norway*'s entertainment indulgence, headliners were booked through New Yorker Hank O'Neal's HOSS Productions, an acronym of Hank's initials and that of his partner/colleague Shelley Shier. He signed comic Norm Crosby, singer Connie Stevens, retired Ruby Keeler, jazz pianist Teddy Wilson, songwriter Sammy Cahn, a Dixieland ensemble from Eddie Condon's West 52nd Street club, Warren Covington and the Pied Pipers, and a string quartet from Baltimore's Peabody Conservatory.

Mary and I recommended to Compton that he try a murder mystery at sea. The late great crime novelist Donald Westlake and his wife, Abby Adams, had already hosted one aboard *Vistafjord*. We had met them during a "mystery weekend" at Mohonk Mountain House in New Paltz, New York. Mohonk was rechristened *S/S Mohonkia* so I delivered some ocean liner talks. A capacity crowd in 1920s garb booked every room. Peter hired Don and Abby to mount a maritime whodunit for *Norway*'s July eastbound and flew them to Miami for a glimpse of the vessel.

Norway sailed not from New York but from Philadelphia's Packer Marine Terminal; it had been deemed not worth dredging Pier 88's slip for one visit. On Wednesday afternoon, 18 July, *Nor-*

way just made it to sea beneath the Commodore John Barry Bridge after six feet had been detached from her mast top.

In command was Captain Aage Hoddavik, a handsome Nordic master nicknamed James Bond; his staff captain was Geir Lokøen. The crossing was incomparable, boasting every traditional perk save one: propeller thunder beneath the stern. But there was an initial flurry of speed for no sooner were we aboard than a mimeographed announcement warned of a possible dockworkers' strike in Southampton that might jeopardize our call. *Norway* would proceed directly to Amsterdam instead.

To ensure that arrival by the twenty-sixth, Aage Hoddavik ran *Norway* at top speed for two days. But once he received word that the strike had been called off, turbines were retarded. Yet even at 17 knots *Norway* seemed to be traveling faster, transformed into a replicated *France*. We reveled in eight unalloyed, uninterrupted sea days across the same ocean for which our remarkable hull had been designed. No St. Thomas, no Nassau, no out island, indeed no warm-weather reminders save open-air pools; anchors remained in hawse pipes and tenders in davits.

One Caribbean holdover jarred. On our first sea day, in kneejerk adherence to cruise mode, an amplified steel band played around the deserted pool. On day two, the band tried again and, again, nobody showed up. On the third, the band was shifted into Club I, of all places. That would be its final, deafening gig until the Norwegian coast.

Back where she belonged, *Norway* was infused with a gloss seldom achieved in cruise mode. We dined with the Westlakes throughout evenings exclusively black-tied; offering one sitting only, Windward reminded me visually, if not gastronomically, of Chambord. It seemed almost like the old days and I was saddened that my son Guy was not aboard to share them.

Every night, Chip's big band played into the small hours in Checkers and *My Fair Lady* played in Saga Theatre. Teddy Wilson performed nobly in Club I, as did the string quartet, more apropos than the unlamented steel band: Haydn, Schumann, and Beethoven contributed peerless midocean serenity.

Don and Abby had devised an ingenious *Norway* scenario, replete with stolen diamonds and an ice-pick murder. After opening remarks, Don introduced a living rogue's gallery of suspects.

After focus groups indicated that Americans were unfamiliar with the term "tenders," they were described, cumbersomely, as "going ashore boats." No wings grace the funnel.

(Tom Graboski collections)

Going Ashore Boats

I played renegade *France* steward Jacques LeFraque, Mary was Henrietta Scarney, a scatty but sinister medium, Roger Ebert became inquiring photographer Rudy Burdock, Miami Dolphin Larry Csonka masqueraded as menacing heavy Wiley Zutton, Warren Covington impersonated off-key musician Lincoln Shayne, and Abby was cast as Amanda Andrews.

Passengers thronged all five sessions. During the third, Henrietta Scarney conducted a séance to identify the murderer. Although Mary did not know it, the perpetrator shared her cabin. Don's confidential letter of instruction to me had begun: "You did it, guy." Two days out of Southampton, the Westlakes unmasked murderer LeFraque to a chorus of hisses, laughter, and applause.

Ideal shipboard entertainment, it was an extended, multiday event that worked on several levels, invigorating the cruise staff and intriguing hundreds of passengers. In sum, exactly the right kind of house party tomfoolery that engendered perfect crossing atmosphere.

Other ocean liner vibes contributed their own magic. Bridge addicts gathered religiously in the card room and midmorning bouillon was circulated. Though horse-racing appeared, bingo did not. Taking a leaf from childhood crossings, I devised a treasure hunt for *Norway*'s children. Movie matinees screened in Saga Theatre included classics introduced by Roger Ebert. British Immigration officers stamped passports in Checkers; their presence, combined with eastbound's twenty-three-hour days, re-created an unmistakable North Atlantic ethos.

In every cabin, public room, and corridor, no one evaded the thrum of *Norway*'s resurgent diligence. Day and night, she maintained a relentless pace toward the rising sun, unmistakably bound on a voyage of purpose rather than pleasure. No landfall appeared over the bow, only an empty horizon beckoned as we persevered on our easterly great circle to the old world.

After entering Great Britain's western approaches on schedule, *Norway* arrived in Southampton early on the morning of 24 July, the strike a no-show. *QE2* occupied the Queen Elizabeth II Terminal so we tied up along the Western Docks at Berth 106. Equipped with bow- and stern thrusters, Aage docked *Norway* himself with a flourish, to pilot Jack Holt's admiration.

Opposite: Wearing a brunette wig, coronet, and a lot of jewels, Anne Slevin Hoehler plays the Queen of Transylvania in *My Fair Lady*'s ballroom scene. (Abby Adams Westlake collection)

The *unusual* suspects line up in Checkers Cabaret (*left to right*): Warren Covington, Mary Maxtone-Graham, John Maxtone-Graham, Abby Westlake, Larry Csonka, Roger Ebert, and Donald Westlake. (Abby Adams Westlake collection)

The vessel was booked solid for the crossing to Amsterdam and her North Cape cruise. The weather remained as peerless as it had been for our Oslofjord entrance four year earlier. "Tropical all the way," exulted James Bond. Extraordinary crowds greeted the vessel at every port. Crossing the Arctic Circle, Aage arranged a special surprise. Three "armed," helmeted warriors, brandishing swords in a miniature Viking craft, were hauled up the ship's side; crewmen launched them and their vessel into *Norway*'s pool.

Southbound, an even more impressive hull was airlifted out from Trondheim by helicopter and deposited aft of number 2 funnel. This was a genuine Viking extravaganza, model of a huge projected vessel called *Phoenix*, Knut Kloster's next dream and perfect *Norway* sequel. Displacing 250,000 tons, she would be larger, accommodating an incredible fifty-two hundred passengers.

Here was yet another Wandborg/Kloster production. In fact, Tage boarded *Norway* at the same time, ready to preach *Phoenix* gospel. Distinguishing his design was a novel inversion: while public rooms remained buried below within two gigantic catamaran hulls, cabins were atop the vessel in superstructure unlike any predecessor's. Four separate cabin towers rose from the strength deck, each tapering ziggurat surrounded by shaded balconies. Along the strength deck were palm trees, sand

At Windward table #34, Maxtone-Grahams on the left and Westlakes to the right are about to dine.

(Abby Adams Westlake collection)

beaches and pools, and, concealed within floodable entrances between the hulls, tenders for whisking passengers ashore on demand. Tage and Kloster were convinced that few would disembark. Why forsake a vessel already a remarkable destination in and of itself?

As I write these words, Royal Caribbean International's giant *Oasis of the Seas* nears completion. Her five-thousand-passenger count is the first, never previously equaled save by projected *Phoenix* more than a quarter of a century ago, a concept years ahead of its time. *Phoenix*'s 250,000-ton displacement anticipated *Queen Mary 2*'s by two decades.

I had glimpsed the project in New York the year previous, invited by Knut to a private reception at the Waldorf. There, he unveiled drawings and photographs of *Phoenix*. It was a staggering, futuristic creation symptomatic of Kloster's vision no less than a perfect extension of the ascending arc established by *Norway*.

Another reason that *Phoenix* had been unveiled aboard *Norway* was to show her to Aage Hoddavik, Kloster's chosen master. A Kloster admirer, he described his employer "not as a man who looked over his shoulder, but ahead." Hoddavik would spend many years as *Phoenix* consultant, promoter, and dashing poster boy. When we said good-bye to him in Miami that September, his farewell to Mary remains in my mind: "Next time we sail together, we'll be high in the air, up with the birds."

After Oslo and en route to Hamburg, Knut asked Per Sopp to show him the forward boiler room. Two more of those superannuated French boilers were being cut up for removal at Blohm & Voss. First glimpse of that Dante-esque inferno was jolting, more smoke and flare than the owner had bargained for. Per Sopp recalls:

When we came in, the whole room looked like it was on fire, from all the blow torches cutting the old boiler drums into pieces. Knut went white in the face and wanted to leave. He asked me never to tell anyone that he had seen that forward boiler room. I told him not to be worried, everything was under control, with firefighters ready continually. It looked more dangerous than it really was.

Mary and I remained in England for a week before reembarking in Southampton for a westbound crossing to New York aboard *Royal Viking Sky* on 6 August. Only after boarding did we encounter

another Kloster surprise. He had just bought the company and its three vessels, lock, stock, and barrel.

Founded by Warren Titus in the early 1970s, Royal Viking was an upscale San Francisco company that seemed an unrealistic companion piece for mass-market NCL. Today, Micky Arison controls a vast armada of nearly a hundred ships encompassing broad social spectra; their relative disparity matters little in 2010 but, twenty-five years ago, cruise lines projected an image reflecting the income, pretension, and taste of their clientele. Accustomed to circling the globe, Royal Viking regulars would have little reason to join Caribbean beginners flocking for a week aboard *Norway*.

Conversely, few of *Norway*'s seven-day novices could afford the time, expense, and social pitfalls of a Royal Viking jaunt.

Much effort would be expended to generate meaningful crossruff between NCL and RVL. I sense that Kloster's democratic idealism clouded his perception of America's hidebound pecking order. Though cruising may be one class, the classes to which individual companies cater are very different. Five years later, NCL would buy Royal Cruise Lines as well, slightly more upscale and somewhat on a par with Royal Viking.

That fall, Mary and I flew back to the UK, rejoining *Norway* for her westbound return to Miami; as though resigned to imminent cruising resumption, an intermediate stop at Bermuda was scheduled. Spectacular entertainment continued, including Le Hot Club de France's jazz violinist Stéphane Grappelli and composer/pianist Michel Legrand.

If one were to plot a performance graph of *Norway*'s two Caribbean decades, the mid-1980s would have been its unequivocal high point. Her blackout propensity neutralized, *Norway* prospered. Throughout 1983 load factor was a buoyant 93 percent, all the more astonishing considering that rival fleets were experiencing a recessionary slump. The following year's crossings and North Cape extravaganza added their own distinction.

Not only *Norway*'s size and glamour appealed, so did the entertainment roster that Compton embarked. Repeat comedians were Flip Wilson, Phyllis Diller, and the Smothers Brothers; a choir of first-rate singers included Tony Bennett, Mel Tormé, Vic Damone, Shirley and Jack Jones, Carol Lawrence, Diahann Carroll, Rita Moreno, and Roger Williams. In addition to Chip Hoehler's aggregation, there were bands galore—Cab Calloway, Lionel Hampton, The Fifth Dimension, and The Captain and Tennille. *Norway* offered an entertainment deluge that dominated the mid-eighties and overwhelmed the competition.

Yet another itinerary disruption emerged in May 1986. *Norway* steamed out of Miami on the evening of her Saturday return carrying a newly embarked passenger load and mountains of electronic equipment. Recruited for the first time were strolling musicians to serenade both dining rooms, accordionist Jon Persson accompanying violinist Paul Culbertson.

The vessel's destination that evening was not St. Thomas but Wilmington, North Carolina. Over one frantic Sunday at sea, technicians wired the ship and revamped her afterdecks. That evening, as *Norway* lay anchored offshore, NCL was primed for a coveted public relations coup: the stars, producers, director, and technicians from NBC's *Today Show* were on board, ready to broadcast. That week's morning episodes would originate from *Norway* as she pioneered an itinerary southward along America's eastern seaboard toward Miami.

The producers were determined to have me in place for Monday's first interview. Mary and I were crossing to England on a Royal Viking vessel, delayed for twenty-four hours by bad weather. After an angst-filled Sunday westbound flight and an interminable drive from Raleigh to Wilmington, we located the tender station and headed into the night to find *Norway* far offshore. We staggered aboard in the small hours and, after three hours' sleep, I was made up and ready to face Jane Pauley on *Norway*'s stern.

There are few reliable means of evaluating the marketing returns engendered by a vessel hosting *The Today Show*; did any of that larger audience ever book a cabin? Perhaps not but the fact that NBC chose *Norway* for that expensive, weeklong remote conveys a sense of the buzz she was generating.

Sadly, those positive vibes did not resonate in far-off Oslo where Kloster was becoming increasingly estranged from his board and Miami's management. The Royal Viking purchase never generated the synergy he had hoped for. Preoccupying his Oslo colleagues was duplication of Ted Arison's resounding success with a 1987 Salomon Brothers IPO that had netted Carnival $400 million. The board was unanimous in not wanting to burden its

October offering with a *Phoenix* proposal—too big and risky a proposition for new investors.

But *Phoenix* turned out not to be the problem: NCL's IPO fell afoul of a plunging market. On 19 October 1987, the market lost 508 points, dropping to 1738. (Remember, the Dow Jones had only recently topped 2,000.) Battered by that financial storm, NCL's offering was canceled.

Knut Kloster had already walked. In 1986, twenty years after founding NCL, he resigned the chairmanship, relinquishing his pivotal role to his younger brother Einar. Later, his son Knut would take over.

The board was content that the only NCL legacy retained by Kloster was his beloved *Phoenix*. Knut would call his new company World City Corporation, A/S Kloster Cruise. In return for handling *Phoenix*'s operations, NCL was allotted 25 percent of the company's shares.

At a last Miami board meeting, forthcoming company strategy was on the agenda. Kloster asked Joe Paige, NCL's senior vice president of marketing and sales, what kind of newbuilding program he would prefer, *Phoenix* or three conventional

Opposite: Touching up paint on number 2 funnel. The Norwegian postal banner overhead indicates that the photograph was taken prior to 1986. (Author's collection)

In 1988, new teak decking goes down on *Norway*'s starboard bridge wing. Once *France*'s 6-inch (15.25 centimeter) legged gratings had been removed, officers standing behind the bridge railing seemed shorter. (Author's collection)

Photo finish: Maxtone-Graham in the hot seat, under the Jane Pauley gun, for *Norway*'s opening segment of *The Today Show*, 18 May, 1986. (Author's collection)

Weatherman Willard Scott jokes with passengers before going on camera to deliver his report. (Author's collection)

newbuildings with the same capacity? Paige's instant response was *Phoenix*. When Kloster asked why, he replied, "Because I know that I could fill *Phoenix* to capacity for at least the first three years without any advertising. The ship's uniqueness, appeal, the great publicity she will get, and the word of mouth would provide all the needed promotion." Was he just being nice to the departing chairman or was he really that keen?

How maritime history might have changed had an enthusiastic *Phoenix* consensus emerged. But most NCL executives were unconvinced, perceiving *Phoenix* as yet another distraction from marketing *Norway* or adding conventional vessels to the fleet.

Phoenix was never built, though not for want of trying. As Einar Kloster wrote: "Knut Utstein Kloster is not a man to let his dreams die." Kloster pursued that one for years, setting up a New York office run by John Rogers, a hard-charging lawyer/front man who bombarded the press with releases, renderings, and projections. The vessel's name and owning company were amended to Phoenix World City in hopes of having it American-flagged. After Rogers died his position was taken over by his associate

Stephanie Gallagher. But a Title XI application for a federal loan guarantee has languished in Washington for years with no letter commitment forthcoming. Beltway inertia or undercover stonewalling? Kloster wonders.

Both he and Wandborg insist that *Phoenix* is contract ready and I am convinced, like Joe Paige, that had that remarkable vessel been built she would have created a sensation. But as years passed moment and momentum were lost. Phoenix World City subsided, irrevocably, into an historic footnote.

In early 1987, the year after Kloster's departure, the board decided to flag out all NCL vessels, switching from Norwegian to (cheaper) Bahamian registry. It was a sad moment when *Norway*'s postal banner was lowered and replaced by the Bahamian flag. No longer would the name OSLO—*Norway*'s home port—be emblazoned across the stern. One American passenger who inquired "what those initials stood for" was advised by a disgruntled captain: "**O**nly **S**ome **L**ost **O**verboard."

The following year brought further erosion of *Norway*'s isolated star power. Bigger cruising rivals came over the horizon as the industry played

Dining with some Royal Viking passengers, Aage Hoddavik and Bjorn-Erik Julseth (*far right in white dinner jackets*) are busy promoting *Norway*.

(Bjorn-Erik Julseth collection)

Hotel director Bjorn-Erik Julseth officiates for *Norway*'s reflagging. The Norwegian postal banner has been lowered, to be replaced by the Bahamian flag. (Bjorn-Erik Julseth collection)

catch-up. In January 1988 the most ambitious contender yet steamed up Government Cut. *Sovereign of the Seas* was Royal Caribbean Cruise Line's first megaship, her displacement exceeding *Norway*'s. She inaugurated her Caribbean career with a competitive itinerary that saw *Sovereign* and *Norway* call at St. Thomas the same day.

When she tied up for the first time at St. Thomas's West Indian docks, Aage Hoddavik and hotel director Bjorn-Erik Julseth came ashore to inspect Royal Caribbean's new giant. After disembarking, they ran into an appealing Norwegian couple on the pier, heavyweight boxer Steffen Tangstad and his new wife, who were honeymooning aboard *Sovereign of the Seas*.

Over a glass of beer, Tangstad asked Aage and Bjorn-Erik what ship they were from. Once *Norway* had been pointed out on the horizon, they seemed dumbfounded that a beautiful ship called *Norway* actually existed. On the instant, Aage and Bjorn-Erik invited the couple to lunch in the master's cabin.

There was a lot to drink, before, during, and after that convivial meal, by which time the honeymooners, dazzled by their hosts no less than by *Norway*, asked if they might switch from *Sovereign* to *Norway* for the balance of the week.

They hastened ashore, packed, and retrieved their luggage and tendered triumphantly back out to *Norway*. It was, Bjorn-Erik later suggested, classic piracy, abducting admittedly voluntary hostages from one Norwegian vessel and returning them to Miami aboard another.

Their *Norway* hosts spoiled them shamelessly. The boxer and his bride were installed in a splendid cabin and, for good measure, Staff Captain Lokøen, robed as a minister in a bedspread, remarried them in his cabin, with acolyte Bjorn-Erik assisting in a purple bathrobe.

It was sad that *Norway* had, in effect, lost her tonnage edge. But the saddest eighties' deprivation was Kloster's departure. He was sorely missed by a host of stalwarts, crew, and staff who had surveyed *France* with him, brought off the Bremerhaven conversion, struggled with the floods and alarums of her maiden voyage, and wrestled with blackouts and fires to follow. If ever a ship personified the imprint of its owner it was *Norway* and Knut Kloster. Without his hands-on presence, *Norway*'s passion and promise began to recede.

A heavy hitter arrives. Royal Caribbean Cruise Lines's *Sovereign of the Seas*, fresh from France, steams up Government Cut on the afternoon of 3 January, 1988. I was on the bridge and, as we passed *Norway*, heard one NCL crewman bawl: "Get a *real* ship!"
(Royal Caribbean International)

Little Norway I is still afloat; *Little Norway II* has finished for the day and ascends to storage position up on Pool Deck. **(Robert and Charles Replogle collection)**

CHAPTER TEN

THE DOWNHILL DECADE

Personally I did not like the plans at all but it was not up to me.
I believe it took away all the beautiful lines of the vessel and she was never the same again.

Per Sopp, technical marine superintedent

Opposite: Senior officers' funnel portrait: taken in March 2001 (*from left to right*) Staff Captain Arne Sommer, Captain Sverre Sovdsnes, hotel director Carl Kitsios, and chief engineer Bjarne Kleven stand atop *Norway*'s number 2 funnel off St. Thomas. (**Sverre Sovdsnes collection**)

To readers who might take exception to the title above, it was selected with reason. Throughout the

nineties and into the millennium, *Norway*'s cruising career continued. Thousands of contented passengers still fell in love with her, flocked ashore at St. Thomas, ate—and drank—their fill in dining rooms and bars, and cheered the entertainment. Occasional eccentrics still embarked, among them an Indian maharajah so besotted with the crew that he threw an exclusive party for them one night in the Roman Spa.

But during those same years, Norwegian Cruise Line entered an era of retrenchment, compromise, and financial shortfall. Things were not helped by a revolving door at Miami headquarters; presidential turnover was endemic. Most worrying for old *Norway* hands was the head office's penchant for lavishing scarce resources on hotel renovations rather than giving desperately needed attention to *Norway*'s engine room.

The vessel started looking tired. By the midnineties passengers could not miss a whiff of drains along certain alleyways as well as scuffed paint, worn carpeting, and balding upholstery in cabins and public rooms. Entertainment budgets were curtailed. The vessel's profile had been amended, Knut Kloster was gone, *Norway*'s flag too, the vessel's Nordic distinction vitiated. Moreover, she was a lesser Caribbean standout; rival

megaships were proliferating. Hence, downhill decade.

In 1987 Knut Kloster III recommended to his board that *Norway*'s revenue be enhanced by adding balconied suites to her upper decks. If nothing else, it was a prescient decision. Shipboard balconies became the rage of the nineties and installing some aboard NCL's flagship would certainly improve her marketing appeal.

One can pinpoint the cusp of cruising's balcony mania by noting the moment when rival Royal Caribbean Cruise Line saw the light. Its first megaship, *Sovereign of the Seas*, entered service in January 1988 without balconies, but two ensuing sisters—1991's *Monarch of the Seas* and 1992's *Majesty of the Seas*—each boasted a balcony row from the beginning.

Tage Wandborg unrolled the vessel's drawings at Knud Hansen and started pondering how best to implement Kloster's request. The only way to add cabins is park them on top. The Cunard Line had bitten that bullet aboard *Queen Elizabeth 2*. In 1972 one deck's worth of balconied penthouses had been added. Five years later, they were joined by two larger, forward-facing suites over the bridge. A second penthouse deck was added in 1987, the same year that steam turbines were replaced.

Tage's installation would be more noticeable. Whereas only thirty-four suites had been added to *QE2*, nearly four times as many—124—would encumber *Norway*, one and a half decks' worth. The lowest and longest, renamed Sun Deck, stretched aft 492 feet (150 meters) from the bridge to the Great Outdoor Restaurant. The "half," formerly Sun Deck, now Sky Deck, was stacked atop the first.

Slightly less than half the additions had balconies. But nonbalconied suites were made distinctive with transparent, floor-to-ceiling outboard walls. Because that accumulation of plate glass would be extremely heavy, Tage specified a new product, Lexan-Margard, a plastic substitute weighing half as much.

Norway's "skyline," as Tage called it, would be changed forever. Her waist became thicker, creating a middle-aged spread the deck house length. The funnels seem to have been half swallowed by superstructural accretion, like birthday candles sinking into a cake's icing.

Bridge scene at the out island. The vessel is at anchor and both tenders have taken most passengers ashore. Captain Geir Lokøen stands at right and Staff Captain Arne Jorgensen talks on the radio at left. (Nelson B. Arnstein, M.D., collection)

Anchored off Great Stirrup Cay,
Norway shows off her amended profile.

Those additional decks also created a vacuum near the stern. During a Southampton refit six years later, new boiler flue uptakes were erected on top of number 2 funnel, narrowed to increase their exit flow so as to loft fumes more expeditiously clear of the decks.

For the fourth time, *Norway* returned to the scene of her conversion, the Bremerhaven yard called now Lloyd Werft. Implementation of that 1990 refit was pegged at $45 million. By the time the work was completed, the figure had just about doubled to $82 million. It was a common NCL truism that *Norway* was a notorious money pit, gobbling millions with ease.

On 23 August 1990, *Norway* departed Miami. In addition to 450 crew, she embarked 239 German

shipwrights to prep the vessel en route. Geir Lokøen was in command, Jan Ottesen was staff captain, and Jan Trollerud the project manager.

En route, first order of business was a scorched earth policy the length of *Norway*'s Sun Deck. Railings and structures were cut away and piled on the after end of Pool Deck; by crossing's end it had become a 150-ton scrap heap. Then load distributors—"foundations" for the anticipated suite modules—were welded in place, obviating the need for further reinforcement. Fjord Deck cabins were equipped with new sewer connections for the suites scheduled to rise above.

Wandborg's and Lloyd Werft's operational setup was exemplary. All 124 cabins had been prefabricated within twenty-one aluminum modules,

Loading new suites aboard *Norway* at Lloyd Werft. (*Above*) A starboardside, forward module is lowered into place. It is a double-decker, the upper balconied, the lower with floor-to-ceiling windows. (Lloyd Werft Bremerhaven)

Aft of the pool a single layer is nearly closed up. Note the perforations made in the funnel's skin, indicating that it is ready for temporary removal. Replacement lifeboats have not yet been embarked. (Jeff Macklin collection)

the forward ones literal double-deckers. Their interiors were almost complete—bathrooms, ceilings, doors, ductwork, cabling, fire detectors, electrical fixtures, carpeting, curtains, even furniture.

Though *Norway* spent thirty days in Bremerhaven, only a tenth of that time was consumed attaching the new decks. One after the other, twenty-one modules were hoisted up, lowered in place, and attached, the installation completed in an astonishing fifty-six hours.

Since the modules increased *Norway*'s displacement by 1,050 tons, 2,000 tons of a special mud ballast were pumped into unused water and fuel tanks in the double bottom forward to preserve stability. Interestingly, the vessel's draft was unaffected, remaining as before at about 10 meters (35 feet).

But new decks were only one item on *Norway*'s 1990 shopping list. In dry dock, three openings were cut through the shell plating. One gave access to the laundry for replacement machinery, another allowed embarkation of a 350-ton evaporator into the main turbine room, and the third created an entry for a new "chiller" (air-conditioning compressor), cooling capability for the new decks. Before leaving dry dock the existing rudder was amplified with what is called a fishtail to improve *Norway*'s maneuverability. Every lifeboat was replaced; manufactured by the Norwegian company Harding, the new craft had been constructed to match original *France* davits. Another first-time task was detaching the vessel's working funnel for cleaning and refurbishment. Only days later, 1,412 cubic feet (40 cubic meters) of sooty ash had been removed.

Aft on Pool Deck, a 240-seat extra-tariff restaurant replaced the Lido bar, designated first Le Rendezvous but subsequently renamed Le Bistro. It was so far aft that it needed its own dedicated galley. Initially, occupants of the new suites were to have been served there exclusively but Kloster quashed the idea; *Norway* was not going to become a two-class vessel on his watch. So Le Bistro was made available to all comers, passengers and crew alike.

Another transformation was adaptation of *France*'s old indoor pool into the Roman Spa, combining it with fitness equipment and treatment rooms to make *Norway* competitive with rival cruise lines. In both dining rooms, individual domed lamps were added to the center of every

table. From that day on, all *Norway* tablecloths were pierced by a central hole to accommodate the lamp bases.

One Bremerhaven spring evening, Tage and Per Sopp dined ashore and walked back toward the yard. Confronted with the illuminated ship, Tage realized that he should have amended *Norway*'s bridge wing slopes to conform with the added decks. But, as Sopp observed, it was a thought too late. Freewheeling 1980 conversion days were no more; ten years later contract parameters had to be scrupulously observed.

No lithographs had been provided for the new suites. So began a game of musical frames: lower-deck cabins were plundered and their pictures distributed up top. To replenish the emptied walls, Alexsandra Sopp was given $3,000 in cash and sent ashore to buy up every framed image she could find in Bremerhaven. The 360 she located were delivered on board and the case of the missing decor was resolved.

Another flap. On the last day a German-speaking caller telephoned a bomb threat. Having recorded it, Jan Trollerud shared it with Bremerhaven police. He and they decided against evacuating the ship; two thousand men were frantically preparing for departure. No alert was broadcast but extra gangways were rigged. Nothing happened. Trollerud suspected that the caller may have been a potential stowaway, creating a diversion to insinuate himself on board.

His suspicion proved correct. A stowaway *did* embark before *Norway* sailed on 16 October. Unlike his maiden voyage forerunner, his weakness was less alcohol than garrulity. A large shipyard team was still aboard, finishing up cabins. Each evening, they and their NCL counterparts met to compare notes. Rather than maintain a low profile the stowaway, strutting about in stolen coveralls, joined the discussion enthusiastically, suggesting provocative if senseless recommendations for further renovations. Neither contingent—yard personnel nor NCL's inspection team—called his bluff because no one was sure to which group he belonged.

Finally unmasked, he was identified as an escapee from a Bremerhaven asylum. Among his possessions were several hundred dollars, indicating that he planned a lengthy U.S. stay, which, in the end, never happened.

As soon as she reached Miami, *Norway* had to be reinspected by the Coast Guard and Tage's

To demonstrate the shipyard's prefabrication zeal, one module's cabin was specially illuminated in flight to reveal two "passengers" and their "butler" already inside. (Lloyd Werft Bremerhaven)

The surface area of *Norway*'s rudder was amplified with a fishtail to improve maneuverability. (Jeff Macklin collection)

Lexan windows were grudgingly accepted. Another weight-saving ploy involved the dividers separating the new balconies. Rather than made of opaque steel they were light, transparent panels. Svenn Dahl suggested to me deadpan that while the partitions did not provide privacy they "certainly improved sociability."

Cruising life resumed with 248 additional passengers. I sailed in one of Tage's glass-walled suites and found it a remarkable aerie; even lying abed the horizon was visible. Another time, we were accommodated in one of the lavish, forward-facing suites. However luxurious, when returning westbound to Miami, afternoon sun spilling through the forward window wall overwhelmed the newly amplified chiller. We learned to close the curtains.

Staff Captain Gunstein Langset recalls an ingenious subterfuge attempted by a devious *Norway* shop assistant one Saturday afternoon. The call came to the bridge on radio channel 16 VHF, a "calling and distress frequency" answered by the officer of the watch.

"Distress" was clearly the caller's operative emotion. Weeping, the woman called just after 4:00 P.M., the vessel's sailing time, with a sob story. Driving to join the ship, a traffic jam had delayed her so badly that by the time she reached Dodge

Island *Norway* was gone. Her question: should she fly to St. Maarten or rejoin when the ship returned the following weekend?

The officer inquired solicitously if she were still at Pier 1. "Yes, I am," she sniffled.

"Then you must be looking the wrong way. *Norway*'s still here. We've been delayed by a late flight from New York and will not sail until nine." Clearly, the malingerer had been caught in a lie, calling in her spurious traffic emergency from home rather than Dodge Island. Rejoining neither in St. Maarten nor Miami, she was fired instead.

Whenever *Norway* was in Miami the radio room shut down. But during every cruise it was in constant operation. Until the mid-nineties, radio officers were a vital and integral part of *Norway*'s command structure. Not only fluent at reading and dispatching Morse, they were also required to monitor all ship-to-shore passenger calls. Telephonic linkage was erratic: connections often broke and had to be reestablished mid-call.

Because of their licensed omniscience, radio operators heard all manner of private and sometimes indiscreet exchanges, aural voyeurism they kept strictly to themselves. In fact, a clause in the Navigation Act of 1934 spelled out their sworn obligation to secrecy.

Far more than passenger foibles came their way. Inside the forever humming radio room behind *Norway*'s bridge, radio officers were privy to all Miami and/or Oslo directives and knew everything that had happened or would happen on board.

We first met radio officer Jarl Nygaard aboard a Royal Viking ship; he later transferred to *Norway* and remained a great friend throughout many cruises. Jarl left *Norway* forever in 1993, swallowing the anchor and joining Oslo's Norwegian Maritime Radio Inspection Office, which he now heads.

The end of his seagoing career was regretful but inevitable. The importance, usefulness, and, indeed, very existence of radio officers steadily diminished. They no longer monitored passenger calls because superior satellite telephones and later cell phones were so improved. Fax machines and the Internet were coups de grâce. Those handsome black shoulder boards with their radio spark logo were phased out, never to be seen again. Final nail in the coffin, in 1999, last Morse transmissions were tapped out from ships and shore stations around the globe. Marconi's pioneering dot/dash threnody, ethereal dispatches of urgency, assistance, or reassurance, was silenced forever.

The year that Jarl Nygaard signed off, *Norway* encountered a frightening storm en route up Government Cut. Storms at sea, where there is room to maneuver, are far preferable to storms within confined waters. For Miami's cruising fleet, that gale was remembered as the storm of the century.

With Hans Meeg in command, *Norway* was inbound to Miami early on the second Saturday of March 1993. NCL's flagship always arrived first. A

Le Bistro, *Norway*'s 1990 extra-tariff restaurant, occupies the former Lido bar. As aboard every vessel with alternate dining, it proved immensely popular with officers, crew, and staff who relish an occasional dressy night out instead of eating in their customary wardroom or mess. (Norwegian Cruise Line)

weather advisory had indicated that a cold front was expected but nothing out of the ordinary.

At 0420 the pilot boarded and, traveling at her customary 8 knots, *Norway* headed for Miami's entry breakwater 3 miles (4.8 kilometers) distant. Once Meeg had adjusted his radar to six-mile range, he picked out the white blip of the approaching front. Immediately assessing its strength, Meeg asked the pilot station for two tugs to meet him at the breakwater. They were readily available on weekend turnarounds because bunkering barges needed maneuvering the length of Dodge Island.

As he spoke, wind velocity increased and *Norway* was already past the channel's point of no return. Meeg increased speed to 10 knots. At the

breakwater, he deployed stern thrusters to improve his turn. Completing the maneuver, he was relieved to see his requested tugs standing by.

Speed retarded to 8 knots again, he started up Government Cut. Suddenly, as though a demon had turned a switch, the front enveloped *Norway* in a howling onslaught, blinding bridge windows with torrents of rain. Meeg likened the effect to a blizzard whiteout. He could do nothing but persevere stubbornly upstream toward the turning basin, even though ranges indicating *Norway*'s course were completely obscured.

Three factors aided his progress: the vessel's deep draft, accompanying tugs, and her recently extended rudder, a combination that delivered

Weight-saving but transparent dividers separated new Sky Deck balconies.
(Author's collection)

FRANCE/NORWAY

Norway successfully into the turning basin. Despite 50-knot winds but abetted by the tugs' muscle, Meeg completed *Norway*'s requisite 180-degree turnabout before heading back downstream.

Bringing *Norway* alongside was difficult. The gale had veered yet again and powerful gusts kept blowing her off the dock. After making fast, a rain-soaked Meeg instructed his equally rain-soaked mooring officers to employ half again as many hawsers. He would keep a bow- and stern thruster running all day as unrelenting winds threatened to break her loose.

Norway had Dodge Island to herself; no other vessels entered port until late morning. Every master, following Meeg's example, requested tug assistance. One captain tried docking without them but changed his mind after nearly being driven ashore on MacArthur Causeway. *Sovereign of the Seas* nearly came to grief. Her shallow draft and excessive flank—a wind-catching sail—wrenched a bollard from Dodge Island's cement; too many hawsers had been attached to it. Until lines were rerigged, a tug braced its bow against the hull to keep *Sovereign* in place.

Norway's passengers disembarked at 0730 but, at the airport, found all flights in turmoil. The storm had made a hash of every schedule. Meeg finally embarked his delayed replacement passenger load late in the evening, returning to sea at about ten-thirty P.M., the end of an exhausting day.

Sea air sharpens appetites, rendering every ship's company preternaturally peckish. Acknowledging that phenomenon raises a question that must be addressed: how did *Norway*'s galley compare with *France*'s? Did a Windward meal ever approximate one of those epic Chambord offerings? Alas, no. A dedicated French chef and his staff, producing meals for a discriminating North Atlantic clientele, achieved levels of richness, sophistication, and presentation to which no Caribbean galley has ever aspired.

Occasionally, retired *France* personnel sampled *Norway* cruising. They mostly enjoyed revisiting their old/new ship, delighted that she had survived and that new passengers were experiencing shipboard within the same hull. Some days seemed reminiscent of *France* cruises: languid subtropical passage, swimming in new on-deck pools, sunning ashore, and absorbing extravagant nightly entertainment every night. But on the topic of food, kudos faltered, dwindling and degenerating into gri-

Jarl Nygaard was kind enough to make a present of *Norway*'s radio call sign mounted on a plaque. LITA, the ship's four-letter code, means "small female" in Norwegian. (Author's collection)

macing shrugs. French cuisine and Frenchmen's attitude toward it is fearsomely specific: they neither understand nor appreciate any substitute.

Maxtone-Graham's *Norway* strategy? Accept the status quo. It is useless agonizing about conditions aboard a former vessel, particularly if it happens to be the same one. Though finding no fault with *Norway*'s galley, I sometimes felt that lunches were superior to dinners. Food always was good and plentiful. Soups were excellent and first-rate grainy, crusty rolls appeared daily from the bakery; the Great Outdoor's teatime tuna fish sandwiches and assorted pastries were memorable; and I share the Norwegian predilection for herring and gravlax. It was aboard *Norway* too that I was introduced to that perennial wardroom staple *gjeitost* (pronounced *yay-toss*), a caramel-hued, semisweet Norwegian goat cheese that, during the Nazi occupation, served as children's substitute for nonexistent chocolate.

Norway's pastry chefs scored high. I always looked forward to an excellent banana cream pie offered at lunch every time we anchored off St. Thomas. There was also a seven-layer cake that, from maiden voyage on, won many friends and sabotaged all dietary resolve.

I sailed with Craig Claiborne aboard *Norway*, on a Caribbean cruise, long after his retirement. Always the showman, he gave a cooking demonstration at sea in the North Cape Lounge. He wanted to show his capacity audience how to prepare chile con carne.

He worked with makeshift equipment at a table in the middle of the dance floor; jury-rigged extension cords powered a huge electric pan. He cut the meat into the cubes he preferred to ground beef, emptied it into an oiled pan, and tried browning it. But the current was inadequate, the pan overfull, cooking anything impossible, and his audience finally disinterested. Out of time, poor Claiborne aborted the whole gig. I am sure his mind strayed longingly back to *France*, where he and Pierre Franey had *compèred* so many of Henri Le Héudé's flawless presentations.

Indeed, sole replication of that era was when French consortia chartered *Norway* for simulacra *France* cruises. In all, six were mounted and the first, in early December 1989, proved predictably the best.

From Limoges came crates of china—a trove of specially designed plates, cups, saucers, and ashtrays. An image of *France/Norway* adorned every one. Most ashtrays and butter plates went missing before cruise's end and the residue was auctioned off. The week following, crew cabin searches recovered a sizable haul of purloined crockery.

At Dodge Island, six yellow-painted, plywood letters spelling FRANCE were arrayed at the base of number 1 funnel and a Moët & Chandon jeroboam was shattered against the hull. Near disaster: the line holding it had stretched overnight and the bottle struck at water level but, thankfully, still broke.

Many of France's most celebrated chef/restaurateurs had handed over their establishments to subordinates while they flew to join *Norway*. Among others, Paul Bocuse, instigator of *la nouvelle cuisine*, had forsaken Lyon, Pierre Troisgros let his brother Jean cope with their Roanne restaurant, and Claude Terrail deserted Paris's Le Tour D'Argent. After poring over his *Guide Michelin*, Bjorn-Erik calculated that fifty-one Michelin stars had embarked.

An animated copse of alien, starched toques bobbed throughout *Norway*'s galley. Competing with the clatter of pan against stovetop, the galley fixture that French cooks dub the piano, jovial French imprecations echoed once again and a remarkable gastronomic renaissance delighted both dining rooms.

Instructed to renounce their customary cruising cool, waiters served "France" passengers more formally. French maîtres d'hôtel ensured that platters were correctly presented. The largely French clientele had paid three times *Norway*'s normal weekly tariff but shrugged off that formidable supplement.

On first and last nights, the hotel director Julseth delivered, in passable French, welcome and farewell addresses respectively. And when Captain Haakon Gangdal descended on gala night, diners stood and applauded.

Second sitting often ran past midnight and signature dishes highlighted some landmark menus: Joël Robuchon's *Gelée de Caviar à la Crème de Chou Fleur*, Bocuse's grandparental tribute *Œufs à la Neige Grand'mère Bocuse*, Claude Terrail's *Foie gras des Trois Empereurs*, and *Assiette des Croqueur de Chocolat* re-created by Pierre Ducroux.

Norway's officers relished those unbelievable feasts, as many as seven courses, from caviar to Cuban cigars. But few mustered the courage to consume the garnish of one chicken dish, a bright red coxcomb and two feet.

That intermittent French invasion apart, a humbler yet incomparable treat was a noodle soup prepared in the Korean mess. That fragrant concoction was topped, if desired, by a fried egg. Uniformly praised as one of the best buys on board, a generous portion cost a dollar. The steaming elixir was dispensed every night, from eight o'clock until three in the morning.

Though captain's dinners aboard *Norway* lacked the flair of their *France* forerunners, they were nonetheless flattering occasions for passenger couples. They assembled aft in a portside corner of Club I where the master joined them for cocktails after two enervating hours of passenger handshakes. (Captain Gunnar Øien always celebrated completion of one sitting's worth of handshakes by turning cartwheels across Club I's carpet.) Then the master led his guests down that celebrated staircase to his Windward table.

Husbands and wives were, inexplicably, seated beside each other, negating the conversational give-and-take of a proper dinner party. Additionally, no special banquet was prepared; one ordered from that evening's menu. In addition to the master, several ship's officers enriched the table, together with visiting company brass. A great deal of wine prompted animated conversation.

Norway's most coveted invitations were for meals taken far from the dining room, banquets scheduled whenever the right visitor/friends mix coincided. Mary and I sailed on a mid-January

An issue of special china for the *France* cruise of 1989: dinner plates and butter dishes as well as cups and saucers were set on all dining room tables, a million-dollar indulgence. (Author's collection)

1990 cruise that included Miami hands Rolf Skjong-Nielsen, former electrical officer Tore Johansen, Per Sopp, and Tage Wandborg. Under our cabin door appeared an invitation from Captain Trygve Vorren for dinner in the bowels of the vessel. The venue? The Chinese laundry.

Alone among *Norway*'s multiple crew nationalities, Chinese laundrymen boasted their own galley and their own volunteer cook. He set helpers to work during much of that preparatory day, cooking and stockpiling quantities of fried rice, shrimp, sweet and sour pork, scallion pancakes, garlic beef, and platters of assorted noodles.

In full operation, a ship's laundry becomes tropical, the thermometer hovering around 100 degrees centigrade. But work was always suspended for the dinner's duration and, once washers, driers, and presses had been shut down, heat and humidity dissipated. Bowing to shipboard's unrelenting pressure, a catch-up washing/pressing binge would be instigated on the morrow; like junk mail, *Norway*'s soiled laundry avalanche never relented.

About twenty guests were invited and, for noncrew, finding the way to the laundry was challenging. Led by an officer, we descended via a battered crew elevator and then persevered through a Dolphin Deck maze and occasional cul-de-sac, as lost as any disembarking Norwegian prime minister.

What gave those evenings their cachet was the juxtaposition of black tie with that honest proletarian surround, indoor equivalent of the opera lovers' *fête champêtre* at Glyndebourne. But instead of lounging on picnic rugs beneath Sussex foliage, we sat on folding metal chairs beneath a tinkling array of wire hangers, evening dresses, tunics, and mess jackets swaying overhead. Four conjoined folding tables were covered with a makeshift cloth, doubtless double bedsheets; laundrymen have their way. The only Chinaman in attendance was our host, the genial laundry master.

Infectious, boisterous conviviality reigned throughout that archetypal Norwegian evening, the meal punctuated by jokes, japes, and laughter. Because the first *France* cruise had sailed a month earlier, residual brandy and liqueur were still on tap and multiple bottles of wine were broached. Hotel director Bjorn-Erik, past master of postprandial games, precipitated gales of merriment. During one previous dinner, he had driven his Harley-Davidson into the laundry with a roar. For another, amply girthed Johannes Kausland, a radio officer who doubled as indefatigable accordionist, provided raucous musical accompaniment.

Those evenings were unforgettable, *Norway* and Norwegian magic alike. But their days, alas, were numbered. Public health inspectors always disapproved of Dolphin Deck's aberrant galley; a live

Opposite, top: Late afternoon, Dodge Island, December 12, 1989: makeshift FRANCE letters are erected at the base of number 1 funnel. (Norwegian Cruise Line)

Opposite, bottom: Captain Haakon Gangdal poses with the rechristening bottle. (Jeff Macklin collection)

In the Windward dining room, the Maxtone-Grahams sit to the right of Captain Trygve Vorren. Nearest the camera on the right, Staff Captain Gunstein Langset with Rolf Skjong-Nielsen two seats to his right. Nearest the camera at left is Per Sopp.
(Bjorn-Erik Julseth collection)

An after-dinner toast in *Norway*'s laundry (*from right to left, seated*): chief engineer Harald Vaagnes, unknown, hotel director Bjorn-Erik Julseth, Rolf Skjong-Nielsen, an assistant purser, Tage Wandborg, the author, Mary Maxtone-Graham, and Captain Trygve Vorren; (*right to left standing*): the electrical officer Tore Johansen, Staff Captain Gunstein Langset, unknown, and, in the pink shirt, *Norway*'s laundry master. Directly behind Wandborg is Per Sopp.
(Bjorn-Erik Julseth collection)

chicken had once been found in residence. Regretfully, it would be closed before century's end and those infamous laundry dinners became history.

Whether originating in Windward, Leeward, or laundry, gala evenings always concluded on International Deck's stylish Café de Paris where espresso, aquavit, beer, and yet more talk flowed freely at a delightful afterparty. That corner remained an inescapable late-night rendezvous for every three-striper and above: captains, staff captains, hotel directors, chief engineers, food and beverage managers, chief officers, security officers, and privileged guests always gravitated there at evening's end.

It was never called the Café de Paris but was code-named instead the shelf or, in Norwegian, *hylle*. Why? One retired officer who cherishes his anonymity volunteered: "This was the place to be seen and to observe what went in and out of Checkers and the traffic flow on International Deck."

Shelf—household locus for display—indicated that the café served as vantage point for inspection and evaluation. For "what went in and out of Checkers" or International Deck's "traffic flow," read attractive lady passengers. The shelf was where *Norway*'s introductions and perhaps assignations were often initiated.

The laundry was only one of several backstage areas we visited. Mary was writing a murder mystery set aboard *Norway* and, having posited a murder inside number 1 funnel, asked chief engineer Harald Vaagnes if we might inspect it.

The chief consented to show the funnel's interior and also suggested a visit to its top. Next morning, while we were anchored off St. Thomas, he handed us boiler suits and gloves. Though unused since 1974, the funnel's interior was grimy with soot.

Mary is acutely acrophobic. But offered that unique opportunity, she gritted her teeth and climbed. From Sun Deck to wing level was 40 feet (12 meters) and getting there involved scaling flights of steep interior stairs, which, near the summit, became a ladder. En route upward, I looked down (Mary did not) and saw, far below, *Norway*'s moribund forward boiler room.

Then sunlight spilled from above and we emerged, standing on the gently swelling convexity of number 1 funnel's starboard wing. The view was breathtaking, *Norway*'s after two-thirds spread out below. Blackened exhausts directed aft had once vented stack gas but the wings on which we

stood no longer served any purpose. Though a handrail adorned the stack, only a pointless, foot-high railing led to wing's end.

Years later I received a surprise present from *Norway* captain Sverre Sovdsnes. Off St. Thomas, he and his senior officers had climbed to the top of working number 2 funnel for a portrait in immaculate whites. I wrote thanking Sverre and, recalling the sootiness of our ascent, told him that I knew he and his fellows had worn boiler suits for the climb.

Another shipboard area I enjoyed was at the bow, on the mooring deck beneath the forepeak's whaleback, as far forward as one could get aboard *Norway*. While under way, it was irresistible to look out through the fairlead. This essential bow feature is a stoutly reenforced hole through the stem casting where cables can be rigged for towing. Leaning out and looking straight down, one was rewarded with the sight of *Norway*'s stem sundering the Caribbean.

That same mooring deck was the place *not* to be during *Norway*'s first departure from San Juan. A maiden Puerto Rican call was made in mid-November, 1990. That evening, at dusk, *Norway* was ready to depart. After raising the anchors the vessel started for sea. In midchannel, making 9 knots, one of *Norway*'s anchors, its cable still not yet secured with retaining claws, dropped precipitously to the water.

It departed the same, apparently jinxed starboard hawse pipe from which a *France* anchor had vanished in 1962. But that San Juan loss involved more than a 15-ton anchor: 80 tons of attached anchor cable followed it. At breakneck, deafening speed, furlongs of anchor chain were wrenched from the locker in relentless, clattering pursuit, dragged by the anchor's weight and the ship's forward momentum.

Undoubtedly, it was the final links, a flailing, whiplash tail of chain, that wreaked the most havoc. The capstan was destroyed. Its vertical steel shaft—22 inches (56 centimeters) in diameter—was fatally split; angle-iron stanchions surrounding it were flattened like grass; dozens of .98 inch (2.5 centimeters) bolts were sheared off as though paper. Thank heavens no crewmen had been nearby. They would have been brained by flying chain.

Six months would pass before that starboard capstan was reactivated. Finding replacement components was difficult. Per Sopp finally located a discarded propeller shaft in Poland of the appropriate

length and diameter that could be machined and installed.

In November 1996, the company put up new funnel livery. Its original cornflower blue was painted in a new navy blue/white configuration—blue above, white below—separated by a boundary line sloping aft. Only a year later it was replaced. (A new president at work?) This time, the structure was overpainted entirely in *Norway* blue—shafts, wings, and caps. Then a logo, *Norway's* first, was added in the form of NCL's corporate symbol, gold NCL initials inside a gold frame.

Corporate decision makers do not really understand funnels. Like cattlemen, they are more interested in branding. Funnels do best with bright, primary colors rather than symbols designed for letterheads or mailing pieces.

In April 1999 *Norway* was back in Bremerhaven for her fifth visit. Three diesel generators were replaced and boilers were partially retubed. That boilers were getting attention was heartening, even though it was scarcely the radical overhaul they needed.

On the 16 May 1999, *Norway* sailed from the yard en route for Marseilles where she would embark a

French passenger load for yet another *France* cruise. The day following, 17 May, was Norway's Constitution Day. Captain Jan Otteson hosted a celebratory dinner on the starboard open deck outside his quarters. It was a warm spring evening and Per recalls the peace and pleasure of that festive meal as *Norway* steamed down-Channel at sunset.

Two weeks later, after a short Norwegian vacation, Per flew from Oslo to Heathrow and changed planes for return to Miami. The plane left the gate and began trundling toward the takeoff queue.

Suddenly, a stewardess was at his elbow, asking him to retrieve his hand luggage and prepare to disembark. The aircraft stopped, the fuselage door was opened, and Per descended to the tarmac where a waiting car returned him to the terminal. There, a telephone call from London awaited him. It was Kristian Siem, NCL's board chairman. *Norway*, Siem told him, was on fire in Barcelona.

Last port of call for the *France* charter, passengers were still on board the partly blacked-out vessel. By the time Sopp landed in Spain the fire was out. It had started in the aft turbogenerator room when a faulty weld in a high-pressure hydraulic line released an oil mist. When it struck the hot

Opposite: The view of *Norway's* number 2 funnel and her after decks. (Author's collection)

Left: A collection of ancient sooty vents points aft. Maxtone-Graham shadows appear on the blue elevation. (Author's collection)

Overleaf: Alongside in Miami in 1997, *Norway* has not only her new upper decks but also new funnel livery. (Tee Adams Photo)

turbine casing flames ignited, badly damaging generators and switchboard. After passengers had been off-loaded and bused overnight to Marseilles, *Norway* was towed from the passenger terminal to a cargo berth for a two-day survey.

I was at sea at the time and had heard nothing about the fire. We were aboard *Grand Princess*, sailing eastbound from Florida to Venice; en route, we called at Barcelona. There, to my astonishment, lay *Norway*, directly across from our berth. We had sailed on her the previous October, repositioning from Barcelona to Miami. Now, she was back in the same port, a desolate, darkened *Norway* berthed at a deserted pier. But out of sight her engine room was a hive of activity as engineers from all over the world repaired the damage. In seventeen days the vessel was ready and Sopp sailed with her to Southampton.

That was, he would discover, his final passage aboard what he always thought of as "my ship." Later that year he had to resign because his son had been employed by a firm with which NCL did business, contravening his signed "noncompete agreement." He resigned almost eighteen years to the day since he joined. Within a week, he was

hired by Caterpillar as service manager for its Engine Division. One last encounter with "his ship" would occur three years after the millennium.

Later that summer of 1999, between July 14 and 22, *Norway* returned to Le Havre, major participant in a local wingding promoted as Havre 99. Apparently, Kloster's contractual 1979 pledge no longer applied. The ship received a gratifying reception, its only downside a wind shift that brought a saluting tug's water plume cascading down onto the forward open decks, drenching hundreds of passengers.

The balance of that European cruise season was canceled and *Norway* returned to Miami for resumption of her Caribbean schedule. I was on board and we rendezvoused with *Norwegian Sun* for a midocean glimpse of a solar eclipse, obscured, alas, by rain.

The low point of that crossing was an appalling renovation of Checkers Cabaret. NCL prided itself on being a sports-oriented line so, cheaply and awfully, they turned Checkers Cabaret into the Sports Illustrated bar, a grievous decorative misstep. A friend, an Englishman named Les Royl, had been charged with the renovation. Daily, I

Bottom left: Back in New York and rainbowed with signal flags, *Norway* has tied up on the north side of Pier 88 in September 2001. Nearly four decades since *France* appeared for the first time in the same slip, that remarkable hull has lost none of its allure. (Richard Faber collection)

Bottom right: A view from the stringpiece. As one entered her Manhattan pier shed, a pillar momentarily obscured the bow's letter *R* so that her name read NO WAY. (Richard Faber collection)

watched in disbelief as the new facility emerged. I salvaged some of Angelo's discarded checked carpet and, at home, fabricated fragments into commemorative coasters, some of which are still in my cellar.

Captain Geir Lokøen served longest in command of any master, French or Norwegian. He had first gone to sea as a fifteen-year-old cadet in 1962, the year *France* entered service. But long before then he was already smitten, devouring every newspaper account and photograph throughout his childhood.

Not until 1977, by then chief officer aboard a bulk carrier bound for Rouen, would he see his dream ship. He recalled the moment.

Everything about *France* was beautiful but most eye-catching of all were her two funnels. They were so large and tall, and stand for me like something solid that holds the ship up and carries her through all dangers, like two guardian angels. They even have wings.

By miraculous happenstance, his opportunity to embark arrived. Sailing aboard *Southward* at the time of *France*'s purchase, Geir requested a transfer, joining *Norway* at Bremerhaven in March 1980. Thrilled to be aboard, he climbed to Sun Deck and gazed up at the funnels. "I was not disappointed. They were really large and tall and I felt very safe."

Established in the vessel's hierarchy, Geir Lokøen scaled the promotional ladder—first officer, chief officer, chief security officer, safety officer, staff captain, and finally captain in the late eighties.

Geir was tall and sported a light beard and rimless spectacles. He was extremely popular with both fellow officers and crew. There is a probably apocryphal story that he once greeted a new crewman on Boat Deck, introducing himself by first name.

"Good morning, I'm Geir," he announced, extending his hand.

"Oh, so am I," the man responded with a grin. Thereafter, Geir stayed with Captain Lokøen. A firm but fair disciplinarian, he was a dedicated seaman and genially good natured. He loved a good story and I have never forgotten the bemused, radiant smile that started infectiously in his eyes.

Apart from his unabashed love affair with *Norway*, Geir Lokøen kept his emotions firmly in check, never revealing anything personal to his

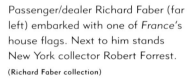

Passenger/dealer Richard Faber (far left) embarked with one of *France*'s house flags. Next to him stands New York collector Robert Forrest. (Richard Faber collection)

Unfurled down the side of the vessel before departure, the flag would be hoisted briefly while departing Halifax, the last time a French Line house flag flew at sea. (Richard Faber collection)

Fairlead view. Despite the intruding anchor, if one leaned far enough out there was *Norway*'s bow, hypnotically impacting with the sea. (Author's collection)

fellow officers or even his family. His only flaw was chronic addiction to nicotine. At many captain's dinners, I recall Geir excusing himself between courses to go outside for a smoke. It was the same on the bridge or at the shelf: invariably, Geir's hand cupped a cigarette.

The love of his life was Sissel Kvåle, born on the island of Osterøy northwest of Bergen, an extremely attractive woman who had once worked as a ship's radio officer. Their daughter Iselin was born in 1978, and in 1984, the year of their marriage, her younger sister Michelle joined the family.

Like all Norwegians Geir loved fish. On 17 April, 1987, while *Norway* was anchored off Great Stirrup Cay, Geir and hotel director Bjorn-Erik Julseth went trolling for lobsters. Wearing face masks and carrying spears, they held on to the stern of one of *Norway*'s man-overboard boats as it towed them across the reef. They could spot lobsters scuttling below. When they caught one, they raised the beast, impaled on a spear, up to the boat where a crewman placed it in a container before returning the spear.

The fishing was good but once, after several passes, Geir noticed that Bjorn-Erik lay on the bottom, staring intently at a coral outcrop. His first thought was that he had adopted a tactic familiar to both of them, lying in wait near a crevasse in hopes of flushing out another victim.

Then Geir realized that Bjorn-Erik's spear had been discarded and that he was lying unnaturally still. Immediately, he let go of the boat and plunged down for a closer look. Bjorn-Erik was unconscious. Geir hauled him to the surface and helped crewmen drag the unconscious hotel director into the boat. Still insensible, Bjorn-Erik was carried as fast as possible to *Norway*'s medical center. His lungs were full of water, his pupils dilated, and his fingernails blue.

To Geir's vast relief, the ship's surgeon restored him to consciousness. "What's your name?" he demanded repeatedly, a question that worried Bjorn-Erik as he struggled back to consciousness. Understandably, the medico was concerned about lack of oxygen to the brain. But, apart from some broken ribs sustained by being dragged over the gunwale, Bjorn-Erik made a complete recovery. What had felled him was carbon monoxide, inhaled from the motors' exhaust as they were towed through the water. Thanks to Geir's rescue, Bjorn-Erik's life was

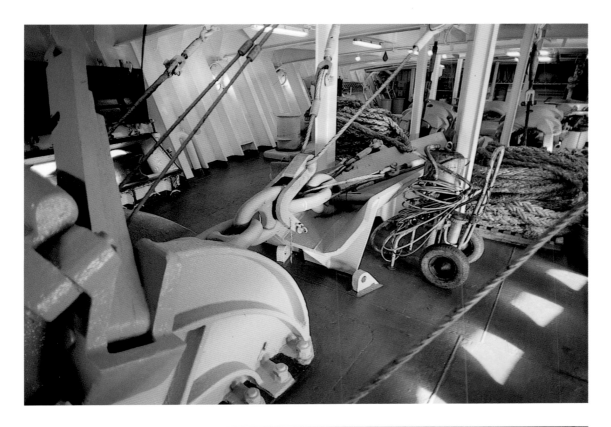

The forward mooring deck in happier times. Suspended from the deckhead by stout cables are restraining claws that, not deployed in time, would have prevented the incident. (Author's collection)

Left: As 1,100 feet (335 meters) of anchor cable were torn precipitously up from the locker, the capstan was destroyed. (Author's collection)

Below: One of its sheared-off mounting bolts. (Author's collection)

Norway undocks and starts to move. Moments later, there was a minor pier collision that scarred the superstructure. (Richard Faber collection)

saved, a harrowing episode that brought the two friends closer.

Of all the world's gamblers, the most rabid are unquestionably the Chinese. Given their all-consuming addiction, it is surprising that neither Hong Kong nor Singapore has casinos. This was not lost on entrepreneur Colin Au, who decided to start an Asian cruise line that would embark gamblers aboard floating casinos for legal gaming at sea.

The beginning of Star Cruises was quite incredible. When he first arrived in Fujian province in 1937 at the age of nineteen, Tan Sri Lim Goh Tong carried a small suitcase and $175. He anglicized his name to Colin Au and founded Genting Group in the Malay Highlands, a hugely successful conglomerate encompassing hotels and apartments as well as paper, power, oil, and gas interests.

In 1993, carrying presumably bigger suitcases crammed with bundles of U.S. dollars, Mr. Au flew to Stockholm where two ships, Finnish-built *Athena* and *Kalypso*, were for sale from bankrupt Swedish Rederi AB Slite.

The Far Eastern visitor was driven to the pier. Ushered aboard *Athena*, an elevator took him to the main lounge. Gazing around, Mr. Au requested politely to see the ship. Informed he was on it, he asked the price and, from his suitcase, produced the requisite amount. Through a window he saw nearby *Kalypso*.

"What about that one?" he asked. Told it was also for sale he paid cash for it as well. Once the vessels had been repositioned to the Far East, they did incredible business. Overnight cruises out of Hong Kong and Singapore sailed at the end of every day. Nonstop gambling started outside the twelve-mile limit. Then, after feverishly all-night gaming, passengers disembarked after breakfast.

The company flourished, becoming the third largest cruise line in the world. Flush with gambling revenue, in 2000 Star Cruises PLC of Malaysia purchased Norwegian Cruise Line.

NCL continued to operate as before but it was a rude jolt to officers that one Star Cruise dictum enforced on board was that officers of three stripes and above were forbidden to drink any alcohol whatsoever, zero tolerance. Aage Hoddavik told me that he grew very tired of what he called "Eskimo Flips," Perrier and ice. Shelf gatherings assumed a contrasting solemnity.

Norway visited New York in September 2001 to embark passengers for what was billed as her last crossing. After reaching Southampton, Star Cruises and NCL had arranged that, following some French cruises out of Havre and Marseilles, the vessel would reposition to the Far East.

She tied up at Pier 88 on 5 September, a bright early fall day. As always, "a last crossing" had gen-erated intense interest. A capacity crowd of passengers surged aboard, including three hundred from France. I had been asked to join as well but, regretfully, had a previous commitment to sail westbound aboard *Sun Princess*.

As *Norway* backed into the Hudson at 5 P.M. a portion of her Pool Deck overhang conflicted with the pier. Steel was rent but, fortunately, the damage was only cosmetic, well above the waterline. *Norway* continued out into the stream, turned, and sailed downriver as New Jersey's afternoon sun brilliantly illuminated her passage past the World Trade Center towers.

In fact, 9/11 aborted *Norway*'s Far Eastern deployment. In its aftermath, as American passengers eschewed overseas travel, NCL decided it made sense to return *Norway* to Caribbean station. As soon as the program of French cruises was over *Norway* deadheaded westbound to Miami to resume her weekly cruising schedule.

For the crew, who had enjoyed the Mediterranean, it was a reluctant resumption. The weather may have been flawless but St. Thomas was not Marseilles and Cancún not Villefranche. Thus the numbing monotony of a Caribbean week infused *Norway* once more.

Even *Norway*'s disappointing funnels look well in that peerless afternoon light. It was 5 September, 2001; six days later, both World Trade Center towers would be rubble. (James Giammatteo collection)

CHAPTER ELEVEN

DEMISE II

The boilers on the S/S Norway have reached a state where a decision must be made.

Memorandum from NCL's port engineer to executive vice president, cruise operations, November 1997

Something had gone very wrong in the boiler room.

Second engineer on Olympic Deck, 25 May, 2003

Opposite: 0630 hours, 27 June, 2003. Flanked by escorting tugs, S.S. *Norway*, incapacitated by its vulnerable boilers, leaves the port of Miami under tow behind oceangoing tug *Smitwijs Rotterdam*. (Captain Robert Bourne collection)

Sunday 25 May began like any other Miami turnaround day. With Haakon Gangdal in command,

Norway and 2,135 passengers returned from the eastern Caribbean, steaming up Government Cut at dawn. As usual, she was first in; three other Sunday ships—RCI's *Voyager of the Seas* and Carnival's *Victory* and *Paradise*—would follow her into port. Their weekly encounters were so routine that no acknowledgments, neither whistle nor wave, were ever exchanged.

In the turning basin, *Norway* began her 180-degree pirouette until her bows were pointing down the cut. From the ship's loudspeakers came end-of-cruise wrapups as delinquent passengers were summoned to settle their accounts.

Norway retraced course downstream to berths 3 and 4. Captain Gangdal stood on the starboard bridge wing; hard-right rudder and judicious surges of bow- and stern thrusters coaxed her sideways and alongside. It was 5:29 A.M.

Messenger lines were hurled ashore and longshoremen hauled blue hawsers across the shrinking gap separating hull from pier. Winches ground and stopped, allowing initial hawser lengths to be

slipped over bollards. Then the capstans reversed, rewinding line back around their revolving drums, as the forward mooring officer directed placement of spring lines.

Down on the pier, forklift operators started their engines and converged on the vessel's open ports, retrieving pallets of her monumental luggage accumulation and shunting them inland to the carousels.

The owners of those duffels, holdalls, golf bags, and bulging zippered suitcases were either packing hand luggage, finishing breakfast, or queuing to have their customs declarations stamped in the Sports Illustrated bar.

Once the earliest suitcases had been transferred to the pier, ship's speakers called for holders of the appropriate color-coded labels to proceed ashore. Roused from public rooms, they shouldered luggage and descended stairtowers to disembark.

At 6:37 A.M. there was what one crewman described as a bump. Chief engineer Steinar Sjøhaug

A view taken from passing Carnival *Victory* shortly before dawn, 25 May, 2003. *Voyager of the Seas*, in the background, is about to moor astern of *Norway*. (Svein Sleipnes collection)

heard two impacts, a small one followed by a larger. A control room engineer suggested simply a "bang." Fiona McKenzie, a Saga Theatre stage manager, remembers that the ship shook and then went quiet; too quiet, she felt. Peruvian assistant purser Rocio Reyna, helping immigration officials, felt the same shake. Edalgo Harris, the captain's Jamaican waiter, was woken up in his Norway Deck cabin by a "jolt," followed by the ship "jostling."

On the opposite side of Government Cut, a couple bound on a cruise later that day were video-taping Dodge Island. Inadvertently, they captured *Norway*'s explosion. Six years later, YouTube still screens it; the image was replayed all day throughout Miami news broadcasts.

It looks like two separate episodes, nanoseconds apart. First, the swift, upward smear of a black column rising straight above number 2 funnel. It was followed immediately by obscene black clouds, jetting outward and upward from wings and funnel top, momentarily obscuring stern and pier.

An off-duty second engineer saw "lots of black smoke from the aft stack." In fact, the black cloud was not smoke but explosively expelled soot, scoured from the funnel's interior.

The explosion precipitated an immediate blackout. Corridors, public rooms, and cabins were plunged into darkness until circuits of emergency lighting flickered on for ghostly illumination. A small fire started and sprinklers in the affected area unleashed torrents of water.

Over the loudspeakers came the emergency signal, that familiar, oft-rehearsed seven-short-and-one-long blast. Gangdal's voice ordered crew and passengers to muster stations at 6:52. "We have experienced an explosion on board," he explained.

Fiona, whose cabin was aft, retrieved her jewelry and life jacket and went to her assigned station at lifeboat 11 on the starboard side. Without air-conditioning, the sun started cooking up Promenade Deck and passengers started complaining about the heat.

British cruise director Kieran Buffrey told Fiona there had been "an incident." From their vantage point above the pier, they could see fire engines and ambulances arriving and walking wounded leaving the vessel.

Megan Williams, *Norway*'s shore excursion manager, overheard on her radio a transmitted snippet between officers: "Two dead." It proved, alas, only a preliminary count.

Not until 8 A.M. were passengers allowed to resume disembarkation. Those in need of help were assisted. There was no panic, no complaints, and no passenger injuries.

Not so for crew. This is what happened. There were four boilers in *Norway*'s working after boiler room, numbered 21, 22, 23, and 24. The numerical code assigned a 2- prefix for the after room's boilers while 11, 12, 13, and 14 enumerated their inactive or removed duplicates in the equivalent space forward.

Of the four, one was shut down for maintenance while the other three remained in harness. It was boiler number 23, farthest aft, starboard side, that ruptured violently at 0637 hours.

Its contents—20 tons of scalding water at 528 degrees Fahrenheit—burst through the space, a rampaging tornado of superheated steam. Four Filipino crewmen on engine room duty were killed instantly and horrifically. Raging upward to Caribbean Deck en route to the funnel, the blast thrust steel bulkheads sideways, crushing and cooking to death three more men in cabins adjacent to the upper flank of that three-deck-high boiler.

Jamaican steward Winston Lewis had just finished breakfast. Opening the mess door to leave, he was mortally wounded by the same steam onslaught. Had he *not* opened the door, his friend Edalgo insists, he might have survived. Passenger Gail Zwakenberg told reporters on the pier later that she had seen a "crewman on fire, his skin melting from his body." Lewis died four weeks later in the hospital.

The blast scalded six more crewmen in corridors and cabins along Slime Alley or I-95, their name for the vessel's working alleyway. After injured crewmen gathered in the main galley on Caribbean Deck, a "Code Alpha" was telephoned to the bridge requesting medical assistance.

Three men rigging a garbage gangway on Biscayne Deck's port side were hurled through the open port into the water, later rescued by a Fire Department launch. Some of their colleagues dropped eight feet down to the pier from *Norway*'s starboard side; one broke his leg. Over a hundred crewmen who ran from the vessel onto the pier were prevented from reembarking by Miami Dade fire officials. During later frantic head counts, so many missing men prompted fears of a hideous death toll.

At 6 A.M., Per Sopp had taken his morning coffee out onto his Brickell Bay Drive terrace. Every Sunday, he still watched the ships come in.

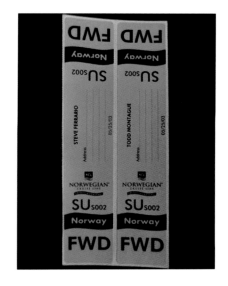

Orphaned souvenirs: NCL luggage labels for the 25 May 2003, cruise that never happened. (Steve Ferrario collection)

On *Norway*'s bridge, Svein Sleipnes, NCL's vice president, nautical and port operations/CSO, poses with Captain Frank Juliussen, in command for passage to Bremerhaven. After the accident, uniforms vanished; only civilian clothing was worn on board. Behind them on the wall is the photograph of *France*'s bridge that the author presented to the vessel in 1980.

(Svein Sleipnes collection)

When he saw *Norway*'s explosion, he muttered, "There went a boiler." Although Per had not worked for NCL for four years, that horrifying eventuality always haunted him. He was a close friend of both Gangdal and Chief Sjøhaug as well as one of the dead, third engineer Ricardo Rosal.

Another two thousand *Norway* passengers were either en route to or had already arrived in Miami for the vessel's next cruise. Steve Ferrario, a U.S. Navy commander from San Francisco, spent Saturday night at the Miami Hilton Airport Hotel. Early next morning he watched coverage of the explosion on television. Later, in the lobby, he informed the NCL man who, at nine, started manning NCL's Hospitality Desk that the ship would not be sailing; he knew nothing about it.

Wayne Mazzotta, the artist who executed this volume's endpapers, had spent two nights in South Beach. He and his fellow New York friends were informed by Pied Piper's owner and group leader, Derek Burgl, that their *Norway* cruise was off.

Derek had spent the night in Fort Lauderdale and been telephoned early by a friend who told him to turn on television. After alerting Mazzotta, he hurried to the pier, stationing himself there for four hours to turn back clients who had missed NCL airport representatives forestalling newly landed passengers.

Some of Derek's group, deprived of their *Norway* week, tried embarking on the other vessels in port. *Voyager of the Seas* had no space but a lucky few who tried *Paradise* were, astonishingly, welcomed on board without charge.

After the passengers had gone, *Norway*'s crew were mustered in Saga Theatre where hotel director Tony Becker, scarcely visible in the emergency lighting, briefed them about the explosion. Fatalities were not mentioned.

The following day, names of the dead circulated among them in stunned whispers. Seven Filipinos and one Jamaican had lost their lives. On Tuesday, the Bahamian flag at the stern was lowered to half-staff and, with a priest from shore officiating, a packed memorial service was held in Saga Theatre. Fiona recalls that some Filipina women concluded movingly with an a capella performance of "My Heart Will Go On."

Without power, cold storage lockers had to have their melting contents removed. Crew members were mustered into a bucket brigade that, lining humid, lower deck staircases, passed cartons and crates up from hand to hand, then down gangways and into refrigerated reefers on the pier. Only after shore mains had been rigged to provide backup electricity were some stores reembarked.

All the crew were moved into passenger cabins and in relays, wearing hazmat suits, were permitted to retrieve jewelry, cell phones, and pictures from their cabins; asbestos-contaminated clothing and luggage were abandoned. They took their meals in The Great Outdoor Restaurant. Future sailings through 28 September were canceled and *Norway* remained in place for more than a month.

From Washington, a National Transportation Safety Board team converged for examination and analysis of number 23 boiler. They took some two hundred depositions from NCL personnel and pored over maintenance records of *Norway*'s deteriorating steam system.

Unlike downed aircraft investigations there was no hunt for a black box. In black and white, incriminating evidence was there for the asking. A chilling record of disinterest and deferral emerged. Throughout *Norway*'s final years, management had repeatedly ignored the parlous condition of the vessel's steam infrastructure. Logs recorded that cracks, pitting, and tube failures were endemic on all four boilers but only makeshift, stopgap, and essentially money-saving remedial work had been grudgingly authorized.

As far back as 1982, cracks had been discovered near boiler number 23's waterwall header, exactly where a lethal fault would fracture two decades later. In June 1988, "Tube failure, boiler no. 23" was logged. In January 2001, two years before the explosion: "Tube leak in boiler no. 23 plugged." Number 23 was not the only offender. Between July 2001 and February 2002, neighboring boiler number 24 prompted four identical entries: "Superheater tube leaks plugged."

I have never forgotten a conversation I once had with a Royal Viking Line chief. He told me he occasionally had to snake sinuously through his engine room's maze of pipes, cabling, and tanks, parodying, in effect, Charlie Chaplin's tortuous machinery crawl from *Modern Times*. "You must be able to examine everything," he explained.

His words came to mind as I read the NTSB Marine Accident Brief describing the difficulty of physically inspecting the interior of boiler number 23. The access manhole measured 12 × 16 inches (30 × 40 centimeters). Although one chief reported that he had wormed his way inside, his relief, who weighed three hundred–plus pounds (135 kilograms) confessed that "it was impossible for him to enter the drums and headers."

One dangerous anomaly uncovered were alien copper beads forced into boiler wall cracks and then ground down. Copper insertions are ineffectual for correcting steel boiler leaks. Among its conclusions, the Marine Accident Brief condemned those "questionable weld repair procedures."

Probable cause of the accident was, the brief concluded, "deficient boiler operation, maintenance, and inspection practices of Norwegian Cruise Line, which allowed material deterioration and fatigue cracking to weaken the boiler."

The report was adopted and signed by four investigators; a fifth recused herself, voting "to disapprove this brief." It was not publicly released until 29 October, 2007, more than four years after the explosion.

Norwegian Cruise Lines, pleading guilty to gross negligence, paid families of the deceased compensation in the amount of $13 million. Judge Federico Moreno also fined NCL an additional $1 million. In May 2009, lawyers for four badly scalded Filipino crewmen asked the judge to allow them to sue NCL for additional damages in the light of the company's "gross negligence" admission.

The vessel's monthlong stay accumulated berthing fees totaling $284,000. It was announced that *Norway* would be towed to Europe. Explained company spokeswoman Susan Robison, "We need to move it to meet our repair schedule."

Captain Frank Juliussen would command a riding crew of fifty. No shipyard had been determined although past preference suggested that Lloyd Werft seemed likely.

Apart from longshoremen and container cargo handlers, *Norway*'s last Miami sailing day, Friday, 27 June, 2003, was a low-key, almost anonymous event—nationally, a nonevent.

The sturdy, 22,000-horsepower salvage tug *Smitwijs Rotterdam* had been contracted for the tow. To prevent chafing and ensure the tow went as smoothly as possible, Sleipnes had recommended that a dockside crane remove both central and starboard anchors. Then the starboard anchor cable was brought inboard and rove out through the bower anchor's central hawse pipe for connection to the stretcher, an adaptable hawser that would serve as cushioning shock absorber under way. Be-

fore undocking, the crane reembarked both anchors to be secured to the fo'c'sle head.

At 0615 hours, four escorting tugs took up station along *Norway*'s flanks for the trip down Government Cut. Predictably, *Norway*'s Miami finale was, like everything else, over the top: the most ambitious tow ever leaving the port.

At 0830 hours the convoy passed beyond the breakwater and, forty minutes later, slowed off Miami's sea buoy. The tugs relinquished their charge to *Smitwijs Rotterdam* at 0915. A quarter of an hour later, the pilot as well as NCL personnel and a group of riding pilots disembarked.

Once the tow line had been paid out to longer sea length, the two vessels started their linked northeasterly crossing. Conditioned to hauling unwieldy oil rigs, tug master Captain Peter Heerema rated *Norway* 's cherished hull an easier tow.

Twenty-three years after her first jubilant arrival, *Norway* limped from Miami and the Caribbean forever. It was a depressing finis for an historic port irregular, her future, at best, uncertain.

The crane operator and crew have just completed juggling *Norway*'s starboard anchor cable so that it feeds out through the bower anchor's hawse pipe as a towing element attached to a cushioning pennant. (Svein Sleipnes collection)

EPILOGUE

BLUE LADY

It's very sad. When you sailed into the sunrise and looked out over that long bow, it was an unbelievable experience. Nothing will ever be built like her.

Jan-Olav Stori, *Norway* bridge officer

Opposite: Probably one-of-a-kind—an improvised *Blue Lady* life ring. **(Peter Knego collection)**

crossing ever, four weeks. During the ten months she remained there, no repairs were undertaken, only cursory shipboard maintenance.

Captain Tommy Stensrud took over as caretaker captain for the month of April 2004 while Gangdal went on leave. Tommy and his Canadian wife, Margo, a former *Norway* nurse, moved into the master's cabin; two young sons, Erik and Evan, were bedded down in the living room. Margo homeschooled them during much of the day.

On board were seventy crewmen—stewards, cooks, cleaners, engineers, and deck hands. Lifeboat and fire drills were held regularly and everyone took their meals in Le Bistro. Instead of ship's provisions, food was delivered from Bremerhaven suppliers. Though electrical mains were connected, sewage mains never were; waste water was off-loaded into tankers.

Norway's exile seemed, in effect, a replay of her Havre layup, moored this time alongside *der Pier der Vergessenen*, a Teutonic "pier of the forgotten." Tommy remembers that his month aboard, even accompanied by his family, was a downer; immobilized, empty, and derelict *Norway* was essentially depressing.

When Gangdal returned in May, the Stensruds were not sorry to leave. Tommy moved on to Pappenberg, overseeing NCL newbuilding *Norwegian Jewel* and so never saw *Norway*'s disappearance from Bremerhaven on 23 May for a second tow, this one to the Far East. Missing from her foredeck were the tenders. NCL still uses them to take passengers ashore at Great Stirrup Cay.

Restoration of the vessel to service had been put on indefinite hold. "*Norway*," an NCL spokesperson explained a month prior to her departure, "does not fit into the company's well-advanced fleet modernization program," corporate-speak for we have no further use for *Norway* and want to be rid of her.

One cannot blame them. Mired in breakdown limbo, the vessel was useless. No passengers and certainly no crewmen would embark. One ruptured boiler had already killed eight of their fellows, a second or third could do the same. Firing up *Norway*'s engine room was like activating a time bomb.

Her only salvation—replacing turbines with diesels, 1979's long-deferred option—would be even more costly nearly three decades later. And though reengining would obviate that Damoclean boiler threat, *Norway* still remained a forty-one-year-old ship in constant need of repair and renovation, an obligation that neither Norwegian Cruise Line nor Star Cruises wished to continue.

Since she could no longer steam, Star Cruises toyed with the idea of anchoring her off Malaysia's Port Klang as a gambling hell. But like Akram Ojjeh's abortive 1979 Florida brainstorm, it never happened.

In spring 2006 a third name, *Blue Lady*, was daubed on her bows. It first seemed a curiously apropos choice for, throughout many Caribbean years, Jamaican crewmen often called their vessel, affectionately, Blue Lady. Perhaps the real purpose in officially resurrecting the name meant that *Norway* could conveniently recede further toward anonymous oblivion.

She had become a very blue lady indeed—idle, rusting, scarred, and neglected, swinging at anchor, less derelict than a kind of prison hulk for her largely Asian crew. Air-conditioning had long since ceased. In search of a breeze, they set up cots along the shady side of Fjord Deck, just aft of the port bridge wing. Heat and humidity were oppressive, swarms of insects besieged those on-deck sleepers, and a reek of mildew and drains pervaded the vessel. Once pristine decks, public rooms, and cabins had subsided into squalor. One promenade somehow stayed clean, the other was littered with signs, cutaways, clothing oddments, vacuum cleaners, and rubbish. Angelo Donghia's crystal-garlanded Triton and Neptune still stared sightlessly from their Club I niches.

Then, in late summer 2006, *Blue Lady* submitted to a third and final tow to the Indian port of Alang, just south of Mumbai. There, like so many superannuated ships preceding her, she was deposited ashore to be scrapped. Without power to drive herself onto the beach, the tug merely anchored her in the shallows on 15 August. At low tide, much of her underwater hull was visible. By eerie coincidence, the day she went ashore, the little gold model of *France/Norway* that had been attached to my key chain for 30 years, suddenly and inexplicably became detached.

The imminent death of a beloved ship always triggers regret and *Blue Lady*-ex-*Norway*-ex-*France*

Above: Bremerhaven interlude. Margo Stensrud and the children on *Norway*'s forepeak. (Captain Tommy Stensrud collection)

Opposite, top left: Erik and Evan perched on the starboard anchor, flanked by tenders to either side. (Captain Tommy Stensrud collection)

Opposite center left: *Norway* head-on just before departure. One of the off-loaded tenders is moored at the pier. (Captain Tommy Stensrud collection)

Opposite, bottom left: *Norway*'s second tow begins, from Bremerhaven to Port Klang, Malaysia. From a distance she looked pristine. (Lloyd Werft Bremerhaven)

Opposite, top right: *Blue Lady* at anchor off Port Klang, Malaysia. In an attempt to escape 'tween-deck humidity, cots along Fjord Deck serve as impromptu dormitory. (Peter Knego collection)

Opposite, bottom right: The desolation of an abandoned passenger cabin. (Peter Knego collection)

15 August 2006: Derelict *Blue Lady* is aground off Alang. (Peter Knego collection)

Opposite, left: One indestructible *Blue Lady* contour that only demolition would obliterate: the sculpturally exquisite sheer of hull plating approaching the bow. (Peter Knego collection)

Opposite, right: Erosion of the profile. (Kaushal Trivedi, Peter Knego collection)

proved no exception. One belated savior, a Canadian shipping entrepreneur, announced plans to reengine her with diesels, but he was too late. *Blue Lady* was aground forever on Alang's toxic sands and no one had the means, the money, or the will to refloat her.

The presence of asbestos on board fomented a Green Peace outcry. The concern was the health of Alang's workforce, yet the workers' fear of contamination was outweighed by the lure of employment. Predictably, the asbestos uproar subsided, a delaying lawsuit was dismissed, and *Blue Lady*, the largest vessel ever consigned to Alang, was scheduled to be cut up.

For months she lay offshore, like burned-out *Morro Castle* stranded off Asbury Park's beach in 1934. One of the first things the scrappers did was pierce the hull in several places so that *Blue Lady* flooded, resting evenly on the bottom without risk of breaking her back as Indian Ocean tides rose and fell.

Most scrapping vessels are moored in grimy backwaters of well-known ports, New Jersey's Port Newark for *Normandie*, La Spezia for *Liberté*, or Rosyth for the first *Mauretania*. Not so *Blue Lady*. She was scrapped Alang fashion, with no surrounding infrastructure, no crane forest, no railed gondola cars hauling away steel fragments, just her isolated presence off a desolate beach.

Thanks to the ubiquity of digital cameras, there was no shortage of images posted on the Internet, documenting *Blue Lady*'s gradual disappearance. My friend Peter Knego did go aboard; for years, scrapped vessels have intrigued him and he was kind enough to share some photographs. A few of Peter's on deck views seem apparently normal. Surrounding views of open sea and beach are deceptively appealing; it looks almost like a day off Great Stirrup Cay, as though *Blue Lady* had come to rest at an imaginary out island.

Loose *France/Norway* ends remain. In spring 2008 I received a surprise letter from Odette Escolier, the *France* hairdresser to whom I had surrendered my boarding pass in Southampton. She had kept it, with my name and Mary's too, all those years and has written a memoir about her three years on board.

We remet in Paris over the summer of 2008, at the Musée de la Marine, appropriately in front of the museum's *France* builder's model. A week later, after our return from a week's research in Le Havre, Odette asked us to her flat to share a bottle of champagne. We brought her a blue, white, and red bouquet, the same color combination with which she had *fleuri*'d *Norway*.

After New Year's of 2009, several containers arrived in France from the subcontinent. Jacques Dworczak, a self-described "collector/adventurer" born the same year as *France* was launched, had retrieved a consignment of furnishings from the scrappers. Returned to the land of their birth, 446 lots would be sold off during a February auction under the auspices of Artcurial at Paris's Hôtel Marcel Dassault.

The catalogue showed, typically, a mixed bag—chairs, lamps, engine room hardware, a Club I chandelier, bar stools, Jean Leleu's library table, a link of starboard anchor cable, four sections of Subes's *grand descent* aluminum banister, tables, bureaus, lamps, sconces, and one cabin bed. Most items originated from the *France* years. The few attributed to *Norway* included captains' bridge chairs as well as some tables from Club I and The Great Outdoor Restaurant.

The largest and most outlandish was described as *le nez du bateau*—the nose of the boat—a substantial chunk of steel, incorporating railed prow above and fairlead below; it had been sliced intact with surgical precision from the wreck.

An equally mixed bag of Parisians descended. One poignant visitor was a retired Breton crewman who came for a look but departed in tears. Dozens more of the curious came to browse with no intention of bidding, outnumbered by hundreds of determined and apparently deep-pocketed aficionados. Similar to grandstand limitations at

France's christening, there were only 250 sale room seats; many either stood or submitted telephonic or Internet bids.

Throughout two consecutive auction sessions, bidding was brisk and prices high, well in excess of those anticipated. The nose, for example, estimated to fetch between $108,000 and $135,000, was snapped up for $371,118 by Jacques Veron, a Norman real estate developer and collector of contemporary art. Repainted now in *France*'s black-and-white livery, Veron's newest "sculpture" has been reerected as the waterfront focus of his latest Deauville development called Blue Bay. By way of home port homage the nose points toward Le Havre.

One of Henri Lancel's first class steel cabin bureaus, pegged to sell from $5,400 to $6,075, fetched twice as much, $11,260. A Raymond Subes banister section went for $36,086, nearly twice its estimate. Some bits and pieces had never been on the vessel at all, random souvenirs bought from other collectors. Among them was the only boat train plaque on offer, the twin of the one Ian and I had removed in 1974; estimated to fetch $2,000, it was finally knocked down for $12,216.

Apparently, St.-Nazairians' pain over the loss of *France* is shared by their countrymen. With no French-flagged passenger vessels in existence, small wonder that they paid hefty prices for remnants of their last. To Dworczak's gain: his final gross amounted to $1,610,722.

One treasure eluded him. Anne Carlu's stained-glass chapel reredos had been removed from the chapel during the 1990 refit, crated, and returned aboard the vessel to Florida. Once there, it spent eighteen years in storage at Goltens Marine in downtown Miami.

Now it has been relegated to meaningful use. Prompted by recommendations from Miami's Norwegian community, NCL donated the glass to Pastor Dag Magnus Hopstock Havgar for incorporation into his new *Sjømannskirken* or Norwegian "seamen's church" at 2950 South Flamingo Road in the town of Davie, west of Fort Lauderdale. Dedication is scheduled for early 2011.

Nothing could be more apropos than incorporating a cherished artifact from a Norwegian ship's chapel into a Norwegian seamen's church's decoration. Pastor Havgar, architect Jerry Clawson, and project manager Thomas Wiig selected a prominent position, centerpiece of the sanctuary between the altar and a glass cross adorning the northeast

wall. Just as it was aboard *France* the stained glass
will be electrically backlit.

That a shipboard relic of such perfect prove-
nance enriches Pastor Hagvar's and his Norwegian congregants' place of worship makes good
sense. Ships are frighteningly transitory; once they
are gone, little remains. Installation of Anne
Carlu's work garners another distinction. To my
knowledge, that stained glass represents Florida's
only publicly visible *Norway* artifact, solitary me-
mento of Miami's pioneering megaship. Of
course, there are two larger ones in the Bahamas,
Tage Wandborg's tenders that ferry NCL passengers ashore to Great Stirrup Cay, still called *Little
Norway I and II.*

In August of 2008 Mary and I took a farewell
northern cruise aboard Cunard's *Queen Elizabeth 2*, our last glimpse of the vessel before she
would disappear to Dubai that fall. One port of call
was Stavanger where we spent the day with two
Norway friends, Bjorn-Erik Julseth and Sissel
Lokøen, Geir's widow. Home between voyages,
Bjorn-Erik still sails as hotel director, not in the
Caribbean but aboard *Finnmark*, one of the Bergen
Line's *hurtegruten* or coastal expresses that ply, year-
round, between Bergen and the North Cape.

Sissel told us that Geir had signed off *Norway* in
1999 and been transferred to *Norwegian Star* while
the NCL newbuilding was under construction at
Pappenburg. Once she entered service, he would
alternate as master between *Norwegian Star* and
Norwegian Dream.

In 2002 he signed off the *Star* in Hawaii and,
back in Bergen the following year, was diagnosed
with throat cancer. After a gallant battle he died
peacefully at home in Norway on 12 May 2004.

Now his widow and his hotel director colleague
have grown close, devoted to each other. Together,
they have built a new house on the island of Sokn,
twenty minutes' drive north of Stavanger. They
moved in over the summer of 2009; right on the
water, Bjorn-Erik insists it is like living on a ship.

That those old *Norway* friends have been
drawn together closes an emotional circle of astonishing diameter. During our morning coffee
and later lunch, both confessed separately that
they are convinced that saving Bjorn-Erik's life on
that lobster-fishing expedition back in 1984
seemed like Geir's mystical, premonitory determination that, twenty years before he died, his
close friend should survive to be a comfort and
companion for widowed Sissel.

The fourth and very special thousand-footer is gone now, its last hull fragment plucked from the shallows and consigned to the smelters. For me, a few cherished souvenirs remain: the little gold key chain model, now firmly reattached, 1974's money clip, a Hermès *France* scarf, and the chrome NORMANDIE sign from the door of *France's appartement de grand luxe*.

One final *France* story boasts a Camelot connection. Throughout 1962, the vessel's first year of life, hundreds of distinguished French passengers booked passage to New York, anxious to sample the delights of the republic's latest flagship. One of the most distinguished was a very special VIP who embarked for a 14 December westbound. Throughout the crossing she never once entered the dining room nor even stirred from her cabin.

The occupant was, in fact, a painting, Leonardo da Vinci's fragile masterpiece *Mona Lisa*. Jackie Kennedy had asked André Malraux, France's minister of culture, if the painting might be displayed at Washington's National Gallery. Acceding to Mrs. Kennedy's request, Malraux arranged for the painting to be packed within a special container and, accompanied by two curators, consigned to a first class *France* cabin. Alternately, one of her two handlers always remained on duty as cabin sentry. Should *France* come to grief, they had been advised, *Mona Lisa's* container was not only waterproof but buoyant.

Midway across, news of the painting's presence was circulated on board and, by the time *France* tied up at Pier 88 on 19 December, there had been games, puzzles, quizzes, and dances in her honor for the balance of the crossing.

France/Norway came to a tragically abrupt end. There was no ritardando, no announced withdrawal, no hyped last voyage, only an unpredicted catastrophe that brutalized everything, like an Edwardian pocket watch rescued from *Titanic* with rusted hands stopped at 2:20.

It was an unhappy irony to resurrect *France/Norway* at my desk at exactly the same time that she was being torn to pieces on the far side of the globe. Though that explosion remains *France/Norway*'s last, lethal image, I feel it should not. Her unique, doubled life deserves kinder remembrance, to be found, I trust, between these covers.

Preserved fragments—money clip from *France's* 1974 world cruise, the *France/Norway* key chain model, and the NORMANDIE suite's door sign. (Author's collection)

GLOSSARY

Throughout the text, readers will find a variety of French and/or English maritime terminology. Herewith, an alphabetized list.

Alleyway. Longitudinal shipboard corridor between cabin rows.

Atelier. Studio or, in French shipyards, workshop.

Bâbord. Starboard, the right side of a vessel facing forward.

Bagages. Luggage

Bagagiste. A porter handling luggage.

Baguette. France's crusty national loaf.

Boat train. Trains shuttling between Paris and Le Havre, carrying westbound passengers for embarkation or bringing eastbound passengers to the capital. Incorporated into boat trains were postal and luggage vans. They were never called ship trains.

Boot topping. Waterline demarcation of a ship's hull.

Café-Grill. *Normandie*'s extra-tariff restaurant, which late at night segued into the vessel's *bôite*, or nightclub. The English word "grill" had (to the displeasure of the Académie Française) insinuated itself into the language, denoting any elegant restaurant, the model probably London's Carlton Grill.

Cambuse. Shipboard provision room.

Chantier. Shipbuilding yard or mercantile supplier.

Chariot. Wheeled vehicle for carrying anything.

Chasseur. Literally, chaser or hunter, perhaps a porter retrieving lost luggage or, in *Normandie* elevators, a supplementary operator who ushered passengers into or out of the car.

Chef. Chief or senior cook in any kitchen or galley. There is only one. Subordinates are described as *sous chefs* (underchefs) or *aides de cuisine* (kitchen helpers).

Chef de bagages. Baggage master, charged with the location and disposition of all passenger luggage.

Chef de deck. Senior deck steward.

Chef de lancement. Shipyard foreman supervising a vessel's launch.

Chef de rang. Literally, ranking chief, not a galley occupant but a senior dining room steward. (See *Commis*)

Chef de Réception. Hospitality chief. Aboard every French liner, the most senior purser, coping with passenger queries or demands, his assistants *sous chefs de réception*.

Chef de train. Official in charge of the boat train.

Cheminée. Funnel.

Classe Touristique. Tourist Class.

Commandant. Master. His immediate inferior—in English, staff captain—was *commandant-adjoint*.

Commis. The term—also adapted as is into English aboard Cunarders—can be translated as "busboy." The most junior French Line busboy was a *commis débarrasseur*, who cleared used plates from the table. A promotion elevated him to *commis de rang*, charged with bringing full trays from the galley.

Commissaire. Purser, the man who looked after the well-being and financial administration of passengers and crew.

Compagnie Générale Transatlantique. General Transatlantic Company, the French name of the French Line. It was often abbreviated to Le Transat or CGT.

Département. A regional subdivision of France, equivalent to Britain's county or America's state.

Dummy. British term for dining room waiters' station.

Femme du chambre. Literally, woman of the bedroom, a French cabin stewardess.

Ferronnier. An artist who works in iron.

Fumoir. Smoking room.

Garçon de cabine. Literally, boy of the cabin, or cabin steward. (See *Femme du chambre*)

Gare Maritime. Literally, Sea Station, the sheltered threshold uniting boat train with ocean liner.

Grande déscente. A French vessel's main staircase; often inaccurately described in English as "grand" staircase, though it often was.

Grand Salon. Main lounge aboard French ocean liners.

Groom. The lowest-ranked bellboy. (See *Mousse*)

Ingénieur. Engineer.

Ingénieur principal. Chief engineer.

Maître d'hôtel. Literally, master of (the) hotel, in overall charge of a dining room.

Marraine. Godmother.

Médecin chef. A French liner's senior surgeon. (See *Chef*)

Mousse. Literally, moss, but aboard French Line vessels a bellboy in buttoned tunic and pillbox hat. Subdivisions include *mousse de sonnerie* (general messenger boy), *mousse de deck* (assisting deck stewards), or *mousse d'ascenseur* (elevator operator).

Newbuilding. New vessel under construction.

Paquebot. Ocean liner.

Passerelle. Bridge.

Pilote de choix. Chosen pilot, preferred senior pilots of any port used by the French Line, selected for his in-port expertise and familiarity with a particular vessel.

Plongeur. Diver, French galley slang describing the deep-sink pot walloper.

Pont. A ship's deck or a bridge (cf. the song "Sur le Pont d'Avignon") but *not* a ship's bridge (see *Passerelle*). Occasionally the English word "deck" was used (see *Chef de deck*), and decks were described thus: *Pont Principal, Pont Promenade, Pont de Soleil* (Sun Deck), etc.

Porteur. Porter.

Première Classe. First Class.

Quai. A quay or dock for mooring liners.

Salle à Manger. Dining room.

Shell plating. Steel side or skin of a hull.

Strake. Horizontal plating row along a hull.

Transat, Le. See *Compagnie Générale Transatlantique.*

Tribord. Port, the left side of a vessel facing forward.

BIBLIOGRAPHY

Arnold, Muriel. *Tiaras and T-Shirts.* Kinloss: Librario Publishing, 2007.

Bannerman, Gary. *Bon Voyage!* Lincolnwood, Illinois: Passport Books, 1984.

Baudet, Vincent. *A Bord du France.* Silver, n.d.

Claiborne, Craig. *A Feast Made for Laughter.* New York: Holt, Rinehart and Winston, 1982.

Croisile, Georges. *En Route pour la Mer: Souvenirs d'un Marin.* Paris: La Table Ronde, 1971.

Garin, Kristoffer A. *Devils on the Deep Blue Sea.* New York: Viking Press, 2005.

Harvey, Clive. *R.M.S. Queen Elizabeth.* London: Carmania Press, 2008.

Hillion, Daniel. *France Norway.* La Falaise: Editions Babouji/MDV, 2006.

Le Huédé, Henri. *The Dining on the France.* New York: Viking Press, 1981.

Jones, Nicolette. *The Plimsoll Sensation.* London: Little, Brown, 2006.

Joubert, Roger. *Palace des Océans.* Maisonneuve and Larose, n.d.

Laver, James. *The Age of Optimism.* London: Weidenfeld and Nicolson, 1966.

Le Goff, Olivier; translated by Roger Jones. *Ocean Liners.* Edison New Jersey: Chartwell Books, 1999.

Maxtone-Graham, John. *Crossing and Cruising.* New York: Scribners, 1992.

——— . *Normandie.* New York: Norton, 2007.

——— . *Norway.* Norwegian Caribbean Line, 1981.

——— . *The Only Way to Cross.* New York: Macmillan, 1972.

Mazar, Pierre. *Les Oeuvres d'Art du Paquebot France.* Geneva: Livror, 1969.

Offrey, Charles, and Louis Morin; illustrations by Pascal Halley. *France: Album Souvenir.* Le Touvet: Editions Marcel-Didier Vrac, 2003.

——— . *Terminé pour les Machines.* Presses de la Cité, n.d.

Ollivier, Frédéric. *Normandie: Un Chef-d'Oeuvre Francais (1935–1942).* Douarnenez: Chasse-Marée, 2005.

Peter, Bruce. *Knud E. Hansen: A/S Ship Design through Seven Decades.* Copenhagen: Forlaget Nautilus, 2007.

Pettré, Christian. *Splendeur et Rouille.* Paris: Editions du Pen Duick, 1978.

Scull, Theodore. *Ocean Liner Odyssey 1958–1969.* London: Carmania Press, 1998.

——— . *Ocean Liner Twilight.* Windsor: Overview Press, 2007.

Warwick, Ronald W. *QE2: The Cunard Line Flagship.* New York: Norton, 1993.

Villers, Claude, and Christian Clères. *France: Un Rêve de Géant.* Grenoble: Editions Glénat, 1996

Readers who would like to order a DVD of the author's The Only Way to Cross, *shot aboard* Norway *in 1981, should send a check for $30 payable to "Crossing & Cruising" to: John Maxtone-Graham, 117 West 78th Street, New York, New York 10024. Sterling checks, payable to the author in the amount of £20, are also acceptable. Postage and handling are included in the price.*

A *France* bookmark given out by the librarian on board. (Author's collection)

INDEX

SS NORWAY | 1 JUNE 1980 – 25 MAY 2003 | NORWEGIAN CARIBBEAN LINE | 66,000 GR